Hearing
the Internal
Trauma

Interpersonal Violence:
The Practice Series
Jon R. Conte, Series Editor

Interpersonal Violence: The Practice Series is devoted to mental health, social service, and allied professionals who confront daily the problem of interpersonal violence. It is hoped that the knowledge, professional experience, and high standards of practice offered by the authors of these volumes may lead to the end of interpersonal violence.

In this series...

Hearing
the Internal
Trauma
Working With
Children and
Adolescents
Who Have Been
Sexually Abused

Sandra Wieland

Interpersonal Violence:
The Practice Series

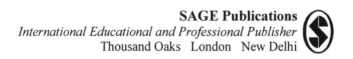

SAGE Publications
International Educational and Professional Publisher
Thousand Oaks   London   New Delhi

For information address:

SAGE Publications, Inc.
2455 Teller Road
Thousand Oaks, California 91320
E-mail: order@sagepub.com

SAGE Publications Ltd.
6 Bonhill Street
London EC2A 4PU
United Kingdom

SAGE Publications India Pvt. Ltd.
M-32 Market
Greater Kailash I
New Delhi 110 048 India

Printed in the United States of America

Library of Congress Cataloging-in-Publication Data

Wieland, Sandra.
   Hearing the internal trauma: working with sexually abused
children and adolescents / author, Sandra Wieland.
      p.   cm. — (Interpersonal violence; v. 17)
   Includes bibliographical references and index.
   ISBN 0-7619-0365-8 (cloth: acid-free paper). — ISBN
0-7619-0366-6 (pbk.: acid-free paper)
      1. Sexually abused children.   2. Sexually abused teenagers.
I. Title. II. Series.
RJ507.S49W54 1997
618.92′858223—dc20   96-10127

This book is printed on acid-free paper.

97 98 99 00 01 02 10 9 8 7 6 5 4 3 2 1

Acquiring Editor: C. Terry Hendrix
Editorial Assistant: Dale Grenfell
Production Editor: Michèle Lingre
Production Assistant: Sherrise Purdum
Typesetter/Designer: Janelle LeMaster
Indexer: Juniee Oneida
Print Buyer: Anna Chin

◆ ❖ ◆

To all the children and adolescents
and to all those who hear them

◆ ❖ ◆

Contents

Preface

Working in a therapeutic setting with children and adolescents who have been sexually abused is intense, frustrating, draining, rewarding. There is so much that I, as a therapist, would like to do for each child I see, and yet I am limited, always, by the environment—both that of the child and that of the center in which I work, by my understanding of what is happening for the child and within the child, and by the child's own personal moment—whether she is wishing to ignore the abuse and all of the distress resulting from it or wishing to deal with both the abuse and the distress.

This book is part of the process of my trying to understand the child or adolescent's experience, both during the time of the abuse and through the months and years that followed. I realized that I needed to be alert not just to symptomatic behavior but also to the child's internal sense of herself and her world. Reading widely in the literature on childhood sexual abuse, child development, early attachment and deprivation, and trauma widened my grasp of the experience. Watching and listening to children and adolescents describe what it felt like inside them highlighted for me the internalizations that occur with an experience of sexual abuse. Listening to adults who had been sexually abused as children talk about their childhood and adolescence and watching them act out their distress from back then supplied labels for these internalizations.

The Internalization Model described in the book is a theoretical model based on a review of the literature and clinical experience. Therapists and other professionals with whom I have worked have found it helpful for understanding children and adolescents who have been abused emotionally and physically as well as sexually.

As therapists, we need to move beyond theoretical models. We need to learn how the effects of sexual abuse can be shifted: how the abuse can become, for a child, a happening in his life and not a determinant of his life. The second focus of the book is, therefore, therapy.

Developing the ideas and techniques included in psychodynamic trauma-focused therapy has been both challenging and fun. I reviewed traditional play therapy and adolescent therapy approaches drawing from each what I found most appropriate for working with children and adolescents who had been traumatized. Then, working together in sessions with a child or with an adolescent, I tried many different ways of approaching and shifting the abuse-related internalizations. Some had no effect, but bit by bit, certain types of interventions proved more successful. These interventions are presented for you to consider and to try.

Perhaps most challenging to develop was the last chapter, as I talked with my colleagues and with myself as to how we, as therapists, hear ourselves. How we hear ourselves affects the way in which we are able to hear the children, adolescents, and parents with whom we work.

Many people have helped me learn how to hear, how to hear the children and adolescents and how to hear myself—Ann Mully, Juliett Hopkins, Jean Turner, and Marjorie Wieland. Colleagues have discussed ideas, shared cases, and encouraged me to keep writing— Thérèse Laberge, Helen Pigeon, Sandy Ages, Lalita Salins, Bev Cimermanis, and Pauline Barrett. A special thanks to Jon Conte for comments and suggestions and to Ellen Berstein and Janet Adams for reading the manuscript from beginning to end, to Marjorie Elwood for editing and encouraging, and to Chris Whelan for all of the above.

Introduction

Acknowledgment of child sexual abuse has increased dramatically in the last 20 years. During this time, disclosures have increased, social agencies and legal systems have shifted their policies and increased their involvement with children and adolescents who have been sexually abused, and special treatment programs have been established.

The literature on adults sexually abused as children has expanded. Books and articles on research, treatment, and personal experience continue to be published at a rapid pace. While the research has tabulated observable effects from early abuse, personal accounts have spoken of a changed internal experiencing of self and others. Literature on treatment for adults who were sexually abused as children has reflected both these areas: internalized shifts and observable behaviors. As knowledge increases, adults find themselves in a stronger position for seeking therapy and for impressing on therapists the importance of listening to the internal experience of abuse.

The literature on children and adolescents who have been abused has not been as extensive. Indeed, it is sadly lacking in some areas.

Children and adolescents have far fewer resources for becoming aware of and expressing what is happening inside themselves. They cannot take themselves to therapy and, for the most part, do not have the skills, once there, to say, "Listen to me and how I, inside myself, experience myself and my world."

This book seeks to do what the child or adolescent cannot do. It presents a conceptual model of the internalizations—the sense of self and world internalized from external events—that occur for a child or adolescent when he or she is sexually abused. The Internalization Model, presented in this book, traces these shifts from the outside event (particular components of the sexual abuse experience) to the internalized effects (abuse-related sense of self and world) to the child or adolescent's behavior (the observable symptoms of sexual abuse). The model also separates out the effects common to all sexual abuse experiences, those that occur to children or adolescents who have been abused by someone close to them, and those that occur when the abuse is extreme. Research findings on child development, early attachment, sexual abuse, and trauma as well as extensive clinical experience guided the development of the model.

The Internalization Model invites clinicians to look at the effects of abuse from a different perspective. Rather than centering on behavioral symptoms, this model highlights the effect of abuse on a child or adolescent's internal model of self and of the world. It is the child's internalizations arising from the abuse, not the symptomatic behaviors, that need to be addressed and changed if the abuse is to be come something that has happened to a child rather than a determinant that shapes the child's life. As abuse-related internalizations shift, symptomatic behavior decreases.

The Internalization Model is designed not only as a conceptual model but also as a therapeutic tool: a framework a therapist can use as she seeks to understand a child's play or an adolescent's conversation. In Chapters 2 and 3, the Internalization Model is used as a guideline for recognizing and understanding what the child or adolescent is "saying." In Chapter 4, it is used as a framework for recognizing the work that needs to be done with a nonperpetrating parent.

The second focus of the book is psychodynamic trauma-focused therapy. I briefly review psychoanalytic, behavioral, and cognitive therapies, both as they apply to children and as they apply to adolescents. I identify the elements of each that are important for working through trauma (in particular, the trauma of sexual abuse) and draw from each of these therapeutic traditions to develop a psychodynamic trauma-focused therapy.

Psychodynamic trauma-focused therapy, as it applies to children, adolescents, and nonperpetrating parents, is described in Chapters 2, 3, and 4. Interventions are described that enable a child, adolescent, and nonperpetrating parent to reach a level of understanding such that the abuse is no longer overwhelming and the experience can be accurately incorporated into the individual's view of self and world. Chapter 4 also presents a process whereby a perpetrating parent can identify and assume responsibility for the abuse-related messages, covert as well as overt, given to the child. Both dyad and family therapy are discussed.

Little research has been completed and even less reported in the literature regarding what therapeutic approaches and techniques work most successfully with children and adolescents. Psychodynamic trauma-focused therapy is presented as an approach observed clinically by therapists, parents, and by the children and adolescents themselves to provide relief from the trauma of sexual abuse. Children relax and begin to engage in normal age-appropriate play and social interactions. Adolescents start to feel better and more sure of themselves; they are able to respect and care for themselves and are able to form more positive relationships. Nonperpetrating parents become more aware of their child and establish or reestablish positive interaction with the child. Perpetrating parents develop behavioral patterns that are nonabusive emotionally as well as sexually.

The last chapter looks at the therapist's own experience within the therapy session. Personal background, professional training, and ongoing stresses affect our abilities to hear and understand what a child or adolescent is presenting to us. The importance of our working through the internalizations each of us formed during our childhoods and our recognizing when personal experience and attitudes intrude into our interaction with a child or adolescent is discussed. The experience within the session is described.

As a therapist works together with a child or adolescent who has been sexually abused, the therapist incorporates numerous techniques and addresses specific issues. It has not been possible, because of space limitations in the present book, to describe in detail several of these techniques and issues. A companion volume, *Addressing the Internal Trauma: Specific Techniques and Issues in Abuse-Focused Therapy*, is planned for publication next year by Sage Publications. The use of imaging, genograms, time lines, and techniques addressing dissociation will be discussed in more detail in that book. Issues related to assessment, sexuality, and resistance are discussed and interventions described.

Whereas the discussion within the present book focuses on the working through of the effect of sexual abuse on a child's concept of self and his world, this does not imply that therapy should be limited to these issues. Trauma-focused therapy must always be combined with sensitivity to and discussion around the other deprivations and anxieties in a child's life. Family issues relating to attachment and communication need to be considered. The physiological effects of hyperalertness (van der Kolk, 1987), dissociation (Perry, Pollard, Blackley, Baker, & Vigilante, 1995), and dysregulation (Friedrich, 1995) must be considered and addressed as well. No matter what area of therapeutic focus a therapist has, being alert to and addressing the child's abuse-related internalizations assists the child in working through his abuse.

The reader will note that the terms *victim, survivor, disorder,* and *sexually abused children* are not used in this book. I feel that it is essential that children and adolescents who have been sexually abused be recognized as *children and adolescents*. They are children and adolescents who have had something happen to them that never should have happened; they do not have something wrong with them. There are feelings and confusions to work out, there are coping mechanisms to recognize and change, there are internalizations to be shifted, but they themselves are okay. They do not have a disorder; they are displaying normal reactions to abnormal and abusive events.

Although more girls than boys experience sexual abuse, and a higher percentage of the girls who have been abused find their way to therapy than do the boys, it is important that sexual abuse and therapy addressing sexual abuse be thought about with both genders in mind. For this reason, both female and male pronouns are used in the following discussion. The gender pronouns are consistent within a section but are applied on an alternating basis between sections. Pronouns are altered in some paragraphs to agree with the example presented or to distinguish the child from the parent.

Case examples are used throughout the book to illustrate (a) the manner in which children and adolescents present their experiences and their internalizations within a session and (b) the manner in which a therapist can think through what is happening and then formulate a therapeutic response. Each example is drawn from an actual occurrence in therapy. All names are changed and, in some cases, the age or scenario has been changed slightly to provide complete confidentiality.

Hearing the Internal Trauma provides a theoretical model of the effect of sexual abuse on a child's or adolescent's internal sense of self and the world. The Internalization Model is then used clinically to provide a framework for understanding and working with a child or an adolescent within a therapeutic session. A therapeutic approach—psychodynamic trauma-focused therapy—is described and illustrated.

Research needs to clarify and to measure abuse-related internalizations and to examine the outcome of therapy using the psychodynamic trauma-focused approach. Until this research is completed, the validity of this approach will need to be considered as tentative. But even as we wait for this to be done, the therapeutic formulations, the clinical approach, and the techniques described in this book can provide, for therapists and other professionals, ideas and techniques as they work with children, adolescents, and their parents.

I invite the reader, whether beginning a new area of study or well versed in the area, to enter, together with me, into an enquiry into the child or adolescent's experience. We shall be exploring the internal processing of that experience and then searching for ways to help the child reprocess the experience.

1

The Need for a Framework: The Internalization Model

Children and adolescents who have been sexually abused have been coming to therapy for decades. It is, however, only during the last two decades, and more particularly within the last 5 years, that the abuse has been part of the known history of the child coming to therapy. Therapists now have the opportunity to address directly this trauma and the effects of the trauma on the child and the child's family. Despite this opportunity, many children who have been sexually abused and who are in therapy are not receiving the help they need in dealing with the abuse trauma.

Children who have been abused are experts at hiding their experiences and pain inside, at disconnecting themselves from what has happened to them. As a result, children often do not play or talk

AUTHOR'S NOTE: To simplify the discussion, the term *children* will be used to refer to both children and adolescents. When the discussion pertains only to adolescents, the term *adolescents* will be used. When the discussion pertains only to children, the specific age group will be designated (e.g., preschool children, school-age children).

1

about these issues in such a manner that therapists can understand easily what is being experienced. Therapists too quickly fall back on the comment, "She isn't ready to talk about it," rather than wondering if they, the therapists, are the ones who are not ready to hear what the child is saying. Therapists need to have a good understanding of the child's experience—not only the sexual touching or distorted family functioning that occurred within the child's objective reality but also the messages that are internalized within the child's inner reality.

Whether one uses the language of psychoanalytic, learning, or cognitive theory, a similar process occurs as a child interacts with her environment. The event—in this case, an incident that has inappropriate sexual and interpersonal content for a child—occurs with specific characteristics: type of touching, relationship with person who touches, emotional atmosphere, physical sensation. This event occurs for a child who has specific personal characteristics: age and developmental level, temperament, concept of self and world, pattern of family functioning, social-cultural context. As the event is integrated by the child, the child's learned responding (Bandura, 1977), the child's personal schemata (Petti, 1991), and the child's internal object world (Klein, 1965) shift. These shifts both reflect and affect the child's inner reality. It is from this inner reality that has been affected by the sexual abuse that the child continues to interact with the world. It is this reality that needs to be addressed if the child is to be able to develop and experience new situations not distorted by the abuse experience. The therapist needs to be aware of this personal inner reality to hear the child's trauma.

A review of the literature on childhood sexual abuse indicates that considerable attention has been given to recognizing the symptoms of sexual abuse (Finkel, 1987; Friedrich, 1990; Lusk & Waterman, 1986; Sgroi, Porter, & Blick, 1982), to identifying and validating the occurrence of abuse (deYoung, 1986; Yuille, 1988), and to specifying the short-term and long-term effects of abuse on children (see reviews by Beitchman, Zucker, Hood, daCosta, & Akman, 1991; Beitchman et al., 1992). Little attention has been given to the child's experiencing of the abuse and processing of this experience. The occurrence of an event and the symptoms or effects resulting from an event are observable and quantifiable. The child's experience of

the event and processing of this experience, being internal processes, do not lend themselves to direct research studies. These
processes do, however, need to be understood within a conceptual
framework and need to be noticed and responded to within the
therapy session if therapists are to be effective when working with
children who have been sexually abused. Friedrich (1990) has
pointed out that "without a model, our understanding of sexual
abuse remains superficial and intervention suffers" (p. 2). If a model
is to assist the therapist as well as the researcher, it needs to consider
not only the initial events and subsequent behaviors but also the
child's internal processes.

The present chapter briefly reviews models that have been developed to explain the dynamics that occur for a child who has been
sexually abused. Although these models have been important in
furthering understanding of abuse, a more complete model of the
child's internal processing of the abuse is needed for the therapist
to have a framework as she works together with a child. An alternative model, the *Internalization Model*, is then presented.

The subsequent chapters apply the Internalization Model to therapeutic work with children, adolescents, and families. In Chapter 5,
the therapist's experience in therapy is discussed.

❑ Models: Processing the Abuse Experience

Several models have been developed over the last decade that assist the therapist in understanding the dynamics and effects of sexual abuse. The traumagenic factor model developed by Finkelhor
and Browne (1985) identified four characteristics of the abuse experience: (a) betrayal (the failure of caretaking and the demand for
secrecy), (b) stigmatization (the shame and guilt created by the
meaning given to the abuse by the child and by other people),
(c) traumatic sexualization (the arousal and confusion elicited by
stimulation beyond the physical and emotional level of the child),
and (d) powerlessness (the experience of not being able to control
what is happening to oneself). These factors were described as al-
tering "children's cognitive and emotional orientation to the world

and creat[ing] trauma by distorting children's self-concept, world view and affective capacities" (Finkelhor & Browne, 1985, p. 531).

Although this model highlights numerous aspects of the abuse experience and the self-perceptions arising from the experience, it does not address the process going on inside the child as he moves from the initial experience of abuse to the changed perception of self. When therapists use this model as a basis for therapeutic intervention, they may miss the child's processing of the abuse experience. If this is missed and therefore not addressed, therapy is all too likely to remain superficial.

Hartman and Burgess (1988, 1993) proposed a model of trauma reflecting neurological functioning, information processing theory, and stress response theory that is helpful in understanding the child's responding to sexual abuse. This model, referred to as the *information processing model* of trauma, highlights the processing that a child does at the sensory, perceptual, and cognitive levels. The initial or pretrauma phase includes the child's background at the time the abuse occurred: age, developmental level, family structure, sociocultural factors, prior traumas. The second or trauma encapsulation phase includes (a) input—the experience itself, (b) throughput—the emergence of coping and defense mechanisms, and (c) output—the sensory, perceptual, and cognitive memory base that leads to future behavior. The third or disclosure phase includes concealment or disclosure, whichever has happened. The fourth or posttrauma phase includes the child's behavioral response. Emphasis is placed on the disruption that occurs within the child when the incoming sensations, perceptions, and cognitions do not match the child's understanding of the world and on the manner in which the child accommodates to this mismatch: for example, denial or dissociation.

Whereas this model helps the therapist think about the child and the effect of the abuse on later functioning, it does not provide a framework for understanding the child's behavior in the therapy session and the linkage between that behavior and the internal sense of self and the world resulting from the abuse.

The posttraumatic stress disorder (PTSD) (American Psychiatric Association [APA], 1994) has also been used as a formulation for viewing the effect of childhood sexual abuse (Herman, 1992; McLeer, Deblinger, Atkins, Foa, & Ralphe, 1988; Terr, 1991). Terr (1988, 1991), in her work with children, and Herman (1992), in her work with adults, have distinguished between Type I PTSD, which occurs following a single traumatic event, and Type II PTSD, which occurs following long-term experiences. The reactions following a single traumatic event cause the classic trauma responses: (a) hyperalertness reflected in sleep and concentration disturbances, pervasive guilt, or intensification of symptoms when a similar situation occurs; (b) a reexperiencing of the trauma through intrusive thoughts, dreams, or feelings; and (c) a numbing or withdrawal from the world (APA, 1994). Reactions following prolonged and repeated trauma include denial and emotional numbing, self-hypnosis and dissociation, and alternations between extreme passivity and outbursts of rage (Terr, 1991). Although PTSD is helpful in describing symptoms, it does not address the child's internal experience that maintains this state of being overwhelmed. As a result, it is insufficient for the therapist in a therapy session with a child.

The coping model developed by Friedrich (1990) highlights the interrelationship between the initial social setting (risk factors, preconditions of abuse, family variables), the characteristics of the abuse (relationship of the abuser, frequency, and intensity), the responses of the child and the parent or parents (initial coping, ongoing coping), and subsequent reactions. This model is helpful in understanding what has happened and in explaining to parents the dynamics occurring for the child and for the parent(s). It does not, however, provide a framework that can assist therapists, as they work with a child, to recognize the child's internal experience.

In his recently presented *integrated treatment model*, Friedrich (1995) addressed the need for a closer look at what is going on within the child. Within this model, attention is given to developmental interactive processes (attachment); neurophysiological, behavioral, and cognitive reactivity to trauma (dysregulation); and the development of sense of self and other as a result of sexual abuse (self-theory). A closer look is given to the child's internal experience and the need for addressing and remediating this experience. Although this model can be extremely helpful to the therapist, it does not provide a framework for understanding the internalizations that arise out of the abuse and for recognizing these internalizations within the child's behavior during therapy.

This internal experience needs to be understood in further detail if a therapist is to be able to recognize and to address the child's trauma. Only then, when the trauma as experienced, understood, and integrated within the child is addressed can the sexual abuse be experienced without trauma and be assimilated into a healthy world schema.

For a model to assist the therapist as she works within the therapy session, it needs to include the child's experience and the processing of that experience. It needs to include the expression of the processing, that is, the resulting behavior. A model will be presented that was developed to explain the child's experience as the abuse occurs, the way in which the child internalizes that experience, and the behaviors that result from what has been internalized. This model has been found by therapists to be helpful when working within a therapy session with a child or adolescent who has been sexually abused.

❏ Internalization Model

As a child experiences her world, the child takes in, both consciously and unconsciously, information with regard to herself and her relationship with the world. Defined in neurological terms, a child's sensations and perceptions become memory, either explicit or implicit. A considerable amount of memory, particularly for young children, is implicit: that is, not constructed with words (van der Kolk, 1994). As a child becomes older and facts and events are recorded in explicit memory, emotional associations, sensorimotor responses, and events occurring under conditions of extreme stress continue to be established within implicit memory (van der Kolk, 1994). New experiences are processed together with previously acquired information, emotional associations, and responses. The processing varies depending on the developmental level, both of cognitive functioning and emotional defending, of the child. The child develops what has been variously described as a cognitive map (van der Kolk, 1994), mental schemata (Piaget, 1963), or an internal working model (Bowlby, 1971, 1973).

Defined in psychoanalytic terms, "the outer world, its impact, the situations the infant lives through, and the [persons] he encounters, are not only experienced as external but are taken into the self and become part of his inner life" (Klein, 1975a, p. 250). Melanie Klein observed that once a situation is internalized, it may become "inaccessible to the child's accurate observation and judgment" (1975b, p. 346) but continues to exist and influence the way the child sees himself and his world even when others tell him that he or the world is not that way. Bowlby (1971, 1973), in his studies of children and attachment, extended Klein's description of the child's internal model. As a child internalizes experiences of self and of self in relation to others, the child creates an internal working model that in turn forms a base from which the child interacts with the outer world.

The taking in and processing of the meaning of outer experiences as they relate to the self I have called *internalizations*.[1] These internalizations become part of the base from which a child responds to or interacts with the outer world.

Just as a child's internalizations are expressed in her day-to-day behavior so also are they expressed as the child plays and as the adolescent talks during therapy. A model focusing on the child's internalizations enables the therapist to understand more clearly, and therefore to address more directly, the child's inner experience. As the abuse-related internalizations are addressed, the negative internal experience of self and world resulting from the abuse shifts and, as a result, the child's future behavior and experience. The model being presented was developed from several sources: assessment and therapeutic work with children and adolescents who had been sexually abused; work with adults as they reprocess childhood sexual abuse experiences; and a review of theoretical, clinical, and research literature on childhood sexual abuse.

The Internalization Model describes (a) the child's abuse experience, (b) the child's internalizations resulting from this experience, and (c) the child's behaviors arising from the internalizations (see Figure 1.1). The experience of an abuse event, as with all events, is a subjective experience. The experiencing of the event is shaped by the child's developmental level, the child's temperament, and the child's present understanding of herself and of the world—that is,

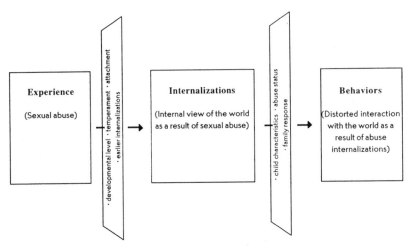

Figure 1.1. Sexual Abuse—The Child's Internalizations

internalizations from earlier experiences. This understanding includes both positive and negative images of self, of parents, of self in relation to parents (attachment), of the world, and of self in relation to the world. For the child whose knowledge of self, parent, and world is primarily negative, the negative experiencing of the abuse is heightened. For the child whose understanding of self, parent, and world is primarily positive, the negative experiencing of the abuse is moderated.

From the experiencing of the abuse, the child's internal sense of self and of the world is altered. These internalizations, the abuse-altered view of self and world, in turn affect the way the child responds to her environment—that is, the way she behaves. The effects of the abuse internalizations on the child's behavior is, in some cases, moderated or, in other cases, intensified by the child's developmental level, the child's other experiences, and the child's temperament. The level of safety now existing in the child's world (is the abuse secret or known) and the types of response from important people in the child's world also affect the impact of the internalizations on the child's behavior.

Discussion will initially center on the abuse experience and the child's internalizations from that experience. Patterns of behavior affected by these internalizations will be discussed in a later section of the chapter. As with all models, the Internalization Model is a simplification of a complex interaction of factors. This simplification is necessary if a model is to provide a framework helpful for a therapist when in a therapy session with a child. Figure 1.2 presents a summary of the model being presented.

The following discussion is organized around Figure 1.2. Each section is briefly described. The discussion of each characteristic of the sexual abuse experience, the resulting internalization, and the behavior arising from an internalization is headed by the appropriate boxed portion of Figure 1.2.

EXPERIENCE → INTERNALIZATION

The effect of an abuse experience differs depending on (a) the relationship of the perpetrator to the child (Adams-Tucker, 1982; Finkelhor, 1979; Hindman, 1989; Russell, 1986)—was the perpetrator someone whose relationship with the child was, and perhaps still is, important for the child—and (b) the severity of the abuse (Burgess, Hartman, McCausland, & Powers, 1984; Elwell & Ephross, 1987; Friedrich, Urquiza, & Beilke, 1986; Johnston, 1979; Sirles, Smith, & Kusama, 1989). To differentiate among the characteristics common to all abuse experiences, characteristics that occur when the perpetrator is in a close relationship with the child, and characteristics that occur when the abuse is severe, the discussion of the abuse experience is divided into three parts: all sexual abuse experiences, sexual abuse experiences perpetrated by someone in a close or trust position, and sexual abuse experiences in which the abuse is extreme.

All Sexual Abuse Experiences

An encounter between an adult or a child who is older[2] or more powerful and a child, carried out for reasons of sexual stimulation, is sexual abuse. This may include touching either of the child or by the child or observation of the child or by the child. For the child, a sexually abusive experience includes four basic characteristics: (a) intrusion: the child's physical self and normal development, both

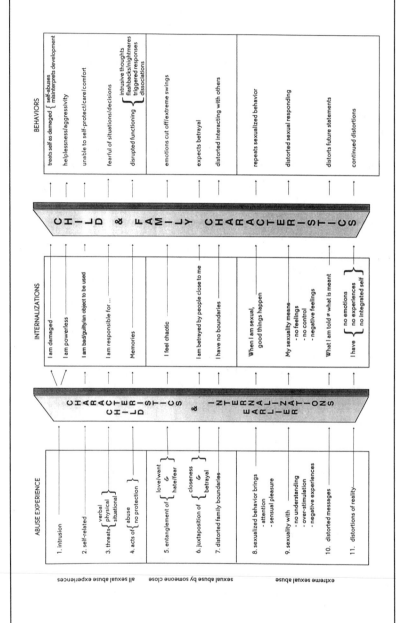

Figure 1.2. Internalization Model: What a Child Experiences When Sexually Abused

sexual and personal, is intruded on; (b) self-related: the encounter occurs to the child herself; (c) threat: the child is placed in an intimidating relationship with the abuser; and (d) memory encoding: memory both of the abuse and of having no protection is encoded.

intrusion As an infant and then the child matures, the self develops. The infant moves from initial awareness of internal sensations to awareness of external perceptions; the toddler moves from awareness of self to awareness of important others; and the child moves from awareness of her own activities to awareness of the world's activities. In all of this, the body serves as an important boundary, a distinction between the self and others.

Yet for the infant to grow and for the child to develop in a healthy way, the boundary of the body must, of necessity, be crossed. Touching and holding are essential for both physical caretaking and emotional nurturing (Harlow & Zimmerman, 1959). Touching that is neither caretaking nor nurturing, that does not consider the child's needs, is intrusive to the child. And intrusive touching is disruptive for the child.

Touching can be described as having both emotional and physical attributes (see Figure 1.3). Each attribute in turn can be viewed as a continuum from positive to negative. The quality of any particular touch depends on where it occurs along a composite of attribute continua.

The first attribute labeled in the figure is *need being met*. In some touching, the child's needs are primary—the older person, usually an adult, is doing the touching to meet the needs of the child (e.g., soothing, feeding, teaching). In other touching, the adult's needs are primary (e.g., picking up a sleeping or happily playing child who is not in need of attention).[3] In many instances, both the needs of the adult and of the child are being met (e.g., cuddling a smiling infant, restraining an out-of-control toddler). Whose needs are considered most important determines placement on the continuum.

Sexual touching by someone older than the child overlooks the child's need for gradual and age-appropriate increase in self-awareness of sexuality. The child's need is disregarded, whereas the

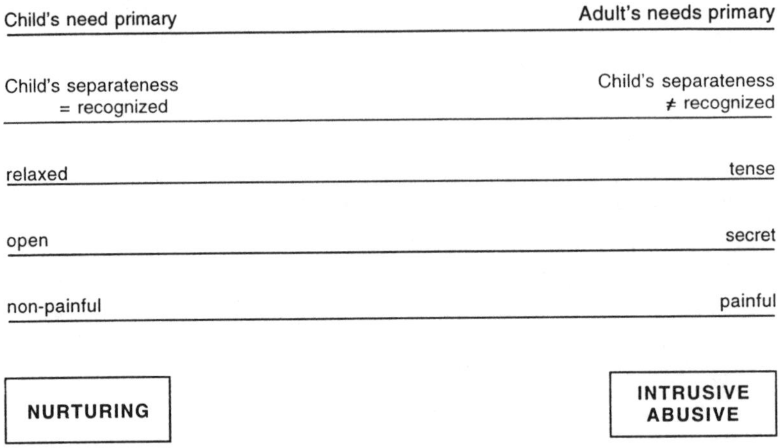

Child's need primary	Adult's needs primary
Child's separateness = recognized	Child's separateness ≠ recognized
relaxed	tense
open	secret
non-painful	painful

NURTURING	INTRUSIVE ABUSIVE

Figure 1.3. Touching Continuum

adult's need for pleasure or domination is met. The touching is intrusive.

A second attribute of touching is the *degree of separateness* recognized between the child and the parent. The parent who sees his child as simply an extension of himself, to be used as he chooses, recognizes no separateness between himself and his child. This parent is likely to involve the child in his own fantasies. Situations of sadistic or ritual abuse are clear examples of a child being forced to participate in the acting out of an adult's fantasy. The abuser who asks a child if she wants to be touched or if she enjoys being touched in a certain way is trying to create an illusion of separateness to justify his behavior to himself. A child or adolescent does not have adequate personal or sexual knowledge to be able to give consent, and thus, there is no participation of a child as a separate person within a sexual abuse activity. When the child is treated as a separate person within an activity, touching is nurturing. When the child is used as an extension of the adult's self, touching is intrusive.

A third attribute of touching is *tension,* with the continuum extending from high tension (relaxed) to no tension. Tension occurs within the context of sexual abuse for several reasons. Tension is a part of sexual arousal. It would be witnessed by the child as the adult becomes aroused and, if arousal of the child occurs, would be experienced by the child. Children often report that the change in the abuser's expression during the sexual act is one of the scariest parts of the abuse experience. Tension would also occur for the child who experiences pain or some other nonpleasurable arousal.

Tension also exists as a result of the perpetrator's and, once the child becomes aware of social mores, the child's awareness that the activity being carried on is taboo. Even the abuser who justifies his actions through cognitive distortion expends considerable effort to keep the activity secret. Distress over what is happening and the need to keep things secret creates tension. When tension does not occur, touching can be nurturing. When tension is high, touching becomes intrusive.

The *openness* with which touching occurs forms a fourth attribute relevant to sexual abuse. Touching that an adult feels comfortable performing in any setting is likely to be nurturing. Touching that is hidden is likely to be intrusive.

A final attribute of touching that is relevant to sexual abuse is the *physical pain* that may be experienced with the touch. Here, the continuum ranges from nonpainful to extremely painful. Painful touch clearly is not limited to abuse situations but also occurs in situations such as accidents or medical procedures. Research on children and their reactions to hospital procedures has shown that the pain experienced can be decreased if the child knows ahead what will occur and thus has a sense of control over what is happening (Visintainer & Wolfer, 1975). Sexual abuse, with its inherent power imbalance, allows for limited predictability and no real control by the child. Thus, the inflicted pain cannot be moderated by healthy coping; intrusion increases.

Touching that occurs along the left end of each continuum shown in the figure is nurturing. Touching that occurs toward the opposite end of each continuum is intrusive. Numerous acts of touching, such as spanking, may be located toward the right on one or more attributes but toward the left on other attribute continua. These acts are higher in intrusiveness than those located to the left on all continua. Sexually abusive acts are located at the right side of the continuum for at least four attributes (needs being met, separateness, tension, openness) and often on all five (the fifth being pain). Sexual abuse is intrusive not just of the child's body but of the child's self.

As the boundary between the self and others is crossed, the infant or young child may have no cognitive recognition of the intrusion. She will, however, experience both emotional (needs not met, lack of separation, tension) and physical (tension, pain) intrusion. The older child who has become aware of the mores of society will be cognizant of the intrusion. This sense of intrusion has been described by children, adolescents, and adults as feeling internally altered or damaged in some way.

> Susie (a 9-year-old fondled by her grandfather) comments, "I know it wasn't my fault, I know I'm not bad and I know my parents aren't angry at me but I just feel this yuck inside, as if something isn't right inside."

This sense that something is wrong inside is internalized from the experience of intrusion. The feeling may range from "yucky" to damaged (Porter, Blick, & Sgroi, 1982), depending on the nature of the abuse (the relationship of the abuser, the extent of the abuse, the frequency and duration of the abuse, the presence or lack of violence (Beitchman et al., 1991) and the child's characteristics (developmental level, temperament, sense of self and of the world). Finkelhor and Browne (1985) refer to this feeling as *stigmatization*, and Friedrich (1995) refers to it as *differentness*. Children who have been sexually abused report themselves as feeling different from peers (Mannarino, Cohen, & Berman, 1994). Although the intensity may vary, the sense that *I am altered . . . I am damaged* is internalized with each experience of sexual abuse.

A second internalization from the intrusion is a sense of powerlessness, of not being able to control what is being done to oneself. The intensity of this internalization varies depending on other experiences, both abusive and nonabusive, that the child has had and continues to have. Particularly relevant are the experiences surrounding disclosure. If members of the child's family or other important people believe the disclosure and are able to be available to and supportive of the child, prepare the child for the investigation and legal procedures, and encourage the child to work through her feelings and reactions from the experience, the child gains a sense of control over these elements of her life.[4] If, however, the disclosure is not believed or the parent is so distressed she cannot be support-ive, if an explanation of what is happening and emotional support is not available as the child goes through the investigation and court procedures, the child's world once again is out of control.

A feeling of powerlessness may also occur if the child experiences a physical response to the abuse. The child who is emotionally attached to the abuser and, thus, feels a pull toward the abuser even when wanting to avoid the abuser, may also feel powerless in relation to the abuse and the abuser.

The child experiences intrusion, both physical and emotional, from sexual abuse. Depending on the child's resources and supports, a sense of damage—sometimes less: *I am altered* and sometimes more: *I am damaged*—and a sense of powerlessness—sometimes less: *I am powerless in some situations* and sometimes more: *I am powerless in all situations*—are internalized.

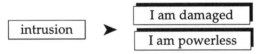

self-related Given the secrecy that surrounds sexual abuse, both before and after disclosure, children are usually unaware of the extent to which abuse occurs to others. The child is aware only that this is happening to him and not to someone else. The question arises for each child, "Why me?" and this leads to "because of me."

> Bob (a 17-year-old abused from ages 8 to 10 years by the Cub Scout leader) says, "Why me? It must have been something about me, or the cub leader would never have centered on me. There were all the other boys, and they didn't get abused."

A child's sense of self is built up from his experiences (Harter, 1983). And as the abuse is experienced or judged as bad, the child judges and subsequently experiences himself as bad, as an object to be used. This is internalized, creating an inner sense of being looked down on or diminished, a sense of shame (Fossum & Mason, 1986; Friedrich, 1995). The child, in many cases, also blames himself for the abuse. This is internalized as having broken some code, as guilt (Fossum & Mason, 1986).

Self-blame occurs in young children as a result of their cognitive processing of the world. The young child has not yet developed the cognitive flexibility to be able to view situations from a perspective outside herself (Piaget & Inhelder, 1956). As a result, the preschool child sees her own activity as the center of what occurs (egocentric thinking). Within an abuse situation, the young child experiences herself as being at the center of what is happening and, therefore, as the cause of the abuse.

As children become older, part of normal sexual development is a curiosity about sex (Rutter, 1971). Thus, when a child 8 to 12 years old is sexually abused, the child is likely to experience curiosity about what is happening. The child, not aware of child development and developmentally normal sexual curiosity but increasingly aware of social mores, blames herself for being curious. She may think her curiosity has caused the abuse and, therefore, may experience a high sense of self-blame and guilt.

As the child moves into adolescence, she seeks to create some order in, or to have some control over, her world (Offer & Boxer, 1991). Particularly in cases of long-term abuse, an adolescent may seek to reverse roles with the abuser (deciding, for example, when and how the abuse is going to happen) to feel some control. The adolescent may "initiate" abuse to secure her freedom of movement at other times or to gain money and favors that lessen the distress she feels. Although an effort to gain control of one's world is a normal adolescent response, the adolescent is likely to blame herself for this behavior.

Self-blaming in children also arises from the abuser's messages: "You're so wonderful"; "I'm doing this because you are you"; "You're making me do this"; "You want this"; "You're a bad child, that is why this is happening to you." Along with the abuser's messages, there are often comments made by other important people in the child's world, such as: "Don't sit like that, it's not proper. You'll get yourself in trouble if you sit like that," or "You're too young. We can't take you with us. You have to stay with the babysitter." The child then believes that the abuse is her fault because she sat in a particular way or because she was so young that she had to stay with the babysitter.

Self-blame is intensified further by the disturbance that occurs to the family following disclosure. Even with extrafamilial abuse, the normal functioning of a family is disrupted, and parents and siblings become anxious and experience stress. The child assumes blame for this distress: "People would not be upset if it were not for me."

The child who experiences physical pleasure during the abuse often blames herself for the abuse. This is particularly relevant for boys in that when the penis becomes erect as a result of being touched, a boy is likely to interpret his physiological response as an indication that he wants the abuse. He then blames himself for the abuse.

The child who sought attention also self-blames, the role of the abuser as the one who turned attention into abuse being overlooked. Even when the role of the abuser is recognized, the child has the experience of being used by another person.

With the increased attention in the media and school prevention programs to discussion of sexual abuse as the fault of the abuser, children are increasingly more able to place the blame with the abuser. The experience of being used by someone else, the sense of internal shame, however, remains.

This view of self as guilty or as used by someone else is internalized: "*I am bad, I am guilty, I am an object to be used.*" The intensity of the internalization varies depending on the child's other experiences and on the reactions of the important adults in the child's life.

self-related ➤ I am bad/guilty/ an object to be used

threats   All situations of sexual abuse involve threats. The obvious threats are verbal ("If you tell, your mother will think you are bad"; "If you tell, your family will fall apart"; "If you tell, I will go to jail"; "If you tell, I will kill you") or physical (the use of weapons or the abuser's size and strength). Threats may also be situational: a mother saying, "Daddy will be home soon; let's make him happy, we couldn't manage without him," or the child being laughed at by others in the family and, therefore, feeling that she would not be believed were she to disclose. For a child whose relationship with an important adult includes sexual touching, telling involves a threat of abandonment for the child and the family.

These threats give a child inordinate power because the child is in the position of controlling what will happen to someone older or to the family. The fact that this power is contradicted by the powerlessness that the child experiences creates a double bind. A sense of responsibility for what happens to the family is internalized by the child at the same time as the child feeling no control over what is happening to herself. When things do happen to people in the family, the child often feels she has not hidden the abuse well enough and, therefore, is responsible for the family's negative events.

Following a disclosure, the disruption in the family frequently parallels the threat that was made, and the child's internalization that she is responsible for what happens to others is reinforced.

> Jane (an 11-year-old sexually abused by her father who threatened that if she told, he would go to jail) reports that the worst part of the abuse was seeing the police take her father away in handcuffs. She feels she has caused this to happen.

> Sharon (a 15-year-old sexually abused at age 9 by a family friend living next door who threatened that if she told, her family would fall apart) completes the house in the House, Tree, Person Projective Test with shaky, broken lines explaining, "It is falling apart." She describes herself as having to try to keep everyone in her family happy and together but as having failed.

The child is unable to recognize these occurrences as a result of the perpetrator's, the system's, or the family's decisions. She holds herself responsible for the distress that occurs.

In other situations, the threat may not become a reality, but the internalized fear and sense of negative power remain. These internalizations affect the child's behavior.

> Tina (a 5-year-old sexually abused by the husband of a baby-sitter who threatened that if Tina told he would hurt her mother) experiences nightmares about her mother being hurt and refuses to leave her mother for fear she will be hurt.

Linda (a 14-year-old sexually abused by her mother's common-law partner who threatened that if she told he would send someone to get her) reports that she feels as if she is being followed whenever she is not surrounded by her friends. She reports that she constantly has to look over her shoulder to be sure no one is there.

The internalization, *"I am responsible for what happens,"* remains with varying intensity within the child.

| threats | ➤ | I am responsible for . . . |

When a child is abused, she experiences two situations: abuse and lack of protection. Whereas the former is recognized by society in the label given to the experience, "sexual abuse," the latter is all too often forgotten. For the child herself, not being protected is keenly felt.

Sally (a 17-year-old sexually abused by her father while living with her father and her step-mother) returns over and over again to questions about her mother, "If she hadn't left . . . ," "If she had taken me with her . . ."

The mother, as the early nurturer and initial attachment figure for the child, is idealized by the child. She is perceived by the child as being able to care for him and being able to keep him safe. When that safety is lost, the child feels that the mother has failed him. The child experiences an act of no protection. This act, together with the act of abuse, is encoded in the child's memory.

Memory encoding occurs, at times, through declarative or explicit memory and, at times, through nondeclarative or implicit-emotional memory (LeDoux, 1994; Tobias, Kihlstrom, & Schacter, 1992; van der Kolk, 1994). Included within nondeclarative memory are skills and habits, emotional associations, and conditioned sensorimotor responses.

Early infant research indicates that memory for sensations begins within the first few weeks of life (Mandler, 1983; Younger & Cohen, 1986). Owing to late myelination of the hippocampus (age 3 or 4 years), the area of the brain in which the verbal component of memories is encoded, early memories, nonabusive and abusive, are encoded through the basal area of the brain in sensorimotor modalities (van der Kolk, 1994). Later in life, hippocampal functioning, and therefore formation of verbal memory, may be interrupted because of the inhibitory effect on the hippocampus by high levels of corticosteroids released by the brain in situations of high stress (Nilsson & Archer, 1992; van der Kolk, 1994). Thus, memories of abuse may be declarative or nondeclarative depending on the age and emotional state of the child when abused. If the child is young or highly stressed, the memories of abuse are unlikely to be encoded with a linguistic component. Affect and body sensations are encoded.

Field research (Drell, Siegel, & Gaensbauer, 1993; Terr, 1990, 1994) and clinical observation (Purdy, 1989) has similarly indicated that early traumatic events are remembered even though a child cannot tell about them—a verbal memory is not available. Early memories for which only the affect and sensory components were encoded are likely to be recalled through these same processes. Terr (1990) reports on a 5-year-old child she interviewed after the parents had been informed that the child, between age 15 and 17 months, had been used for child pornography. The child could not "remember" the events but talked about being scared by a "finger part" and pointed to the spot on her body that matched the spot touched by a penis in a photograph. The child expressed a fear of baby-sitters and drew naked people with detailed genitals. There is also clinical evidence of specific early memories coming into a child's awareness as she matures (Drell et al., 1993; Purdy, 1989; Terr, 1990, 1994).

Memories encoded emotionally or verbally may stay active, may be suppressed (not thought about or felt on a regular basis but still available to active recall), repressed (not available to active recall but still part of the core self), or dissociated (not part of or available to the core self). Repression and dissociation are defense mechanisms used when the knowledge of what has happened is too difficult for the individual to tolerate (Herman, 1992; Terr, 1990). The form in which the memory is held—active, suppressed, repressed, dissociated—becomes part of the child's inner reality.

Although the memories may be repressed, the emotions (anger, fear, sadness) often remain, and the child is left with a general negative feeling but no act to which to attach this feeling. At other times, the emotion is repressed but can be triggered when something occurs that is similar to the original event. This similarity may or may not be consciously recognized.

If the memories are dissociated, the knowledge of the event and the emotions around the event are held within separate ego states or separate selves (Herman, 1992; Kluft, 1984a; Putnam, 1989).

> Doris (a 4-year-old abused by her grandfather who had sexually abused, together with physical restraints, his own daughters when they were young) undresses the girl doll, wraps string around and around the doll, hits the doll, and then pushes it into the shower along with the naked grandfather doll. When asked if anything like that had happened to her, Doris looks up in amazement and, with no indication of anxiety, says "no."

Because the memory and the emotions attached to the memory are not part of the child's core internal world, they are not as readily available for modification by future experiences.

Because the memories of lack of protection do not have the intense sensory and emotional characteristics that are attached to abuse memories, they are less likely to be repressed or dissociated. When the memory of the abusive act is repressed, the child is then left with a memory of lack of protection without a knowledge base for this memory. The child may feel hostility toward his mother or may become easily angered with her without understanding why this feeling is happening.

Although memory itself is a physiological process, the pressures on the child and within the child determine the way the memory is held—active, suppressed, repressed, dissociated. *Memories of abuse and lack of protection*, in active, suppressed, repressed, or dissociated form, become part of the child's internalized world.

The discussion to this point has concentrated on the experience at the time of the abuse. There are also powerful emotions that are evoked by the abuse. The emotions of fear, anger, and rage are discussed in the literature (Jones, 1986; Porter et al., 1982; Terr, 1990). Discussed less frequently but consistently reported by children and by adults who were sexually abused as children, is a feeling of confusion (Friedrich, 1995). This confusion existed during the abuse—what is happening, why is it happening?—and exists after the abuse—what was happening, why did it happen? The nature of the abuse (presence of threats, force, or pain), the context in which the abuse happened (game playing, denial of what happened, punishment), and the child's sense of support from her world affect the child's level of fear, anger, and confusion.

A child who has been sexually abused will internalize some level of *"I am damaged"*; *"I am powerless"*; *"I am bad, guilty, an object to be used"*; *"I am responsible for what happens to others"*; *"memories of abuse and lack of protection."* This occurs whether the abuse is intrafamilial or extrafamilial, whether the abuse is one occasion or repeated occasions, whether the abuse is gentle or sadistic. When the abuser is someone who is close to the child or in a relationship of trust with the child, the experience has additional characteristics that lead to further internalizations.

Sexual Abuse Experiences
Perpetrated by Someone
Close or in a Trust Position

When the perpetrator is someone close to the child or in a position of trust with regard to the child, the child's experience, in addition to the four characteristics already discussed (intrusion, self-related, threats, acts of abuse and no protection), includes three further characteristics: (a) loving or wanting to be close to the person and at the same time hating or fearing that person, (b) experiencing trust and betrayal in close juxtaposition, and (c) living with distorted interpersonal boundaries. Each of these characteristics affects the child's internal sense of self and world.

$$\text{entanglement} \left\{ \begin{array}{l} \text{love/want} \\ \& \\ \text{hate/fear} \end{array} \right.$$

When the abuse is by someone important, the love relationship is not broken; the holding environment is broken. The love attachment continues. This is particularly true for children in situations where the abuse may have been the only attention they received. For these children, the dynamics around the abuse—for example, receiving special attentions, influencing family decisions—may even strengthen the love relationship. Abuse may be perpetrated by someone with whom the child does not have a love attachment but who is in a position where a positive relationship is expected—for example, Cub Scout leader, teacher, stepparent, husband of a baby-sitter.

When the abuse with its intrusion and sense of threat occurs, the child, in most situations, experiences fear, hate, or both. These feelings present minimal difficulty for children when there is no attachment to the abuser. The feelings can be experienced and acknowledged. When, however, these feelings occur together with feelings of love and want, as they do when the abuser is someone close, the child is left in emotional confusion. The child feels both love-want and hate-fear toward the same person. The child becomes unsure of what she is feeling and often ends up hating herself for loving the abuser and hating herself for hating the abuser, a total double bind.

Ambivalent feelings[5] are also experienced toward the nonperpetrating parent(s) (Porter et al., 1982). Love from the attachment relationship and rage from not being protected exist together. This is particularly true when the child has told the parent(s) and has not been believed or when, following disclosure, the abuse experience is minimized by the nonperpetrating parent(s).

The stress of conflicting feelings is compounded by dynamics that occur within incestuous families. Attachment in families where maltreatment occurs has been found to be, in a majority of cases, insecure (Friedrich, 1995; Karen, 1994). These families are often socially isolated, and communication inside the family is limited (Alexander, 1985; Trepper & Barrett, 1989). Negative feelings are not to be expressed by women or children, and positive feelings are to be expressed even if they do not exist. The child is left not being able to sort out conflicting emotions and experiences an internal chaos. *"I feel chaotic"* is internalized within the child. As with the other internalizations experienced, the intensity of this feeling of chaos varies depending on the abuse scenario, the family dynamics, and the child's temperament and earlier experiences.

| entanglement | $\left\{\begin{array}{c}\text{love/want}\\ \&\\ \text{hate/fear}\end{array}\right.$ | ➤ | I feel chaotic |

| juxtaposition of | $\left\{\begin{array}{c}\text{closeness}\\ \&\\ \text{betrayal}\end{array}\right.$ |

Sometimes, the closeness between the abuser and the child is verbalized: the abuser saying, "I love you"; "You're the most important person to me." Sometimes, the closeness simply exists as part of the unspoken expectations within family relationships: a parent, grandparent, older sibling is understood as loving the child. Sometimes, the closeness is stated by others: "Go kiss your grandfather, he loves you so much"; "Auntie [the baby-sitter] is such a special person for you."

> Sally (an 18-year-old sexually abused at age 6 years, when her family first immigrated, by the father in the sponsoring family) reports that she would say that she did not want to go on visits to the sponsoring family. Her father would reply, "They have been so good to us. Of course you want to go and it's really important. We owe this to them."

Following the statement of closeness or goodness, abuse, a betrayal of that closeness, occurs. There is a betrayal of both trust and caretaking (Finkelhor & Browne, 1985). When two experiences occur close together, they become linked for the child. The child experiences betrayal or hurt as something that happens when he becomes close to someone or when someone is important to him. The child internalizes betrayal and hurt as a characteristic of people who are close. This is particularly strong when the abuser is the individual who is also the primary attachment figure.

The strength of the internalization, *"I am betrayed by people close to me,"* may be such that it applies to all future relationships or such that it applies only to intimate relationships.

juxtaposition of { closeness & betrayal } ➤ I am betrayed by people close to me

distorted family boundaries   Child sexual abuse within a family or an extended family system indicates that at least one, and often several, of the boundaries within the family are distorted. Healthy boundaries place parents and children in different subsystems, with the parents attending to each other's needs and attending to and caring for the children (Minuchin, 1967). Healthy boundaries permit each individual in the family to have his or her own personal space that other family members respect. At the same time, healthy boundaries encourage the flow of information between family members and between the family and society in general. Incestuous families have been described as being either overly enmeshed or overly structured, as being isolated from the outside world, and as having poor communication skills (Alexander, 1985; Dadds, Smith, Webber, & Robinson, 1991). These situations, situations that may also occur in families where no sexual abuse occurs, affect a child. The child does not have an opportunity to develop personal boundaries, a "sense of self in contradistinction to other" (Briere, 1996, p. 142).

When a parent uses a child as a sexual partner, the parent moves the child out of the child subsystem into the parental subsystem. The child is put in the position of having to care for the needs of adults.

> Terri (a 9-year-old whose father had her masturbate him over a period of several years) reports that her father would ask her if what they were doing made her happy. She would reply that it did not make her happy but that if it made him happy, she would do it. Father continued to abuse her and continued to ask her if she was happy.

In many situations, the child who is abused ends up taking care not only of the perpetrating parent but also of the nonperpetrating parent and the other children (Pelletier & Handy, 1986). "Parentification" of a child can occur with dysfunctional family situations other than those of sexual abuse. Indeed, for many abused children, the role as parent results from a combination of pressures.

When a sibling abuses another sibling, the boundaries of individual private space within the family are similarly distorted. The boundary between the siblings becomes too permeable, whereas the boundary between the abused child and the parent is too opaque. The parent is unable to see the child's distress, both the distress from the abuse and the distress the child is experiencing from not being protected by the parent. Sibling abuse has been found to occur primarily in families that exhibit other inappropriate sexual activities and interpersonal relating (Loredo, 1982; Smith & Israel, 1987). These distorted boundaries lead to situations in which the child either is unable to tell the parent about the abuse in a way that can be heard—that is, understood—or the parent is unable to follow through and protect the child in an appropriate manner. The child is left having to take care of others in the family, not just her sibling but also the parent who cannot respond adequately to the abusive events.

When a child is sexually abused by someone close to her, the child does not have an opportunity to internalize healthy self and generational boundaries. She experiences herself as being without boundaries and as needing to care for those who should be caring for her. What the child internalizes is, "*I have no boundaries.*" This may permeate all future relationships or may be limited to close relationships.

| distorted family boundaries | ➤ | I have no boundaries |

The child who is sexually abused by someone close to him or in a trusted position internalizes not only a sense of damage, of powerlessness, of being bad, of being responsible for others, and memories but also a sense of being crazy, of betrayal occurring with people with whom he is close, and of having no boundaries. One further situation of abuse needs to be considered: abuse that is extreme.

Sexual Abuse Experiences in Which the Abuse Is Extreme

Extreme sexual abuse is difficult to define. What is experienced as extreme by one child, owing to the child's temperament, earlier experiences, and sense of self, may not be experienced as extreme by another child. Within the present discussion, *extreme* is considered any abuse that severely affects the child's sense of sexuality and reality. This generally occurs when either the content (penetration) or the duration (a year or more) of the abuse is extensive.

The extreme sexual abuse experience includes additional characteristics: (a) special attention or sensual pleasure for the child, (b) overstimulation, (c) messages that do not match reality, and (d) coping mechanisms that distort reality. These experiences are internalized along with those already discussed and form a part of the child's sense of self and the world.

sexualized behaviors { attention sensual pleasure } The touching, looking, or talking that occurs during sexual abuse is attention. Indeed, for some children, this may be the only special attention they receive. There will be certain ways of moving, standing, or sitting to which the abuser pays more attention. The abuser may have taught and then rewarded a child for positioning herself in a particular way: for example, sitting on the adult's lap so that the adult's genitals were touched. This way of sitting will then be repeated by the child to have someone pay attention to her.

As the child's body is touched and rubbed, the child may experience arousal and the pleasure inherent to arousal. This pleasure encourages the child to repeat the behavior that leads to the creation of the sensation—for example, cuddling up to the abuser, asking for the "special" game.

In addition, sexualized behaviors by the child create, for the child, paradoxical power. The child, being intruded on, is in a powerless position while at the same time experiencing, within a specific abuse scenario, power over the abuser and the abuser's behavior. This so-called power helps to reassure the child and, thus, reinforces the sexualized behavior. The behaviors may be used by the child to avoid punishment or to keep the abuser from becoming emotionally abusive to her and others.

Because sexualized mannerisms or behaviors become linked with receiving attention, with feeling good physically, with a sense of power, or with people being happier, the child internalizes, "*When I am sexual, good things happen.*" Depending on the amount of sexualization that occurred during the abuse, this internalization may encompass a wide variety of behaviors or just a few behaviors.

When a child is sexually abused, he is stimulated sexually at a physical and emotional level beyond his developmental level. Children who are not abused are able to experience and learn about their bodies and their sexuality as they develop. The sexual experiences they have (e.g., masturbation, "I'll show you mine if you show me yours" games, curiosity and peeking, sharing stories with friends) fit the level of emotional and cognitive understanding of the child at that time. The level of physical stimulation from these experiences is within the range for which the child's physical system is prepared.

With sexual abuse, the sexual experience is very different. The experience is controlled by someone older and, thus, is geared to a level of sexual response beyond that of the child. Particularly for children who have an orgasm and experience a sensation of losing control without any knowledge of what is happening to them, the sexuality of the abuse can be extremely frightening. This out-of-control feeling is intensified if the abuser makes comments such as "I knew I could get you to," "See, that's what I do to you," "You wanted this, didn't you?"

Even when the child does not experience sexual sensations, she is forced to witness the abuser's sexual arousal and, in many cases, orgasm. These behaviors (facial expressions, sounds, body movements) do not fit the child's day-to-day perception of that person and can be frightening.

For these children, sexuality becomes linked with a sense of fright and of being out of control. For children who cut off body feeling, sexuality becomes linked to a lack of feeling or a sensation of freezing and rigidity in the body. Depending on the nature of the abuse, sexuality may become linked to pain or other negative experiences. When abuse is carried out through bribes and manipulation, the child associates sexuality with these behaviors. The child internalizes, "*My sexuality means no feelings, no control, negative feelings.*" Depending on the abuse scenario, negative responses may be linked to all sexual experiences or only to sexual experiences with a particular type of person or with a person within the family—for example, after marriage when a partner is now a family member (Gelinas, 1983).

Although this internalization may appear to contradict the internalization that good things happen when she is sexual, in reality it does not. Specific sexualized behaviors are rewarded and thus are perceived by the child as positive. At the same time, the child's experience of being sexual or of her own sexuality, including feelings and reactions, may be negative.

sexuality with $\left\{ \begin{array}{l} \text{no understanding} \\ \text{over-stimulation} \\ \text{negative experiences} \end{array} \right.$ ➤ my sexuality means $\left\{ \begin{array}{l} \text{no feelings} \\ \text{no control} \\ \text{negative feelings} \end{array} \right.$

distorted messages   A child is told that she is going on a walk in the woods to look for fall leaves, but then she is raped. Neighbors ask about a spot on the carpet and are told that ketchup was spilled there, but the child knows that the stain is from her blood. The adult preaches that people are not to hurt, and yet the child sees the adult doing just that. In these situations, the child experiences that what adults say does not match reality.

Some level of distortion occurs with most situations of sexual abuse: for example, the adult does something and the child is blamed; the child is told that grandpa will help and grandpa abuses. These distortions are reflected in the child's internalizations around guilt and betrayal. With extreme abuse, the distortion of messages becomes more pervasive. "*What I am told is not what is meant*" is internalized and becomes part of the child's inner reality. For some children, all statements made by others will become suspect, whereas for other children, only those statements made by people in a position similar to that of the abuser will become suspect.

distorted messages   ➤   what I am told ≠ what is meant distortions of reality The severely abused child is placed in situations that are nightmarish because of the events that occur, the emotions evoked, or the pain inflicted. As with nightmares, the child wants to escape. For the child, however, there is no physical way out of the sexual abuse scenario. In a few cases, the child's tenacity, perhaps as a result of temperament, perhaps as a result of some positive support in the child's world, allows the child to maintain emotional-cognitive contact with the abuse reality. Often with severe abuse, however, the child needs a way to escape. The only option open to the severely abused child may be an emotional-cognitive flight.

To create this escape, the child may deny the meaning of what has occurred with thoughts such as, "This is a loving activity," "This happened only because she was drunk so it doesn't really count," or may deny that the situation happened at all (Femina, Yeager, & Lewis, 1990). For others, some parts of or the whole abuse experience is repressed (Briere & Conte, 1993; Herman & Schatzow, 1987). Repression appears more likely if the abuse occurs at an early age, multiple perpetrators are involved, physical injury occurs, or the child is quite frightened (Briere & Conte, 1993; Herman & Schatzow, 1987).

> Diana (a 14-year-old who experienced a sudden emergence of sleep problems when her older half-brother moved back home) reports that her mother has told her that when she was 4 years old, she had come to her mother telling mother that her half-brother had hurt her between her legs. No more was known about the incident or incidents than that, and Diana herself remembers nothing.

Another escape mechanism sometimes used is that of dissociation. The child emotionally ("It didn't bother me") or cognitively ("Nothing happened to me") disengages from what happened. Briere (1992) defines dissociation as "a defensive disruption in the normally occurring connections among feelings, thoughts, behavior, and memories, consciously or unconsciously invoked in order to reduce psychological distress" (p. 36).

Children describe this experience in many different ways. Some talk about themselves as shriveling up inside, thereby having the abuse occur to the outside body, not to them. Others describe themselves as going outside their bodies and watching the abuse happen to someone else. The form dissociation takes appears to vary according to the child's individual style of processing and the abuse dynamics.

> Estelle (a 17-year-old abused by her brother from age 6 to age 15 and not believed by her mother when she disclosed at age 7) talks about a screen that comes down in front of her eyes. This screen allows her to watch what is going on but, at the same time, to turn off her mind so that nothing that is happening has to be processed—after all, she had been told that what happened hadn't happened.

As the child experiences dissociation and the subsequent lowering of distress levels, she learns that this is a successful way of coping with a scary world. The child finds dissociation more successful than saying "no" because she may not be listened to, more successful than disclosing because she may not be believed and may be ridiculed, more successful than crying because she may be hit, more successful than hiding because she may be found and then hurt more severely. Because children continue the style of coping that works, this child will continue to dissociate.

For some children, the dissociative defense becomes linked with a part of the child's self, thereby creating a dissociated part of the child. This dissociated part has the potential of creating an alternative personality for the child (Kluft, 1984b). Kluft (1984b) describes four conditions that are prerequisites for the development of a dissociative identity disorder: (a) an innate ability to dissociate, (b) a traumatic experience—for example, severe sexual abuse—that initiates dissociation as a defense mechanism, (c) the linkage of the dissociative defense with a part of the self, and (d) a lack of supportive people within the individual's environment who can help her make some sense of her world and of the abuse experiences.

The child whose experience of sexual abuse is such that she has had to distort her experience, internalizes this distortion. The child internalizes, "*I have no emotions, no experience, no integrated self.*"

A child's internalizations, a result of the child's experience of sexual abuse, affect the way the child behaves in future situations, both outside therapy and inside therapy. For a model to be helpful to a therapist as she works with the child, the behaviors emerging from the abuse-related internalizations need to be included. It is these behaviors that help a therapist recognize the particular internalization that needs to be addressed at that point in the therapy.

INTERNALIZATION → BEHAVIOR

The extent to which internalizations affect future behavior varies considerably depending on a number of factors: the child's developmental level, earlier experiences, temperament, level of safety, and the response of other people in the child's world. The child's developmental level determines the manner in which the child expresses distress. Research has indicated that young children who have been sexually abused are more likely to internalize their distress, whereas school-age children are more likely to externalize their distress (Finkelhor, 1987). New experiences may counterbalance abuse internalizations (e.g., "People who are close do *not* hurt") or may reinforce abuse internalizations (Finkelhor, 1987). The child's temperament also affects the child's response (Carson, Council, & Volk, 1989). A tenacious child might decide, "I am not going to be beaten, I will not lose power over the other parts of my life," whereas a timid child might decide, "I'll just keep out of sight, there's nothing to be done." Whether the abuse has been disclosed and safety has been established, the abuse has been disclosed and the child still feels unsafe, or the abuse remains a secret affects the way the child behaves. In addition, the reaction of other people to the child following disclosure influences the child's subsequent behavior (Gomez-Schwartz, Horowitz, & Cardarelli, 1990). The child who is treated as normal yet as having emotions and confusions that need to be worked through behaves differently from the child who is seen as a damaged child or a potential abuser.

The following discussion will consider the way in which a child's internalizations resulting from sexual abuse affect future behavior. No behavior is the result of any one internalization but rather is affected by the complex whole of the child's internal world: abuse-related internalizations and non-abuse-related internalizations. The present discussion, in which a group of behaviors is presented as arising from a specific internalization, simplifies a complex interaction. This simplification is necessary to provide a framework helpful to professionals in this field and, in particular, to therapists when they are working in a therapy session with a child. This simplification can help a therapist identify the primary internalization that needs to be addressed when a particular behavior is observed in the child's play or conversation.

The extent to which internalizations affect a child's day-to-day functioning varies depending on the intensity of the internalization (*"I am altered"* being less intense than *"I am damaged"*) and, as discussed, on characteristics of the child and of her world. The present discussion centers on the general effects occurring as a result of abuse internalizations.

The child who has experienced intrusion senses himself as altered or damaged. His sense of self and his body image become negative, with the internalized image having far more effect on how he experiences himself than any external view in the mirror.

Santostefano and Calicchia (1992) describe the distortion of body schema that occurs with abuse as occurring on an unconscious level and therefore not open to corrective cognitive experiences, such as the child being told that he is attractive and worthwhile. When the child experiences himself as being yucky or damaged, he treats himself in that way; he becomes self-abusive. Self-abuse such as alcohol, drug use, self-mutilation, or suicide attempts can readily be labeled. Other forms of self-abuse are more difficult to identify.

> Sharon (a 15-year-old sexually abused by a family friend living next door and not believed when she first disclosed) is asked by the therapist if she hurts herself in any way. She looks away and says, "Well, I bump into walls a lot and I trip down the stairs. I tell my parents I'm just uncoordinated, but I know that's not it."

Some children self-abuse by withdrawing from friendships, by becoming involved in abusive relationships, by engaging in promiscuity, by behaving in ways they know will be punished, by overexerting their bodies, or by neglecting their bodies. Academic failure or overachievement, to the extent that the child does not have time for other activities, may also reflect self-abuse.

The response of the child's family and other important people to a disclosure can have considerable effect on how the child views himself. Sometimes a family considers that the child, particularly if female, has been "ruined" by the abuse and treats the child as such, thus reinforcing the negative message of damage. Even when the family does not respond negatively, increased worry and protectiveness and a change in the way the child is disciplined tend to reinforce a child's sense that something is wrong.

Although these children may not recognize the link between the way they are feeling and the abuse, the feeling that something is wrong pervades their sense of self and what they do.

> Jack (an 11-year-old boy sodomized by several of his mother's boyfriends) insists that because the abuse is all over, it doesn't affect him anymore. He does, however, withdraw from contact with peers, dresses in a way that indicates gender confusion, and scratches at his arms. He comments that he would like to do his own thing but that it never seems to be right—he is simply no good.

Another effect of an internalized sense of damage is the disruption of normal development of sexual awareness (Hindman, 1989). As the child matures sexually and begins to experience normal sexual curiosity as well as sexual sensations and arousal, he is likely to misinterpret both the curiosity and the arousal. Rather than being able to be fascinated with these reactions, the child is likely to believe that the reactions are proof that there is something wrong with him.

> Bob (a 17-year-old sexually abused from age 8 to 10 years by his Cub Scout leader) states that he is perverted. He comments that when he sees a pretty girl, he feels aroused.

Feeling that there is something about themselves, and especially their sexuality, that is altered or damaged, children who have been sexually abused do not have a chance to enjoy an unfolding of sexual awareness. They attach a sense of damage or wrongness to the normal changes in their body and to normal learning about sexuality—for example, experimenting with touching and hugging.

The child who experiences himself as damaged is reinforced in this perception by the media that highlights the abuse background of abusers. Adolescents, particularly males, who have been abused are all too likely to identify themselves as potential abusers.

The second internalization resulting from an experience of intrusion, "*I am powerless*," affects the manner in which a child responds to subsequent events. Response to powerlessness has been observed as both learned helplessness (Seligman, 1975) and acting-out behavior (Friedrich, 1995). These response patterns often appear to be gender specific. Girls are more likely to respond in a depressive (Goldstron, Turnquist, & Knutson, 1989) or helpless mode, which, in turn, makes them vulnerable to further abuse.

> Heather (a 16-year-old sexually abused by her father prior to age 5 and then, in a foster family, made to watch the foster father physically abuse her siblings) explains that each time someone makes a statement or demands something of her, she feels unable to counter it in any way. She goes along with the statement or the demand even when she does not agree with it.

Boys are more likely to respond by trying to exert excess control over their environment. This was described by Anna Freud (1936/1966) as identification with the aggressor whom the child sees as being able to avoid powerlessness. It represents the child's effort to become invulnerable.

> Bob (a 17-year-old abused from age 8 to 10 years by the Cub Scout leader) keeps a rifle in his room that he brandishes in front of his mother. Mother feels terrorized but also afraid of what Bob might do if she put him out of the house.

The aggressive acting-out by some children who have been sexually abused most likely reflects the interaction between the physiological and psychological effects of trauma. Owing to the changes that occur within the autonomic nervous system with extreme trauma (Perry et al., 1995; van der Kolk, 1987), people respond to minor stimuli as if a major danger were imminent. Friedrich (1995) describes children who have been abused as experiencing "dysregulation" that emerges in the form of oppositional defiant behavior or passive avoidant behavior with explosive outbursts.

The expression of powerlessness (helplessness or aggressiveness) may appear in all facets of the child's life or may only appear in sexual situations. Some adolescents may be assertive in most areas of their lives and yet find that they react in a helpless manner when a situation becomes sexual. Other adolescents may interact in a sharing manner within most relationships but become excessively controlling when a relationship becomes sexual.

Whether a child responds with learned helplessness, with aggressive behavior, or with a combination of the two, a sense of powerlessness leads to feelings of fear. Fear also arises when children have been frightened by some aspect of the abuse. This fear may show itself as a fear of the perpetrator, a fear of the type of situation in which the abuse occurred (e.g., going to sleep when mother is not around), or a fear of objects used in the abuse (e.g., belts). Because of the pervasiveness of this feeling of powerlessness, the fear related to the abuse may go beyond a specific person, situation, or object. The fear may grow to include all people of the same gender, similar types of situations (e.g., going to sleep), or similar objects (e.g., anything that can be used to tie things). This fear may pervade the child's life, affecting day-to-day behavior, or it may exist at a more subconscious level, emerging from time to time in anxiety attacks.

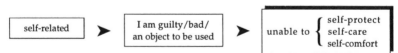

When the child feels she is to blame for the negative situations that occur, she starts to make a connection between negative events and herself. She feels that the way she is and the way she behaves led to the events. Both girls (Mannarino et al., 1994) and women (Gold, 1986) who have been sexually abused have been found to attribute negative events to themselves significantly more often than individuals who have not been abused. Even events quite separate from the abuse situation are viewed similarly—if negative, the individual caused it; if positive, someone or something else receives the credit.

Children who have been sexually abused, particularly those who have been abused by several abusers or have experienced emotional or physical abuse (or both) in addition to the sexual abuse, come to view themselves as objects. These children lose a sense of their entitlement to themselves and their right to determine what happens to them; this is not just a sense of powerlessness but a sense of being diminished (shame) (Fossum & Mason, 1986) and of having no right to power.

When the child perceives himself as negative and without entitlement to his own ideas and decisions, he does not believe himself to be deserving of protection, care, or comfort. This leads to a disruption in the development of *self-systems*—self-protection, self-care, self-comfort—within the child.

The child who feels he is not worth protecting does not develop the normal self-protective strategies that emerge in nonabused children. As a result, the child who has been abused places himself in risky situations: for example, associating with individuals who can be violent or engaging in unprotected sex. Because he does not protect himself, the child finds himself in situations where abuse is likely to recur,[6] thereby compounding the child's sense of guilt and sense of being an object to be used. The child may also not protect his right to his own thoughts and ideas, his right to have others listen to him and allow him personal decision making.

The abused child who sees himself as an object may either not care for himself physically or may place all the emphasis on outward appearance with little care for the way he feels inside. A number of abused individuals dress neatly on the outside and yet wear dirty or worn-out underwear. Some abused children refuse to bathe, and others become obsessive about dirt and bathe many times a day.

The third self-system, self-comfort, enables the child to tell herself that she is a good person and that things will turn out all right. Briere (1996) refers to this as self-modulation and includes self-soothing and self-distraction. When this system is disrupted, the child is unable to recognize and process positive messages from the outside world as well as internal positive feelings.

When the child's general environment is supportive and the people important to the child treat him as someone who is not at fault, who is a good person, and who is able to cope, the disruption of the development of self-systems is less.

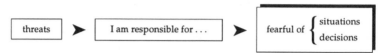

The abused child is placed in a paradoxical situation. Although the child is powerless to stop the abuse, she feels responsible for it. Because of the threats—verbal, physical, situational—surrounding the abuse, she feels responsible for what happens to others. Within the abuse, children become accustomed to meeting the needs of those older than themselves, whereas the adults, who are supposed to be responsible for what happens in a child's world, do not stop the abuse. Thus, the child who is already confused and feeling powerless and guilty is left believing that she is the one who determines what happens next: to the abuser, to the people close to the abuser, to the people close to herself, and to herself.

Although the child may not disclose verbally, she usually does disclose by her behavior.

> Judith (an 11-year-old sexually abused by her adoptive father between the ages of 6 to 9 years) describes some of her behavior during those years. She would "pee" down the heat vent, become aggressive with other children, and was often violent toward her adoptive mother.

When the nonverbal disclosure is not noticed, the child believes no one else will take responsibility for the craziness in her world. She has to continue living with two separate realities—my world is all right; I am being abused.

When the disclosure does occur, parent(s) do become upset (Hooper, 1992; McIntyre, Manion, Ensom, Wells, & Firestone, in press). They are upset by their failure to keep the child safe, by their failure to be good parents, and, with intrafamilial abuse, by their loss of financial stability and of an important relationship (Hooper, 1992). All too often, the child views herself as the cause of this upset. If the child had been threatened by the abuser that her mother "would go crazy" if she told, she now feels that she is responsible for this happening.

The child who discloses as well as the child who does not disclose takes on responsibility for consequences far beyond her control. Needing to do something about a situation yet not being able to keep the world safe, the child becomes fearful of situations and of making decisions.

Abuse and lack of protection are encoded explicitly or implicitly within the brain (van der Kolk, 1994). For some children, the memories remain active or are suppressed; for other children, they are repressed or dissociated. In whichever form they exist, they are internalized, and from there, they affect the child's functioning.

If the memories are active but the emotions connected to them are not worked through, the child is likely to experience intrusive thoughts.

> Marie (a 12-year-old fondled on one occasion by her grandfather— her mother had also been abused by the grandfather but did not disclose until after her daughter was abused) reports that thoughts about the abuse, her grandfather, her mother, and what might happen next keep coming into her mind. Not only do the thoughts appear if something connected to the abuse is mentioned, but frequently they come into her mind when she is with her friends or by herself.

Intrusive thoughts create problems with concentration, with participation in activities, and with being aware of and believing in the positive aspects of the self.

Flashbacks and nightmares may also result from memories. Flashbacks differ from intrusive thoughts in that they are more experiential and less cognitive. Flashbacks may include emotions or sensations with or without a cognitive recognition of the underlying incident. They may also include a total experience in which the individual loses touch with where he is now and feels caught in a recreated experience.

> Sally (an 18-year-old abused by her father between ages 7 and 14 years) pulls back into the corner of the sofa and starts to tremble. "No, no," she says, as she turns her head sideways, "I don't want to, please don't." Her voice is like that of a young child and there is a look of fright on her face. Her eyes are focused on a space just in front of her.

Memories can also cause trigger responses. Trigger responses are emotions and behaviors in the present similar to the emotions and type of responding the child experienced at the time of the original abuse. They occur when something about the present environment is similar to a characteristic of the original abuse. A recall of the abuse is triggered, and the child responds at the emotional and behavioral level he was at, at the time of the abuse. This recall, however, is usually at the unconscious level. A young childlike response, inappropriate for the present situation, occurs without the child being aware of any connection to the abuse.

> Ann (a 17-year-old sexually abused by her uncle between the ages of 4 to 8 years, when the family visited the uncle's cottage—the uncle would ask his niece to sit next to him on the couch, would pull up the blanket, and would fondle her under the blanket while the rest of the family continued with their activities in the same room) reports that over the weekend, she had been with some friends, and one of the males had started to harass her, making sexual innuendoes and touching her more than was appropriate. At the beginning of the evening, she was able to handle the situation well, telling him to stop bothering her and, thereby, stopping most of his behavior. But later in the evening, she was no longer able to say anything directly to the boy or to move herself away from him when he approached her.
>
> Ann then talks about the events of the evening. At one point during the evening, she had been sitting on a couch with friends. The boy who was harassing her tossed a ball toward the couch. One of her friends pulled up a blanket to shield them from the ball. It was from that point on that Ann found she was no longer able to cope with the boy's advances. She was no longer responding as a 17-year-old but instead was responding as a 4-year-old.

Trigger responses can be recognized by the fact that the child behaves in a way that does not fit his usual way of behaving—for
example, acting like a young, frightened child rather than a more
competent adolescent.

When the memories have been dissociated, the child may experience a sense of "not being all there," of something being missing, or
of not being present when particular types of situations occur or
topics are discussed. Thus, the child loses a part of her experience.

The child who was abused by someone close to him has additional
abuse-related internalizations. As a result, his subsequent interaction with the world, with people important to him, and, in particular, with a therapist is affected in additional ways.

When a child loves and hates the same person, wants to be with
but is afraid of that person, he ends up feeling chaotic. Because the
child cannot trust his feelings, in that he experiences feelings that
are exactly the opposite of what he thought he felt or thought he
should feel, he is likely to cut off feelings. Depending on the severity
of the abuse and the amount of support the child receives from his
home environment, the emotional cut off may be limited to people
of the same gender as the abuser and may occur only when the child
begins to feel close to someone, or it may occur with all people
regardless of gender and in all interpersonal situations. The child is
left with a limited emotional base on which to form relationships.
Sexual encounters, intellectual conversations, or self-destructive
activities may become the child's only ways to create relationships.

Some children who experience strong conflicting emotions around
the abuse are able to retain an awareness of their emotions. These
children tend to experience extremes of emotion, swinging from
depression to rage to euphoria. Because incestuous families tend to
be families in which negative emotions are not allowed to be expressed or not allowed toward those who control the family dynamics (Alexander, 1985), the child often does not have a release for the
feelings he experiences. The negative emotions that cannot be ex-

pressed toward the person who has been abusive or the person who places the child in an abusive situation are likely to be acted out toward those who are caring for the child or acted inwardly toward the self.

> Toni (a 13-year-old sexually abused by her stepfather between the ages of 9 to 12 years) is now living with her father and stepmother after the courts found her stepfather innocent, and mother decided to continue to live with him. Toni sits around doing nothing and waits for her mother to call her. Following the few times mother does call, Toni becomes extremely angry, yells at her stepmother, and uses nails to scratch herself.

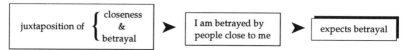

The child who is abused by someone close to her experiences and internalizes betrayal as a characteristic of people when they are close to her. Girls who have been sexually abused have been found to have less trust in others than girls who were not abused (Mannarino et al., 1994). If the nonperpetrating parent(s) believe the child and are able to support and remain close to the child, this internalization is limited to certain types of people or types of situations rather than to people or situations in general. Where there is not a moderating factor, the child's expectation of betrayal and hurt is broader.

This expectation is, all too often, fulfilled. Patterns of the past are repeated because individuals who expect betrayal tend to choose friends or partners who betray. The child, believing she is damaged and, therefore, not deserving of people who are kind and supportive, moves toward people who are not supportive. Even when the child has chosen a friend or partner who is not likely to betray her, she may see betrayal where it does not exist (projection). A third scenario consists of the child believing that she is going to be betrayed and, therefore, treating her friend as if he or she has betrayed her. The friend, reacting to this behavior, ends up turning against the child (identifying with the projection).

In adolescent relationships based primarily on sexual interrelating or on emotional neediness rather than on healthy emotional interrelating, adolescents may feel close when actually being distant emotionally. When the distance becomes evident, the adolescent feels betrayed, perhaps by the boyfriend or girlfriend or perhaps by his own strong feelings that have left an emptiness.

Experiences of betrayal and hurt also occur and recur within the family. As the child continues to turn toward a nonsupportive parent for support, either from habit or from the hope that this time the parent will be supportive, the parent, also behaving from habit, does not provide support. The abusive parent may not admit to the abuse or may minimize it by rationalizing what happened. With disclosure, the nonabusive parent may feel pressured from both sides, both from the abuser and from the child, and as a result may not support the child, thereby further betraying the child's trust in her.

> Keri (a 13-year-old who lives with her mother and brothers while her father, who abused her between ages 11 to 13 years, is living outside the home on a court order) asks her mother to do something for her just as mother is on her way out to spend the evening with Keri's father. The mother, irritated by the demand at that moment as well as by the pressure of having to manage the house alone, yells at Keri, saying that if it were not for Keri, father would be at home and she, mother, would not need to go out.

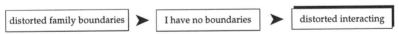

The child who experiences intrafamilial sexual abuse lives with distorted family boundaries and roles (Alexander, 1985; Porter et al., 1982). The boundaries between the child and the abuser are blurred or nonexistent, while those between the child and the nonabusing parent may be impermeable or reversed. The child frequently ends up taking care of the people who should be caring for him.

The child who has experienced a lack of privacy or respect for his personal boundaries is likely either to withdraw from others to prevent further threat to privacy or to become overly intrusive with others. The latter may occur because the child, not having been allowed his own body and personal privacy, is unaware of others' need for privacy or because the child, trained in taking care of the needs of others, continues to do so even when it is inappropriate.

The child who was "parentified" in the incestuous family takes on the role of caring for others while ignoring his own needs (Courtois, 1988). This behavior may continue long after disclosure and, indeed, may be encouraged further if the nonperpetrating parent falls apart. The child may nurture others to excess and not nurture himself enough. Although the excessive nurturing may be a conscious choice made by the child, there is often hidden resentment that feeds an anger toward the very people he is caretaking. For some children, this resentment leads to less nurturing of others, but for many children, the resentment leads to even more caring for others and less caring for themselves.

> Patti (a 16-year-old sexually abused by her stepfather between the ages of 4 to 10 years who moved out of the home at 10 without disclosing, moved back in at 11 because she missed and worried about her siblings and disclosed at 13, following her mother and stepfather's separation) rushes home each day after school to be there when her siblings arrive home. She worries about her mother being lonely and watches movies with her or talks to her during the evening.
>
> When Patti's boyfriend gets into trouble with the law and is kicked out of his home, he moves in with her. She goes with him to all his hearings and assures him that everything will be all right. Patti decides that she does not have time for therapy and, in any case, therapy is not really that important.

The child who becomes the pseudoadult not only becomes trapped in adultlike behavior but also loses normal childhood experiences. He does not have a chance to be cared for by others, to live without fear, and to develop relationships in which the other person is trustworthy. As pointed out by Porter et al. (1982), once a child moves into the role of an adult, he distances himself from his peers and thus is left with few appropriate social outlets.

Children who have had no experience of positive attachment continue to seek attachment (Main, Kaplan, & Cassidy, 1985). When a child has no sense of personal boundaries, this seeking of attachment can become indiscriminant, leading to promiscuous behavior and the tolerance of abusive relationships.

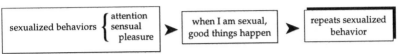

The child who has had extensive positive experiences (attention, gaining rewards, avoiding punishment, sensual pleasure) when behaving in a sexual manner, internalizes sexualized behaviors as positive. And behaviors experienced as positive are repeated by children. Indeed, the occurrence of sexualized behaviors has been consistently found to distinguish children who have been sexually abused from children with other psychiatric problems (Beitchman et al., 1991; Friedrich et al., 1986; Friedrich et al., 1992; Gomez-Schwartz et al., 1990).

These behaviors may include masturbating in public, reenacting sexual activities with dolls or with other children, rubbing (either overtly or in a hidden manner) the genitals of adults, making sexual sounds or motions, dressing in a provocative manner, using sexualized language, or exposing genitals (Friedrich, 1990). For adolescents, sexualized behaviors often appear as promiscuity (Beitchman et al., 1991). These behaviors may be used to create pleasurable sensations or to get attention. They may be behaviors that the child consciously chooses, such as telling other children in the school yard about sexual activities, or behaviors engaged in unconsciously, such as standing or walking in a sexual manner.

Candice (an 18-year-old sexually abused by two of her brothers over a period of 10 years) reports that males accuse her of being sexually provocative when she is not aware of any sexualized behavior on her part. She talks about males approaching her on the street or giving her sexual-type looks. Her friends have noticed that when a male, who is not well-known within the group of girls, joins the group, he always seems to attach himself to Candice. Candice feels that there must be something weird about her and what she is doing that these things happen.

The fact that these behaviors were part of the abuse scenario is seldom recognized by a child. What the child repeats is the wish for attention and pleasure. The behaviors that brought this in the past are repeated.

At the same time that positive meaning is attached to sexualized behaviors, negative attributes may also be linked to the behaviors. This is particularly true for older children and adolescents who have internalized social mores related to sexual behaviors and children who have been punished or ridiculed for sexualized behavior. The child finds herself repeating behaviors that she condemns.

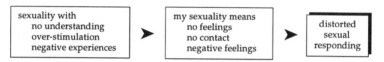

When a child has negative experiences, such as being hurt, feeling manipulated, or experiencing a frightening reaction, connected to her body and to sexual activities, she internalizes sexuality as negative. This internalization disrupts normal sexual development. The child does not have a chance to develop understanding, appreciation, and respect for her body and for her body's physical responding. She does not have a chance to learn that bodily responding can be a way of being intimate and caring with herself and with others. Future sexual situations become distorted.

The child who has been sexually abused has little chance to shift this negative internalization because she is likely to block out healthy discussions of sexuality, whether the discussions occur with friends or during sex education classes.

Carolyn (a 12-year-old sexually abused by her stepbrother between the ages of 10 to 12 years) explains that during sex education class at school, her mind wanders to other topics. She explains that kids were asking questions about or the teacher was talking about things that she had experienced and this made her feel really weird, so she just wouldn't listen. Her mother had given her books to read but they just made her ill, so she did not read them. If her friends started talking about boys, she was scared to say anything because they might guess what "she had done." She would daydream, and soon the discussion would turn to another topic.

Discussions that emphasize the negative aspects of sexuality—for example, sexuality as a way to be powerful or manipulate others—fit the child's experience and tend not to be blocked.

When negative experiences, such as pain, fear, and violence, have been connected with sexuality, the child's future sexual responding may remain linked to these types of situations. Sexual disturbance or dysfunction has been the most consistent long-term effect in children who have been sexually abused (Beitchman et al., 1992). This disruption to the development of normal sexuality may take the form of a lessened or complete lack of physical feeling during sexual contact, a fear of sex, an inability to have enjoyable sex with someone for whom one cares, inability to have enjoyable sex following marriage (the partner has become a member of the family), inability to become aroused if pain does not occur, or loss of sexuality as a way of expressing caring and intimacy.

Heather (a 16-year-old abused by her father between the ages of 4 and 6 years) explains that having sex with a boy means nothing to her. She would not, however, kiss a boy with whom she went to bed. Kissing a boy means she really cares for him.

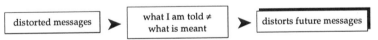

As the child experiences and internalizes that people do not mean what they say, he begins to question and distort comments made to him.

Tommy (a 6-year-old sadistically abused at ages 4 and 5 years by his baby-sitter who used to give him treats following the incidents of abuse) is told by his mother that she will buy a treat for him just for the fun of it. Tommy understands this to mean "You'll get hurt" and becomes very scared. His behavior deteriorates to that of a 4-year-old.

Val (a 9-year-old severely sexually abused between the ages of 3 to 9 years by her father) is being driven to her new foster home. The social worker comments, "Your foster parents are looking forward to having you with them." Val understands this to mean, "They are going to do something to me."

Similar but less extreme distortions may be made by children who experience less severe abuse. For example, children are often told by the perpetrator that the abuse is a way of having fun or showing love. For these children, future fun situations may be experienced as dangerous. If a boy says he loves a girl, the girl may become anxious.

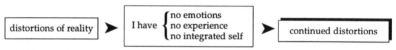

The methods of coping that develop during episodes of sexual abuse are internalized as a part of the child's interactive pattern with her world. The sense of relief experienced when a child denies the meaning of abuse is substantial and encourages the child to use denial when other upsetting situations occur. This is the child who insists that everything is all right but yet is dropping out of school or is unable to keep friends.

The child who represses memories of abuse may also use forgetting with other events. Some children who have been abused grow up with no memories for extended time periods of their childhood.

Dissociation, by disrupting the connections that normally "occur among feelings, thoughts, behavior, and memories" (Briere, 1992, p. 36), enables the child to survive trauma without becoming upset. Because not being upset allows the child to be better accepted in a family, and particularly in incestuous families, the child repeats this mechanism. Dissociation, owing to the positive effect for the child, will be used by the child more and more frequently and, in time, may be used in situations that are not traumatic. As a result, the child fails to learn positive ways of coping with negative situations. The child becomes increasingly dependent on and skillful at dissociation.

The negative side of dissociation for the child is the hole it creates in the child's awareness and knowledge of her world and herself.

The child loses opportunities to learn positive methods of relating to her environment.

> Estelle (a 17-year-old sexually abused by her brother between the ages of 6 to 15 years and not believed by her mother when she first disclosed at age 7) dissociates when her mother becomes angry with her. Estelle's mother says that she can see Estelle "fade out" at a certain point in their discussions. This makes mother furious, but she tries to talk to Estelle about what is happening. Estelle's eyes become more and more unfocused. The relationship between Estelle and her mother deteriorates.

For children who develop a dissociative identity disorder (Kluft, 1984b; Peterson, 1991; Putnam, 1993), the internal disconnection is even greater. Young children report feeling that there is more than one of them, one or some being "bad" and one or some being "good." Adolescents report internal voices, experiences of feeling that they are trying on other personalities, and internal sabotage. When things go wrong, they switch personalities rather than finding a solution to the problem. Thus, the child does not have opportunities to develop healthy ways of coping.

❑ **Summary**

When a child or adolescent is sexually abused, she has an experience of herself, of the people important to her, and of her world that is different from previous experiences. As this abuse experience is internalized, her previous sense of self and world shifts. The abuse-related internalizations now form part of the child's internal working model (Bowlby, 1971, 1973), the base from which behavior develops and the filter through which future events are experienced (see Figure 1.2).

Previous theoretical models, by looking at the dynamics of trauma, the child's cognitive and emotional processing, and the effect of child and family resources, have helped to clarify the dynamics and effects of sexual abuse. They have not, however, clarified what occurs within the child and how this internal experience can be recognized. The Internalization Model, discussed and shown schematically in Figure 1.2, provides a framework for identifying (a) the destructive characteristics of the abuse experience, (b) how these characteristics affect the child's internal sense of self and world, and (c) the behaviors arising from abuse-related internalizations. In this way, the Internalization Model not only helps the therapist by clarifying the child's experience but also by providing a framework for recognizing, from the child's play, conversation, and behavior, the internal abuse-distorted sense of self and world that needs to be addressed.

This model has been used clinically by therapists working with children and adolescents who have been sexually abused. Therapists report that the model helps clarify their thinking as they work with a child and enables them to be more specific in their work. As internalizations are identified, therapists address the internalizations and provide new experiences—that is, new and healthier internalizations for the child. Parents and therapists report a positive shifting in the child's attitudes and behaviors.

Measures are being developed specifying abuse-related internalizations that can be used in pretreatment and posttreatment testing with children and adolescents who have been sexually abused. Research based on these measures will help clarify the dynamics of internalizations and the effect of therapy based on the Internalization Model.

The next three chapters discuss working with children, with adolescents, and with the parents of children or adolescents who have been sexually abused. The Internalization Model is used as a framework for understanding the child's or adolescent's or parent's behavior within the therapy session, for identifying the distorted internal sense of self and world underlying the behavior, and for addressing the abuse-related internalizations. The last chapter looks at the therapist's experience within the therapy session.

❏ Notes

1. Within psychoanalytic literature, *internalization* has been used to refer to the creation, within the mind, of external objects or others and of relationships between self and others (Laplanche & Pontalis, 1973). As used in the present discussion, internalization refers not only to the internalizing of relationships between self and others but also of the self in relation to the self.

2. The age span indicated in most state and provincial laws on childhood sexual abuse is 4 or 5 years.

3. See Fraiberg (1980) for a discussion of the disruptive effect on an infant when the adult's needs are primary.

4. Positive response and support from the mother to the child has been the best predictor of positive outcome for the child following disclosure (Gomez-Schwartz et al., 1990) and participation in court procedures (Sas, 1995).

5. Ambivalent feelings toward caretakers are not unique to the abused child. They are, indeed, part of all close relationships. This ambivalence is, however, heightened significantly by the occurrence of abuse.

6. In a review of research on long-term effects of childhood sexual abuse, Beitchman and colleagues identified revictimization as being more likely to occur for women who had been sexually abused in childhood than for women not abused in childhood (Beitchman et al., 1992).

2

Understanding and Expanding the Play: Children

Sexual abuse is internalized by a child in many ways: a sense of damage, of not being able to control the world, of being bad or guilty, and of being responsible for other people. Memories of abuse and of no protection are held inside. Some children also experience emotional confusion with both positive and negative feelings toward the same person, anticipation of betrayal, and inappropriate boundaries. When the abuse has been extensive, children may unconsciously adopt sexualized behaviors, connect negative emotions or events with sexuality, be unable to believe what people say, and distort reality to live with reality. Fear, anger, and confusion are part of these children's experience. If these internalizations and feelings are not addressed, they will affect the child's understanding of future experiences. They will affect the way the child perceives herself in future situations and responds to these situations.

Although the internalizations and feelings that need to be addressed in therapy are fairly clear, knowing when and how to address them is not as clear. A young child seldom has either the understanding or the words for talking about abuse or the internalizations from abuse. The child's language is play. And it is through this language of play that abuse-related internalizations are presented in the therapy session.

Winnicott (1971b) referred to play as the interface between a child's intrapsychic reality and the outer world. Klein (1932/1975b) stated that the play of a child was equivalent to free association by an adult. Play, like free association, does not have to fit reality and can, therefore, occur without being censored by conscious thought. Play is a more direct and more complete portrayal of a child's internal world than is verbal language. Through the use of play objects (toy animals, dolls, a ball, craft materials), children present their experiences and their internalized sense of self and of the world. Through the use of play objects, children ask questions and try to find out about themselves and their world.

Children do, indeed, tell the adults (parents or therapist) about their world. The important issue, when working with children, is not whether children can tell but rather whether adults can recognize and understand what it is a child is telling. At times, the play of a child who has been sexually abused will clearly express the child's experience—the child tries to put objects into his own bottom or into the bottom of a doll. At other times, the meaning behind a child's play may be disguised—the child who hopes her father will be back home for Easter draws Easter eggs but does not ask the question; the child who became aroused during the abuse makes a "tickle tool" and wonders how it feels for the therapist but does not tell about her feelings of arousal. Even the child who denies the abuse or has repressed memory of the abuse will present abuse issues in her play—tails of baby animals are placed in the mouths of the parent animals, the father doll's trousers are repetitively fastened and unfastened.

Children who have developed a healthy sense of self and the world and have experiences appropriate to their developmental level are able to play through their issues and questions. When, however, the experience affecting a child is an experience at a developmental level beyond the child's understanding, the child does not have the developmental ability to play through that experience. Pynoos and Nader (1993) have described four conditions necessary if play around abuse issues is to provide relief—that is, to permit processing: (a) the child needs some control over what is happening, (b) the child needs to be able to express prohibited affect, (c) some cognitive reworking needs to occur, and (d) a satisfactory ending needs to be achieved. A child with a healthy sense of self and considerable home support who experiences a limited sexual abuse situation may be able to provide by herself, or together with a parent, a play experience that includes each of these conditions. Unfortunately, for most children, the abuse scenario is too traumatizing, the child's own sense of self is too limited, or the home environment is too critical or reactive to the abuse event for self-processing to be possible.

Terr (1990) defined *trauma* as a situation that has overwhelmed the individual—cognitively, emotionally, physically. Sexual activity by an adult or an older child is at a physical, cognitive, and emotional developmental level beyond that of the child. As a result, it cannot be assimilated into the child's worldview nor is the child's world able to accommodate the experience (see Piaget & Inhelder, 1960). A replaying of the abuse experience cannot, therefore, by itself provide relief. If the child, in her play, experiences once again something beyond her understanding, she can be retraumatized (Terr, 1990).

A child is aware at her own developmental level of what happened during the abuse. She is not aware of the objective reality. Because of egocentric thinking, the young child feels that the abuse is a result of her own activity. The child is aware of how she feels inside—the touching felt good, so I am guilty. She is not aware of the reality of the abuse situation—body responding is normal and healthy; someone older imposing or allowing touching is not normal and is not healthy. Children need an expanded information base about abuse, about themselves, and about their world if they are to begin to understand the trauma that occurred (Terr, 1990).

Because children are concrete in their thinking and individuals under stress become more concrete, this information also needs to be concrete—that is, experienced, not just told. The child needs not only the opportunity to express feelings and to talk about the abuse but also an opportunity to reprocess, in a concrete manner, the sense of self and the world internalized from the abuse experience. For example, the yucky feeling inside can be drawn and then given to the perpetrator, because that is where the yuck was—with the perpetrator, not the child.

When the child's information and experience base with regard to the cognitive, emotional, and physical aspects of the abuse increases to a level that the experience can be assimilated or accommodated— that is, it is no longer overwhelming—the traumatic aspect of the experience diminishes. The abuse becomes a happening: one that never should have happened but a happening and not the child. The child is then able to move on with the normal tasks of development.

An understanding of trauma and trauma reduction, together with an understanding of the internalizations resulting from abuse experience, has been found clinically to provide an effective model of play therapy for children who have been sexually abused.

The present chapter briefly discusses models of play therapy that have been used with children who have been sexually abused and the advantages and disadvantages of each model. A psychodynamic trauma-focused play therapy model, based on the Internalization Model (see Figure 1.2) and trauma theory, is presented. The type of play patterns likely to occur in the play of children who have been sexually abused, how a therapist can recognize and understand the child's abuse-related internalizations, and how these internalizations can be addressed are described.

❏ Play Therapy

Children who have been sexually abused have received therapy based on a variety of play therapy models. The first three models to be discussed—psychoanalytic play therapy, nondirective (humanistic) play therapy, and structured play therapy—are used with children having a wide variety of diagnoses. A fourth model, guided play therapy, was developed more specifically for working with traumatized children. The model being presented, psychodynamic trauma-focused therapy, borrows from each of the models described earlier.

Psychoanalytic play therapy, as developed by Anna Freud (1926/ 1974) and Melanie Klein (1932/1975b), provides a theoretical framework that emphasizes intrapsychic functioning and a therapeutic model with carefully observed boundaries (space, time, roles), child-determined content, recognition of transference reactions, and therapist interpretation of the child's conflicts (Freud, 1926/1974) and internal world (Klein, 1932/1975b). Although the psychoanalytic model provides careful attention to and interpretation of a child's perceptions and defenses, which is important for a child who has been abused, it does not provide the information or experiences a child needs to form a context within which a trauma can be understood and processed.

Nondirective play therapy was developed by Axline (1947) from humanistic theory and treatment (Rogers, 1951). As the child plays, the therapist reflects the feelings being expressed, thereby assisting the child in understanding his experiences and his behavior. Although respectful of the child and the child's own process, reflection without interpretation may, for a child who has been manipulated by adults, heighten a child's anxiety without providing any resolution for the feelings. The information and experience needed to process trauma that has occurred is not provided.

Structured play therapy, based on social learning theory (Bandura, 1977), creates activities that direct a child's thoughts and actions to particular issues or behaviors. A child who was sexually abused learns more about himself and the normality of his responses to the abuse. New information is given—for example, adults are responsible for what happens in situations with an adult and a child; sexual feelings are a result of physical functioning, not the child's wishes. As the child incorporates the information, it forms a context in which the child can begin to understand what occurred. This approach, with its prepared activities and exercises, is particularly helpful for working in groups.

One of the dangers of structured therapy, however, is that the issue presented by the therapist may not be the issue relevant to that child at that particular point. A child who was traumatized as he watched his father removed from the home in handcuffs is not going to be able to profit from discussing his anger at father until the distress related to father going to jail is addressed. A second danger is that a therapist may assume that once the activities on a particular issue are completed and the child is saying he feels fine, the child actually is fine. Children who have been abused are skilled at providing what adults want to hear and at cutting off their own feelings. When emotional health is judged on the basis of completed exercises, it is all too easy to assume that the child is doing better than he really is.

Guided play therapy (Gil, 1991; James, 1989) evolved from working with children who had been traumatized. Therapy encourages, through specific activities, direct discussion of the traumatic event, recognition and expression of feelings, and chances to learn how to play. Through guided activities, the child learns information about abuse and the normality of his responses to the abuse situation. Although the activity itself is guided, the timing of the activities is determined by the child's behavior and play inside or outside the session and not by the therapist's predetermined schedule. Therapists working in this context emphasize the importance of addressing the needs of the other people in the family for the child to have an overall reparative experience.

Although guided play therapy addresses the child's need for more information about himself and the abuse and for more time and space for processing this information, attention is not given to the child's internal processing of the experience. Although the traumatic effect of the abuse may lessen, if abuse-related internalizations are not addressed, the abuse will continue to affect the child's life. The child will experience future situations through an abuse-related sense of self and world.

❏ Psychodynamic Trauma-Focused Therapy

Psychodynamic trauma-focused therapy draws from each of the therapies described earlier. In addition, and important to the success of the therapy with children who have been sexually abused, psychodynamic trauma-focused therapy is based on trauma theory

(Herman, 1992; Terr, 1990, 1991) and on the Internalization Model described in Chapter 1.

RELATIONSHIP AND SETTING

The relationship between the therapist and the child is, as with psychoanalytic play therapy, a working, not friendship, relationship. This is important so that the child be able to express negative as well as positive feelings toward the therapist (transference reaction).

The boundaries of the therapy setting and the therapy relationship are carefully adhered to in order to provide a consistent and appropriate experience. The distorted family boundaries experienced by many children who have been sexually abused have meant that the child has not internalized boundaries of self and other. Thus, carefully established and adhered to boundaries within the therapy setting are important. Therapy is scheduled at the same time each week, with the session starting and stopping on time. The same room is used, with consistent rules regarding the use of objects in the room and the child's work staying in the room. The boundaries of the relationship place the therapist in the role of being responsible for safety and for identifying and encouraging the working through of issues. Although the relationship would provide a new attachment experience (Friedrich, 1995), it is not a friendship in that the child does not participate in the caretaking of the therapist.

Based on psychoanalytic therapy, the room is as nonintrusive as possible. A room with a small set of toys and the child's craft box can be far more productive as a therapy setting than a playroom full of toys. A surplus of toys can be distracting and slow down the process of therapy, particularly with hyperactive children. A set of small family dolls (baby, children, parents, grandparents) whose clothes can be removed (detailed anatomical dolls, if used in the investigation, are not recommended); several families of farm animals; several families of wild animals; a few dinosaurs; a car and a vehicle related to rescuing; a hard rubber ball and a soft foam ball; a set of fencing; a baby bottle; and puppets, including a girl, a boy, and one or two animals, are sufficient. A dollhouse, particularly one in which the walls are removable, is useful. Large pillows and a large, soft stuffed animal (a teddy bear is recommended) are helpful.

In addition, each child has a box of craft materials (plain paper, colored paper, white glue, scissors, pencil, eraser, markers, several colors of plasticine, adhesive tape, string, pipe cleaners) that is carefully labeled with the child's name and that is not used by anyone else. All of the work done in the session is kept in the box. Children often want to take home pictures or other things they have made. Maintaining the boundary that everything done in the session remains in the room helps a child know that the distress around the abuse issues can be contained and does not need to "follow the child everywhere." It also helps to clarify that the work in the session is confidential. The difference between *confidential*—the child can choose to tell about the session, but the therapist will not tell—and *secret*—no one tells—should be clarified for the child.

An assessment, including separate time with the child and the parent(s), should precede the beginning of therapy. The child's pictures, play, and responses (verbal and behavioral) to standardized questions about relationships, behaviors, and in particular posttraumatic behaviors, and the abuse provide information on the child's present functioning and the most pressing abuse-related internalizations (Wieland, 1996). An interview with the parent(s) provides developmental and temperament information with regard to the child and information on how supportive the parent will be able to be. The interview provides an opportunity for the therapist to reinforce the importance of the parent's role with the child and to establish a working partnership with the parent(s). The assessment provides information for the therapist and a baseline against which changes during therapy can be compared.

PROCESS

Similar to psychoanalytic, nondirective, and guided play therapy, in this approach, the therapist does not initiate an activity at the beginning of a play session. The therapist observes the child's behavior and play to determine the issue that is relevant for that child at that time. At times, the meaning of the child's play is clear.

At other times, the therapist may need to watch quietly for quite a while or to enquire about the child's activity: "Tell me about your drawing."

To identify the issues being played out by the child, it is helpful for the therapist to have several "information tapes" running inside his head. One tape would include the child's abuse experiences. A second would include the family situation and the child's early history. A child's experience and, therefore, play dynamics, will include relationships (for example, attachment patterns) and events (for example, witnessing violence, kidnapping) beyond those related to the sexual abuse. When a child wraps string around two dolls, it will have one meaning for the child who is distressed by his parents' separation and another meaning for the child who was tied up during abuse. When the therapist remains aware of the child's experiences, distresses are more accurately recognized. The third tape that needs to be running inside the therapist's head includes the abuse-related internalizations. Keeping these in mind helps the therapist recognize play reflecting an internalization.

Once the therapist recognizes the issue or internalization behind a child's play, she responds. This response would be verbal, not behavioral, to move the issue into the child's conscious awareness. To help the child process this issue, the therapist's response is more complex than nondirective reflection and more concrete than psychoanalytic interpretation. Interpretation of the child's play would include three steps: (a) noting what it is the child is doing: "I'm noticing how you are blocking all of the doors of the play house . . . ," (b) linking the child's action to the situation of the abuse: "You may be thinking about R coming into your bedroom . . . ," and (c) relating the child's action to her emotions or internalizations: "and feeling really angry that mom was not there to stop what happened." All three steps may not be necessary and, indeed, may not be appropriate all of the time. Depending on the child's reaction to (b), it may be best to stop at that point and let the child expand on what happened and what it was like for him. This would allow the child space to process memories of the abuse or the nonprotection. If the child shows anger at that point, it may be best to proceed to (c). The previous content of the session (e.g., pushing the mother doll to the bottom of the toy box) or recent behaviors reported by the mother (e.g., hitting out at mother) would help the therapist determine whether the anger is connected to the perpetrator or to the nonperpetrating parent(s).

Although an interpretation can be helpful to a child who is distressed, it is seldom enough for a child who has been traumatized. The child needs help in understanding himself and his world—in particular, the dynamics around the abuse—if he is to be able to incorporate the abuse as a happening, not as him, within his world schema.

Similar to therapists using structured and guided play therapy, the therapist may give information at that point. "You know, all children expect their mothers to know what is happening, even if the mother is not around, and to keep them safe. When that doesn't happen, kids do get angry." Stating that anger is expected in a particular situation helps to normalize it. This allows the child to be less scared of his anger and, therefore, have less need to deny it, project it onto someone else, or split it off from himself. It also helps the child assimilate the anger into his own understanding and, as a result, decreases the sense of being overwhelmed. The therapist may comment further, "Of course you would be angry; even though mom did not know R was touching you, you would wish that she had known and had protected you, so, yes, you would be angry."

The child may become angry with the therapist at this point. Relying on the psychoanalytic play therapy model, the therapist could recognize this anger and the child's wish that the therapist would make everything safe (transference reaction). The therapist could make a limited interpretation of the child's behavior: "Yes, pretty angry at me and the fact I can't make everything safe, protect you from all the questions and feelings inside you," or a more complete transference interpretation: "Angry at me for not protecting you, like you are angry at mom for not protecting you."

If the discussion of anger had not moved into a transference situation, the therapist, based on trauma theory and the guided play therapy model, could create a more concrete experience for the child. The therapist might ask the child to draw the anger, tell the mother doll about the anger, or let out the anger by hitting a pillow or yelling. If the child remains stuck in what he is doing—that is, there is no change in affect or play pattern—then more work needs to be done around that issue. If the child feels some relief, his play content will move on, and the therapist is once again in the position of the observer.

In this way, the therapist uses the Internalization Model and trauma theory for understanding the child's play and determining interventions. The therapist borrows ideas from all modes of play therapy and uses them to assist the child with the working through of early experiences, feelings, and internalizations. The next three sections further describe the process of recognizing meaning from a child's play, recognizing abuse-related internalizations, and helping the child shift these internalizations.

❏ Working With the Child

Before a therapy session begins, the therapist needs to check that the room is the same as it has been before and that the child's box is open and ready. A quick review of the notes from the past session, the child's early history and abuse scenario, and whether this is a particular point in the child's therapy (initial session, sessions before and after breaks in therapy, termination sessions) will help the therapist be alert to particular issues that may come up in the child's play. If the parent and therapist have spoken during the week, this information should also be reviewed. The therapist needs to be clear on what information the child knows was told to the therapist. Because a child can feel betrayed if information is passed on without her knowledge, it is important for parents or group home workers to tell the child what they will be telling the therapist. Only then can this information be used within the therapy.

In addition to this review, the therapist needs to spend a brief moment eliminating any personal issues he may be feeling. Personal feelings related to the therapist's own life can affect the meanings he sees in the child's play as well as his emotional reaction to the child's play (countertransference).

As the play progresses, the therapist watches carefully. The following sections will describe how the child's experiences and internalizations are expressed within the play and how specific abuse-related internalizations can be recognized. Ideas for working through these internalizations are discussed.

RECOGNIZING MEANING
WITHIN THE CHILD'S PLAY

As the therapist watches the child play, she needs to note (a) unusual use of play objects or craft materials and unusual play themes, (b) repetitive play, (c) comments or play not related to the ongoing play, (d) unusual movements by the child, (e) objects or activities that are avoided, (f) the child's use of the therapist together with the therapist's reaction to the child, and (g) events in the child's life. These activities and events indicate important meaning for the child. They need to be thought about in terms of the child's experience and abuse-related internalizations.

Unusual use of play object, and unusual themes. Play, movement, or activity that differs from that seen with most children of the child's age needs to be noted by the therapist. In particular, the therapist notes any unusual use of play objects or craft material.

A 5-year-old takes out the cow family and sets up the cow and one calf over at the side, placing the bull and the other calf in the middle of the table. As he sets a piece of fencing between the bull and the calf, the fencing falls over. The therapist notes that this configuration is distinctly different from the usual grouping of animals made by young children.

The therapist recalls that the mother in the family had given her son little attention. The abuse had been from father. The play may reflect the child's experience and internalization of distorted family boundaries.

A 7-year-old makes a paper basket by cutting and gluing the corners. When she reaches the last corner, she finds that she cannot glue it together correctly, talks about not being able to fix it, becomes discouraged and states that the basket should be thrown away. Because the child has already demonstrated an ability to construct corners, this difficulty has particular significance.

The therapist recognizes that the child may be feeling that the abuse (that is, she) cannot be fixed and, therefore, feels that she should be thrown away. The child may be expressing the internalization of damage.

Repetitive play. Particular attention should be given by a therapist to play that is repeated within a session or over several sessions.

A 9-year-old places the members of the family in the dollhouse and then takes the grandmother and places her in the rocking chair out on the front porch. Although the general arrangement of the family dolls varies from session to session, grandmother is always placed on the porch. When the child is asked about it, she comments that the grandmother is just there watching.

The therapist notes the child's need to have someone "on watch" and recalls that although mother had been told by child protection that the children were to have no contact with father, he had been back to the house. For this child, mother not protecting appears to have been internalized as an active memory (she often talks about it). Her need to be watchful may be a reaction to the memory.

A 6-year-old, when placing the dolls and furniture around the house, repeatedly places a piece of furniture in front of the bedroom door. Although the therapist has talked about the child's memory of the abuse and the fear she experienced when stepfather came into the room, the play pattern continues.

The therapist reviews the home living situation with mother and learns that stepfather is coming over to visit the younger children in the family. An ongoing situation and fear is being represented in the play.

Unrelated Comments or Play. At other times, a therapist may note a comment or a play activity that is not related to the ongoing play themes. By their unusual content, these comments or activities provide information for the therapist.

A 10-year-old sets up a family scene in the sand tray and has the dolls arguing with each other, a common theme for him. He then takes the baby doll and pushes him down in the sand. He goes back to the other dolls and the arguing escalates and dominates the play.

The therapist notices the separation of the baby from the rest of the family and wonders if this represents the child's denial or dissociation (a distortion of reality) from the family violence.

An 8-year-old is busy with craft materials but suddenly looks up and asks, "Is that a knock on the door?"

The therapist is startled and about to reply that there was no knock when she realizes that this comment, by its unusualness, represents a particular concern of the child's. Intrusion into the child's space is an important issue for the child. The therapist will need to determine the meaning of this intrusion (a sense of powerlessness over his world, a memory of the abuser coming into the room) for this particular child if she is to be able to address accurately the internalization from which the child is presently responding.

Unusual movements. A therapist will also need to be attentive to the child's movement and, in particular, movement related to the therapist.

A 5-year-old draws a picture of a boy and a snake. When the therapist asks what that would be like for the boy in the picture to have a snake so close, the boy shrugs. The therapist comments that that could be scary. At that point, the therapist becomes aware that the child has shifted in his chair and that his back is now blocking the therapist's view of the picture.

The therapist recognizes that a child turning his back to a therapist often represents anger at the therapist or a wish to avoid something. Relating back to what has just been mentioned, the therapist reflects that the child may be angry that the idea of being scared has been brought up or that it may feel safer to the child to be angry than to be scared. Not only can the feelings be talked about but also the sense of powerlessness over what is happening—now, in the therapy, and earlier, during the abuse.

An 8-year-old places the family of dolls in the bed. As he does this, he puts his left hand just inside his pant waistline.

The therapist notices the child rubbing his hand down toward the stomach and realizes that placing the dolls together on the bed has probably caused some arousal sensation. The therapist can comment on this as a normal response to being touched or to thoughts about touching, to reassure the child. The therapist can then enquire further as to what the child thinks about when he gets those feelings. Understanding the child's thoughts will help the therapist know what internalizations need to be addressed.

Avoiding objects or activities. The therapist will also want to be alert to play objects or activities that are avoided. When play does not show distress, this does not necessarily mean that something is being avoided; these activities may be good, healthy play. With this play, there is a sense of relaxation in the room. With avoidance, there is a sense of tension, fatigue, or deadness in the room.

> A 7-year-old undresses all of the dolls and then picks up a ball and asks the therapist to play ball with her.
> The therapist notes the sudden change in activity and recognizes the level of anxiety created in the child by the undressing of the dolls, a memory from the abuse.

> A 9-year-old starts a game of catch as soon as he walks into the room.
> The therapist thinks back to the last session and realizes that they had been talking at the end of the session about the child's big brother who had abused him. She realizes that the child may be trying to protect himself from the memories or feelings that would have come up with that discussion.

Transference-Countertransference. An additional source of information is the manner in which the child interacts with the therapist (transference) and the therapist's reaction to the child (countertransference). Davies and Frawley (1994) have described four transference-countertransference relationships that occur in therapy with adults who have been sexually abused. These relationships occur with children as well. At times, within each of these relationships, the child takes on the role of his parent or other influential adult with the therapist ending up with the child's experience, and, at other times, the child takes on the role she experienced and the therapist finds himself in the position of behaving like the parent. It is important that the therapist be aware not only of how he is being used and but also of how he is responding so that the child's earlier experience can be addressed and a new relationship experience can occur.

The occurrence of sexual abuse within the family, or abuse outside the family that is not disclosed, means the child has been unseen and neglected and has experienced an unseeing or uninvolved parent. Davies and Frawley (1994) describe the individual who has been abused as presenting herself as uninvolved in therapy while the therapist works hard to engage her, just as the child had tried to engage her parent. When the child remains uninvolved, as did the parent, the therapist has to be careful not to become frustrated and withdrawn, thereby recreating the child's early experience of parental abandonment.

> Nina (an 8-year-old neglected and abused sexually by both parents from infancy to age 5) comes into the therapy room, picks up the stuffed bear, and lies on the sofa with her back to the therapist. This continues for quite a while.

> **Therapist:** [Feels excluded and also hurt because she has put so much energy into the therapy with Nina. She then realizes that Nina, by being self-involved, is playing the role of her parents.] Your being with the bear leaves me alone and lonely. And how lonely it must have been for you when no one paid attention to you when you were little.

The individual may at other times play the role of the unseen, neglected child who, in self-protection, pretends not to have needs (Davies & Frawley, 1994). In this relationship, the therapist has to be careful to see the needs that are not shown if she is to avoid the role of the unseeing parent.

> Nina curls up in the space behind the file cabinet. She is quiet and nothing seems to be happening.

> **Therapist:** [Waits for something to happen but soon finds that her mind has gone off on other thoughts. As she realizes this, she recog- nizes that something is happening.] It may feel as if you are neglected here, my not noticing you and your quietness. It is my job to notice you. I notice . . .

Another abuse relationship—the sadistic, impulsive abuser and the helpless, impotently enraged victim—may also be played out

(Davies & Frawley, 1994). The child, wishing to avoid the helpless position, takes on the role of the abuser and becomes intrusive, often attacking the therapist. The therapist, as did the child, feels helpless in this situation.

> Nina throws the pillow at the therapist and, when the therapist is startled, laughs a raucous laugh. Nina then prances around the room chanting, "Can't catch, idiot!" and waving the pillow above her head.

Therapist: [Feels the thought processes draining out of her mind. She realizes some dynamic is going on but just cannot piece together what is happening. It is not until after the session, when thinking back on what happened, that she is able to recognize that Nina's abusive-type behavior had elicited in her the very helplessness that Nina would have experienced during the abuse. She hopes that next time she will be better able to respond.]

The opposite positions, the child as helpless and the therapist as intrusive and abusive, may also occur and is, indeed, fostered by the nature of the relationship and the therapist's wish "to get to the material."

> Nina colors with red crayon all over a piece of paper.

Therapist: The red reminds me of the kittens you were talking about last week, the kittens that were bleeding when your mother killed them.

Nina: Let's play baseball.

Therapist: We can do that later, but it is all right to talk about the kittens here. What do you remember?

Nina: I'm going to get some water. [She runs out of the room.]

Therapist: [Reviews what happened as she waits for Nina to return. Clearly, the topic had scared Nina. Then, she realizes that Nina had introduced the red color. It wasn't the topic that was so intrusive but the way she had gone about pursuing it.]

Also encouraged by the therapeutic setting is the role of idealized rescuer for the therapist and entitled child for the individual (Davies

& Frawley, 1994). The danger within this relationship is that the therapist will step in to protect the child from frightening feelings rather than being available for the child as she works through feelings.

> Nina builds a tunnel with pillows and sofa cushions and crawls inside, telling the therapist to put a pillow across the opening.

Nina: It's dark, I'm scared.

Therapist: [Moves forward to remove a pillow and then stops herself.] Yes, scary like when you were locked in the closet as a little child. Scary and you couldn't do anything about it. You are here now. There are pillows, not a locked door. Do you want more time with the dark or do you want to knock down a pillow or do you want me to take away a pillow?

In the turnabout positions, the child moves in to care for the therapist, and the therapist, feeling exhausted from the struggles within the therapy, welcomes the child's concern and support.

> Nina gets a cup of water and props up the cushions in a chair for the therapist. When the therapist switches to that chair, as requested by Nina, Nina asks if she is comfortable.

Therapist: [As the therapist starts to respond, she pauses.] You seem to feel you need to take care of me. And at home you did a lot of taking care of your mother. But I am an adult, like your mother is an adult, and it is our job to take care of ourselves, to take care of you, and to help you learn how to take care of yourself.

The fourth relationship dynamic discussed by Davies and Frawley (1994) is that of the seducer and the seduced. The child and the therapist, through discussion of sexual topics, description of sexual scenes, and expression of sexualized thoughts or behaviors, act out the roles both of the seducer and the seduced.

> Nina, working at the table with her back to the therapist, moves her chair next to the therapist's chair and then shifts the way she is sitting so that she rubs against the therapist.

Therapist: [Feels as if Nina is finally reaching out for some closeness; she feels tempted to put her arm around Nina. Then she thinks more about the movement, that the movement was done almost secretively, that the rubbing was happening without any recognition of it happening. The movement had a seductive, not a close, feeling to it. Should she say something?

But if this movement and touching is positive, she doesn't want to ruin it. A close, positive experience will be so important for Nina. She is sure it is positive. She starts to move her chair closer. This wish of hers, for the contact to be positive, starts to feel seductive.] I notice that you have moved your chair until you are touching, rubbing me. If you would like to lean against me or have a hug, you can ask. And then I can decide if that feels right and I can tell you. Rubbing, in this way, is not appropriate between an adult and a child.

Ongoing events. Even with careful attention to the content of the play or crafts and the atmosphere in the room, there will be moments when the therapist feels—and indeed is—lost as to what is happening. It can be helpful at that point to review the session from the beginning and to review what has been going on for the child during the week.

A 12-year-old stands and looks out the window. She asks the therapist where her car is.

Therapist: [Not able to understand any meaning in this. She then recalls that on the way down the hall, the child asked whether the bear was still in the room. She also remembers that during the week, the child had been switched to a new foster home with no forewarning. The child may be worried as to whether the therapist is going to continue to be there. The child's recent experience of loss raises further the fear of betrayal.]

The content during a play session can provide the therapist with information. Some play and craft activity is quite easy to follow and understand, whereas other activities are less clear. Knowledge of the internalizations resulting from sexual abuse alerts the therapist to what may be happening for the child and, thus, helps the therapist recognize the content being played out.

RECOGNIZING THE
ABUSE INTERNALIZATIONS

The Internalization Model alerts the therapist not only to what may be expressed in the play but also to what needs to be addressed if the child is to work through the abuse and reclaim a sense of self and world unaffected by the abuse. In this section, the Internalization Model will be used as a framework for recognizing what the I am damagedchild is expressing through play.

| I am damaged | During sexual abuse, children experience an intrusion of their bodies and their privacy. This intrusion leaves behind a sense of internal damage.

Cindy (a 10-year-old sexually abused by her uncle between ages 8 and 9) starts scratching herself and says that she is dirty and is trying to get the dirt out.

Therapist: [Notices that there is no dirt on the child, and therefore, she is talking about internal dirt. She also notes the word "out," clearly indicating that Cindy is talking about something internal.] Listening to you talk about dirt inside, I'm wondering if you are feeling that there is dirt inside from the abuse. [Cindy nods.] How big is that feeling of dirt?

Cindy shows a small size with her hands and then a larger size.

Therapist: That dirt doesn't belong there. The dirt belongs to the abuse, not you. And the abuse is out, over, so let's get that feeling of dirt out, over. You could draw it, model it out of plasticine, what do you want to do with it?

Cindy picks up a pencil.
Therapist tapes together two pieces of paper to accommodate the size Cindy had indicated.
Cindy scribbles all over the paper.

Therapist: What now? You could tear it, cut it, squish it, or something else. What do you want to do?

Cindy tears it up, stamps on the pieces, and then with a big smile, puts them in the garbage.

Terry (a 9-year-old sexually abused by her father between ages 5 to 7) comes in and takes out a paper on which she had written "Terry to Sandra" the week before. She adds "I love Sandra" and then erases the "Terry" and adds "love Mommy."

Therapist: [Notices that the very common 7-year-old activity of writing "to" notes and "love" notes had been altered in a way that eliminated the child's name. The child seems not to be able to link herself with love (it might also have been noted that the child did not link herself with "loving mommy," and that would have led to a different and possibly as valid an interpretation).] It seems as if it is really important for you to love me and love Mommy. But I'm also noticing that you erased your name. Do you love yourself?

Terry shakes her head.

Therapist: Close your eyes for just a moment and imagine yourself. Now give yourself a hug. [This was an error by the therapist because it did not first address the internalization expressed in the play.]

Terry: Yucky, yucky.

Therapist: Where's the yuck?

Terry: In the heart.

Therapist: [Goes over to the blackboard and draws a heart and then draws some scribble lines inside the heart.] This is the yuck in Terry's heart. I am going to take the yuck out because it doesn't belong to Terry. [Miming taking the yuck in her hands, she turns to the child.] Where shall I put the yuck?

Terry: In da—no, to the devil.

Therapist: [Goes over to the empty chair in the room.] Hi, Daddy, Terry got all this yucky feeling from your touching her. She wants you to know how it felt. [Holds out hands as if putting the yuck in the chair, then after a moment, with a hand movement, takes the yuck back.] OK, do you know now? [Terry, in her comment, had made it clear that it would have been too threatening to her and her love for her father at that point for the yuck to be left with the father. Moves back to Terry.] What shall we do with it now?

Terry: Throw it away.

| I am powerless | Within the abuse situation, someone else controlled what happened to the child. Because the nature of the abuse (the sexual content) was beyond the child's level of understanding, the world would have seemed even more out of control, and the child is left feeling powerless.

> Tommy (a 5-year-old sexually abused by mother's boyfriend at ages 4 and 5) repeatedly attacks the doll in the bed and throws the baby dolls down the stairs.

Therapist: [Notices not only the destructive acts on the baby and child figures but also the repetitiveness of the activity. The child's motion has a quality of not being able to be controlled or stopped.] I'm noticing how the dolls are getting hurt over and over again. Seems like you are letting me know what it was like when you were unable to stop Carl from hurting you. You didn't have lots of ways of stopping things then. You know what? You do have some ways of stopping things now. What are some of the things you could do now?

Tommy: Yell, I can run.

Therapist: OK, let's practice. Let me see you run . . . What do you think I would do? . . . Let's practice that.

> Karla (an 8-year-old sexually abused by her mother's partner at age 7) asks if she can take home something from her box.

Therapist: [Feels unsure as to why this has come up again at this time.] You would like to take home some of what we do, but everything we do here stays here. At our last session together, you can choose one thing to take home.

Karla: What will you do with the box after I leave?

Therapist: [Reminds herself not to answer the question because answers only cut off what the child is thinking.] What do you think I will do with the box?

Karla: Will you keep it for when I am abused again?

Therapist: [Realizes that the child is talking about her fear that the abuse will happen all over again. This would explain why, week after week, she has blocked the door of the playhouse, even though they have talked about her fear of dangerous things.] It seems that you are afraid that the abuse will just go on and on and you won't be able to stop it.

Karla: What if Mommy and Rick get back together?

Therapist: Rick will have learned how to behave with children. [The therapist then realizes that that is not what Karla is talking about; Karla is talking about a fear of not being able to control what her mother does, what Rick does, what happens to her.] Let's say Rick did come back and he did come into your room and start to touch you, what would you do?

Karla: Scream.

Therapist: Let me hear your scream. . . . What would happen then?

Karla: Mommy would wake up.

Therapist: Let's practice again. . . . That's something you didn't know about before, so now things could be different.

| I am guilty/bad/an object to be used | A child, because of egocentric processing of experiences, because of what abusers and others said to him, and because of his wish not to be powerless, blames himself for the sexual abuse. He sees himself as bad. If the perpetrator was an important person, especially mother or father, the young child wants to protect the perpetrator and, to do this, takes all the "badness" on himself.

Ricky (a 6-year-old sexually abused by his mother between ages 2 and 5) plays at being a young child. He tells the therapist to hit him because he is bad.

Therapist: [Notices that the child has placed himself around the age that the abuse started and is defining himself as bad.] Seems like you think you are bad, that you were bad as a little boy. No, babies aren't bad. When things like abuse happen to children, they aren't bad. It is the person who does the abuse who is wrong. [Therapist carefully chooses the word *wrong* rather than *bad* because for most children, it is important to preserve their parents, particularly mothers, as good. Using the word *bad* for mother could push a child into taking on even more "badness."]

Ricky: Yes, I was bad. [He picks up a toy car and throws it across the room.]

Therapist: [Notices that the child is saying he is bad at the same time as doing something that is normally labeled as bad. The fact that he is doing something may mean that he is thinking of the things he did during the abuse rather than the things done to him.] Throwing the car is not bad if no one has taught you not to throw it. You, as a young child, needed to be taught a lot of things. You needed to be taught that hard objects are not thrown, and you needed a chance to learn that your body is private to you. And it is my job as the mom in our play to teach you not to throw hard things. Here is a soft puppet, that's all right to throw, and I'll take away the things that can break.

> Ricky throws the puppet.

Therapist: And look how well you learn. It was your mom's job to teach you that your body is private, her body is private, and that adults do not touch children. She didn't teach you, so you didn't have the chance to learn. Doing something that you have not been taught about does not make you bad. Now you are being taught new things [Realizes importance of Ricky being clear on learning a new message about privacy of other people's body if he is not to become sexually intrusive with other children] and are learning not to touch other people's breasts or vaginas or penises. Touching them would not be fair to them. Their bodies are theirs, just like yours is yours. You know you can touch your own penis to give yourself a good feeling [Recognizes the importance for Ricky that self and others be differentiated], and when you are grown up and love someone, then you'll want to share touching with them. [Begins the process of distinguishing between sexual abuse and sexuality.]

| I am responsible for . . . | Children are often threatened with the idea that something will happen to themselves, their parent, or their pets if they tell about the abuse. Even when the threat is not verbalized, the power of the abuser in the family is such that children feel a threat. Then, when people become upset following disclosure, it often seems to the child that the threat is coming true. A child becomes frightened, both of things happening and of making decisions.

> Tina (a 5-year-old sexually abused, including being tied and gagged, by the husband of the baby-sitter) tells about a nightmare that she has had of things happening to her mother.

Therapist: [Realizes that children are often threatened that if they tell, something will happen to mother and knows that dreams often represent fears.] What did Arnold say would happen if you told about the things he was doing to you?

Tina: He said he would hurt my mother if I told.

Therapist: And it seems that that was what you were dreaming. But how is Mommy today? . . . Why don't you draw a picture of your mother?

Tina draws the picture. (If Tina had not been able to draw the picture and the mother was in the waiting room, the therapist might have asked the mother to come into the therapy room.)

Therapist: Is she hurt? All right, what are some of the things that might hurt mother?

Tina: She could fall down.

Therapist: Yes, she could. But that would not happen because of Arnold, that would happen because she tripped. What might she trip on?

Tina: I don't know.

Therapist: When you fall, what have you tripped on?

Tina: A toy, she could trip on a toy.

Therapist: Yes she could, and then she would fall. What else could happen to her? . . . Yes, Arnold told you that he would hurt your mother, but you know something, he isn't able to do that.

Kimberly (a 6-year-old sexually abused by mother's common-law partner between ages 5 and 6) plays out, for the second week in a row, having the mother and grandmother dolls die and go to heaven.

Therapist: [Realizes from the repetition that this is a major concern for the child. Last week, she had commented that maybe Kimberly was afraid of something happening to important people, but because the play was returning in such similar form, that may not have been the central part of Kimberly's issue. She then recalled that Joe was quite a violent man and wondered what he had threatened.] I was wondering what Joe said to you when he told you not to tell?

Kimberly: He said he would kill Mommy and Nanna.

Therapist: And that is something you are really scared might happen. But he is not going to kill them—he is a long way away, and the police are protecting Mommy and Nanna. When is it that you think about it?

Kimberly: I see it when I am asleep.

Therapist: [Realizes that the child needs a new experience; his saying a threat will not happen is not enough to alter something really frightening.] Tell me about that picture that comes into your mind.

Kimberly: Well, Mommy and Nanna are sitting in the kitchen, and Joe walks in. And there he is with a gun in his hand.

Therapist: All right, hold that picture in your mind for a moment. Do you have it there?

Kimberly: [nods] He is pointing the gun at them.

Therapist: Now I want you to take Sergeant Lewis into the picture. Is he there? . . . Watch Sergeant Lewis, what is he doing?

Kimberly: He's chasing Joe, he is chasing him out of the house.

| memories | Abuse always leaves behind memories—memories of the abuse and memories of no protection. These memories may be pushed out of the child's awareness or may be dissociated, but they are still within him.

> Amy (a 6-year-old who was sexually abused by several boarders in the home and possibly by stepfather) places the grandfather doll on a chair and the girl doll in his lap. She then pours glue over the doll and calls it "cowboy milk in the middle of the night."

Therapist: [Notices the similarity between something white from a male during the night to semen ejaculation. The placement of the dolls also indicates a possible reenactment of an abuse scenario.] It seems that you are thinking of the times men held you and the white stuff, the semen, from them went on you.

> Amy starts to rub the glue into the male doll's face.

Therapist: You want him to know how it felt. Tell him how it felt. What words will you use to tell him how it felt?

Amy: Yucky! Yucky!

Sonja (a 4-year-old sexually abused by her father over the past year) starts to rock back and forth in a sexualized manner with the large teddy bear and whimpers, "Mommy, Mommy."

Therapist: [Notices the sexualized movement and remembers that the child has done this before, and they have talked about the child's experience. The whimper this time indicates that she is thinking about mother, and the wistful tone of voice seems to indicate a wish for mother. (If there were any indication from the history or the child's tone of voice that the mother might have been connected with the abuse, the child should be asked directly.) This sounded more as if the child was wishing for something.] You may be thinking of the time when Daddy rubbed you and put his finger in you and remembering that Mommy was not there to stop Daddy. Sounds as if you were wishing that Mommy had been there to stop it.

Sonja looks at the therapist.

Therapist: It would have been really scary for you when Mommy wasn't there. (If mother has the resources to respond well . . .) Shall we ask Mommy into the room so you can tell her you wish she had been there? (If mother would not be able to respond well . . .) Tell me what it was like when Mommy wasn't there.

I feel chaotic   When a child is abused by someone important to him, his fear and anger do not replace his love for that person. They exist alongside the love. Opposite feelings for one person do not make sense to a child, they create an emotional chaos.

Sonja (a 4-year-old sexually abused by her father over the past year) takes pieces of plasticine out of her box. She names the large black piece "Daddy," the smaller brown piece "Mommy," and the smallest red piece, "baby." She takes bits of the black off the larger piece and calls them "poisonous string." She then takes those bits and goes over to the waste basket and throws them away.

Therapist: [Notices the identification given to the plasticine shapes and that the parts the child does not like came from the daddy. He also remembers that the child had reported to her mother, but not to the police, that her father had tied her. He wonders if poisonous string might refer to penis or semen or might perhaps refer to a rope, if she was indeed tied. He quickly reminds himself he is not investigating. As a therapist, he is there to help the child with the issues.] Seems like you are thinking of Daddy and of something about him that hurt you. [The abuse had been described by Sonja as hurting, so it was appropriate for the therapist to use this term. If the child had not used it, the therapist should not, because it might not accurately describe the child's experience.] And that thing you would like to get rid of.

Sonja: I miss Daddy.

Therapist: [Recognizes the ambivalence in Sonja's feelings.] Yes, you do miss Daddy and all of the special times that you had with Daddy. And Daddy has a job now to get rid of the behavior that hurt you and to learn how to behave with children.

Sonja: He knows now. He won't hurt me again. I want him to come home.

Therapist: Yes, you do want him to come home. But it is important that he learn how to behave with children first. And that is his job. You could even write him a letter telling him that. [Sonja nods.] You tell me what you want to say and I will write it down.

Sonja: Tell him I miss him and want him to come home.

Therapist: All right, and what were you telling him when you took the bits of poisonous string off the Daddy piece and threw the bits away.

Sonja: I didn't do that.

Therapist: Yes, they are there in the waste basket. And it makes sense that you want Daddy to get rid of the parts of him that hurt you and scared you. [Therapist phrases this very carefully because it is important that the job of "getting rid of" is assigned to Daddy and not to the child.] How can we tell him that?

Sonja: I don't know.

Therapist: You could tell him about the bit of plasticine called "poisonous string" that you put in the wastebasket.

Sonja: Get rid of the string!

Jessica (a 9-year-old sexually abused by her stepfather between ages 5 and 7) makes a card on which she writes "I love sister, brother, my gerbils, my teacher, Julie, the sun, God."

Therapist: [Notices the common 8-year-old activity of making cards but also notes that the person to whom children most often direct their cards (mother) is not listed. This might indicate that the child is remembering that mother was not there when she needed her. Because the child has used an activity that is linked with expressing love, the anger at mother and the child's ambivalence around that anger is probably more relevant at this point.] I am noticing that you have everyone's name there except your mother's. And, yes, you would be angry at mother, angry at her for leaving you in the house with your stepfather.

Jessica: I love my mother.

Therapist: And you can love your mother and also hate her, or be angry at her, for not protecting you.

Jessica draws a picture of herself with an open smiling mouth and sharp teeth in the mouth.

Therapist: Yes, angry but trying not to show the anger. Angry at me for talking about you being angry at mother, angry at mother, and angry at having to come and talk about the abuse.

| I am betrayed by people close to me | For the child who has been abused by someone close to him, a connection is formed for him between being close and being abused.

Josh (a 5-year-old sexually abused by mother's common-law partner between ages 3 and 4) puts a tiger in the lap of the boy doll. The doll pets the tiger and then the tiger attacks the doll, then the tiger is quiet again and the doll pets the tiger again.

Therapist: [Notices that it is the tiger and not the boy doll who is changing behavior; first the tiger is close, and then the tiger attacks. If the child were expressing his own shifting feelings, then the child would probably have used the doll to do the alternating behavior.] I'm noticing how the tiger sometimes is sitting very quietly and close with the boy and sometimes the tiger is attacking the boy. I guess that's like Michael. Sometimes you had good times and close times with him and sometimes he abused you. Seems as though it was really hard to know what would happen next.

Josh takes the tiger and throws it off the table.

Therapist: Yes, really angry at him, and you should be angry with him because he did something he should not have done, he touched you in a way he should not have touched you.

Josh then throws all of the animals off the table.

Therapist: Seems as though when the tiger is unsafe, all the animals become unsafe. But, no, it is the tiger who attacked the boy doll, not all of the animals. Let's look at each animal. How can we tell which animal is safe and which is unsafe?

Josh pushes all of the animals away.

Therapist: At this point, all of them seem to feel unsafe. Some other time we can look and see which is safe and which is not safe.

Debbie (a 7-year-old sexually abused by her father at age 4) looks at *A Very Touching Book* (Hindman, 1985). Each time she sees a picture of genitals, she says, "Gross."

Therapist: [Remembers that Debbie has, for the last 3 years, denied that any abuse occurred. He wonders if the denial is connected with calling genitals gross.] For so many years, you have needed to pretend that your father did not touch you, but it seems that a gross feeling about private parts has stayed with you. Father's touch felt gross but your private parts aren't gross. What would help the gross feeling go away?

Debbie starts to play ball by herself and then looks at her watch.

Therapist: [Notices Debbie withdrawing from the session.] I notice that after I talked about private parts and the feeling of gross, you started playing ball by yourself and now you are looking to see how much time is left in the session. Seems as if you are really angry at me for talking about private parts.

Debbie: No, I want to know if my mother set my watch correctly.

Therapist: [Realizes from the wording that Debbie is dealing with issues of trust.] Seems like you are wondering if you can trust mom, if you can trust me.

Debbie starts throwing the ball with the therapist. She then throws it onto the therapist's desk knocking over the clock.

Therapist: [Keeping the trust issue in mind, realizes that the clock is the only valuable thing on the desk and that it is the one thing that got hurt but at the same time, realizes that the clock may link to Debbie's watch.] You may be wondering if you can trust me to keep things safe and to watch the time. I'll move the clock so it can't get hurt. It is the adult's job to keep special things safe. Children want to hug and play with fathers and it is the father's job to be sure that the child's private parts —your breasts, vulva, vagina—are not touched, are safe.

Debbie: I didn't hug him, he hugged me.

Therapist: And he should not have hugged you in that way.

| I have no boundaries | The child in the incestuous family does not have an opportunity to learn appropriate boundaries between himself and others. He is placed in the position of having to take care of the needs of the perpetrator and of the nonperpetrating parent(s).

> Angie (a 7-year-old sexually abused by mother's boyfriend over the last year) has the child doll feeding the mother doll and the father doll.

Therapist: [Recalls that mother has been depressed for a long time, and that the depression has become worse since the disclosure. Angie makes coffee and toast in the morning for her mother and takes it to her.] I am thinking about how you have had to take care of other people, of John, of your mother, like the child doll is feeding the other dolls. You are right, you have had to do this, but it is not your job. It is the adult's job to take care of herself and to take care of you. How could the mother doll take care of the child doll?

Angie: She doesn't need to, the child can do it.

Therapist: Yes, the child may be able to, but it's not her job. And maybe the mother can learn how to take care of the child. Let's see, what could I teach her? [Realizes importance that the child not do the teaching. That would, again, be an inappropriate role.]

> Ricky (a 6-year-old sexually abused by his mother between age 2 and 5) notices a scratch on the therapist's arm and begins making a bandage for it.

Therapist: [Becomes aware that the child is taking care of her and that she is allowing this reversal of roles, just as a reversal of roles had occurred in the child's home.] You are very busy taking care of me today. But that is my job, my job to take care of my scratch, like it is Mom's job to take care of herself. I will look at the scratch and decide what it needs. If it were open or bleeding, I would put a bandage on it, but it is not, so I shall just be careful not to hit it on anything.

Ricky goes on to play. (If Ricky's concern had continued, the therapist would have needed to pursue the issue of caretaking further.)

| when I am sexual, good things happen | During the period of abuse, the child is given special attention for mannerisms that the perpetrator finds arousing. This attention and the sexual stimulation that some children experience reinforce sexualized behaviors.

Amy (a 6-year-old sexually abused by several boarders living in the home and possibly by her stepfather) announces that she is going to take her shirt off.

Therapist: [Realizes that Amy is repeating behavior that she had been taught and needs now to be taught new and more appropriate behaviors.] You were taught that people want to look at your body, that people like you when you show them your body. But no, your body is yours, and because it is private for you, I don't want to look at it. I like you when you show me the way you make things or the way you play.

Amy: I'm going to take it off. [She starts pulling off her shirt.]

Therapist: I'll turn my chair around while your shirt is off because your body is private. [Therapist turns the chair around.] And then, let me know when your shirt is back on so I can watch you making things or playing. I like to do those things with you. . . . Seems like it is really hard for you to believe that I don't want to see your body. Yes, it would be hard, because other adults taught you to show them your body and to touch their bodies. Those adults were wrong. Your body is for you and not to be shown to other people. Let's see what could you show me—I remember the airplane you made. I liked it when you showed me that.

Jessica (a 9-year-old sexually abused by her stepfather between age 5 and 7) comes in on a cold day in March in a short skirt, no tights, and a sweater that is so big that it slides off her shoulders. Pulling the sweater back up, Jessica says, "I don't know why I wore this."

Therapist: [Realizes that this outfit exposes the child's thighs and, at times, her breasts and that such exposure would have been encouraged by her stepfather.] You know, when you were abused, you were taught to show your body. You were taught that showing your body gets attention. And that seems to have become a habit. But your body is private and you don't need to show it to get attention. Let's see, what are some of the things you do here to get attention? . . . At home? . . . At school? . . . In the schoolyard?

my sexuality means	no feeings no control negative feelings

Sexual arousal during abuse occurs in combination with other experiences: secrecy, pain, fear, manipulation. Even when these negative characteristics do not occur, the arousal raises questions and fears in the child's mind.

Cindy (a 10-year-old sexually abused by her uncle between ages 8 and 9) says that she doesn't like coming and thinking about the abuse.

Therapist: [Feels unclear as to what Cindy may be talking about right now but does recognize her dislike of this whole process.] And it makes sense that you don't like it. It isn't fair that you are left with the thoughts. Do thoughts about the abuse come into your mind when you aren't here?

Cindy: When I'm on the merry-go-round in the play yard.

Therapist: [Thinks about the playground merry-go-round and remembers that the twirling can cause arousal sensations.] I guess twirling on a merry-go-round would give you a tingly feeling between your legs. And when Dan rubbed you or when he put his penis in you, that may have given you a tingly feeling. And tingly feelings feel good because that's the way our bodies are made. Having those feelings with Dan doesn't make the feelings bad. You can enjoy those feelings on the merry-go-round or when you rub yourself, and when you are grown up, you can enjoy them with someone you love and want to share feelings with.

Cindy listens intently but doesn't say anything.

Therapist: What we could do is practice your having those feelings without any thoughts of Dan coming in. Does that sound all right? [Cindy nods.] All right, close your eyes and just let yourself go back there, back to the merry-go-round, the merry-go-round in the playground, and to yourself on the merry-go-round. When you see yourself there, nod your head to let me know. . . . Describe that picture to me. . . . Now let yourself feel that good tingly feeling, just a bit of it maybe, between your legs, and while you feel it, keep looking at the merry-go-round, at your hands on the handle bar of the merry-go-round, at the playground around you. . . . What comes into your mind as you are twirling and as you feel the tingly feeling? [If thoughts of the abuse or the perpetrator come in, the therapist would do the imaging again with more details in the scene and more prompting for concentrating on them. If the intrusive thoughts continue, the child could work on where she would like to send those thoughts while she is twirling.]

| what I am told ≠ what is meant | During the abuse, the perpetrator and sometimes the nonperpetrating parent(s) say things that are not true: for example, "I won't hurt you," "You will be safe with grandfather." The child experiences a mismatch between statements and reality, and this mismatch is internalized as a part of their experience with other people, especially when statements have to do with emotions or closeness.

Jim (a 10-year-old neglected and sexually abused by both his parents between the age of 2 and 6) complains that the things in his box are different from what was in his box last week.

Therapist: [Realizes that this has to do with trust but also remembers that Jim has said, in other sessions, that he does not believe what the therapist has said.] I told you that your box was just for you, and no one else goes into your box. But it seems that it feels to you that that isn't true. It seems as if what I say isn't what happens. I know that your mom and dad told you things that were not true. That was your mom and your dad. This is here.

Jim: The things are different and you said they would be the same.

Therapist: [Stops herself from pointing out that things are the same; that is not the issue.] Really hard to believe that what I say will be true.

Jim: People lie all of the time.

Therapist: Let's check; have I lied? It feels like I lied, like Mom lied, like Dad lied. But other people aren't the same as Mom and Dad, I'm not the same as Mom and Dad.

Jim: I guess we might as well go on with what we were doing.

Amy (a 6-year-old sexually abused by several boarders living in the home and possibly by her stepfather) pours glue on the therapist's hands and then roughly presses the therapist's hands together. She asks if it hurts.

Therapist: [Realizes from the way that the child is pressing her hands that this is relevant to the abuse and to hurting and that straightforward information is needed.] Yes, it hurts.

Amy: No, it doesn't. I don't care.

Therapist: It seems that when people told you to say if their touching hurt and you said that it hurt, they kept right on hurting you. They hurt you and they lied to you. That makes it really hard for you to believe me, believe someone else when they say something.

Amy stops pushing and starts to wipe off the glue.

I have $\begin{cases} \text{no emotions} \\ \text{no experience} \\ \text{no integrated self} \end{cases}$ To survive something that is overwhelming, a child pushes (represses, dissociates) some of the experience or feelings connected to the experience from his awareness. In this way, the child limits what is remembered. This method of coping is internalized as part of the child's interactive pattern with his world. The next time the child is stressed, he is likely to use the same process (repression, dissociation). As he does, he loses much of himself.

Ricky (a 6-year-old sexually abused by his mother between age 2 and 5) picks up the boy doll saying that he had had a twin but the twin was bad, so he sent him away.

Therapist: [Notes the term *twin*, remembering that it is sometimes used with imaginary playmates and sometimes with dissociated parts. Because Ricky has used it to take badness, it likely refers to a part Ricky has dissociated.] Seems like you wanted to get rid of the bad happenings, the bad feelings from the touching, so you pushed them into another part of you. That's a really important part of you. That part of you, the twin, with the bad feelings, why doesn't it tell us about those feelings? What would that part say?

Ricky: He did bad things.

Therapist: You had bad things done to you. And we need to listen to all the parts of you telling about those things. You did what you were taught to do, and that's not bad; the teaching wasn't fair. We need to listen to all the parts of you tell about those things and those feelings.

Ricky takes the boy doll and starts to hit the dinosaur.

Therapist: Really angry and lots of reason to be angry. All right to be angry, all right to hit the dinosaur, not all right to hurt people but all right to be angry.

Judith (a 7-year-old sexually abused by her uncle at age 6) puts the girl doll and the father doll in the bed together.

Therapist: [Recognizes the abuse scenario and carefully stays with a description that fits the disclosure Judith had given.] You may be thinking of the time when your uncle came into your bed at night.

Judith: No, he didn't do that.

Therapist: [Feels tempted to go along with what Judith has said but realizes that that would reinforce Judith's internalized denial.] It may feel easier to think it didn't happen. But it did happen. But it is not happening now, and you're okay. [Recognizes that it is easier for Judith to talk about the dolls than about herself.] What do you think the girl doll would be feeling when the man doll climbs into the bed?

At some point within the therapy, each of the first five internalizations (feeling altered or damaged, feeling powerless, feeling bad and guilty, feeling responsible for others, having memories of abuse and no protection) need to be identified and discussed. The other internalizations need to be discussed with those children for whom they occur.

This is a discussion that may have words on both sides or may have words only on the therapist's side and play on the child's side.

In the latter case, it is important that the therapist verbalize what is
being played to help the child process the abuse on the conscious as
well as unconscious level.

In addition, feelings of anger, sadness, fear, loss, and confusion
need to be addressed. The event of abuse should be discussed but
not investigated.

ASSISTING THE CHILD WITH
WORKING THROUGH THE ABUSE

As the therapist is aware of the child's play and of the internalizations likely to be expressed through the play, she can become
increasingly aware of what a child is saying. Where does the therapist go from there?

The steps within a play interpretation—noting what the child is
doing, linking the child's action to the situation of abuse or other
earlier experience, relating the child's action to her emotions or an
internalization—were discussed earlier in the chapter. Although an
interpretation (all three steps or only one or two steps) may be
helpful to a child, it is seldom enough for a child who has been
traumatized. Because trauma is an experience that overwhelms a
child, the child needs more than an interpretation. This is an experience that she has not been able to integrate within her world
schema. She needs to have her understanding of the abuse and her
understanding of the world in which the abuse occurred expanded.
This can be done through a variety of activities. As this occurs, the
child, through assimilation or accommodation (Piaget & Inhelder,
1960), can start to integrate the abuse experience. The trauma factor
of the abuse decreases.

Even as trauma decreases, however, the abuse-related internalizations may remain if they are not addressed directly. If the child's
future experiences are not to be affected by the abuse, these internalizations also need to be addressed. The relationship and activities
within the therapy can address and, therefore, start to shift these
internalizations.

A therapist can provide information or encourage the child to
practice new behaviors. Role play, puppet play, talking within the
metaphor, and stories can help the child work through old experi-

ences and gain new ones. Drawing, craft activities, and imaging can also be used to help a child tell about experiences and feelings and to start to feel more in control. The therapist reacting appropriately with the child provides a new experience. Each of these activities is discussed in more detail.

Providing and incorporating information. The child's experience of the abuse is formed by her knowledge and perceptions at the time the abuse occurred. Because of age and developmental level, the child's knowledge and perceptions were inadequate for making the abuse understandable. Even as the child grows up and learns more about abuse, the early perceptions often remain attached to the abuse experience. An important part of making abuse understandable is providing new and accurate information and linking this information to the personal experience.

This information would include the fact that adults and older children are responsible for what happens between them and younger children, and, in particular, how the child's abuser was older and responsible. A therapist would let the child know that children are not "asking" or "letting" adults do things; rather, children do what they are taught to do. The therapist and child would work at figuring out what the child had been taught. The therapist would note that when children want attention or to feel good, they are asking for attention and to feel good, not sexual touching.

Information also needs to be given about the child being the same child she was before the abuse, that the abuse has not irreparably altered or damaged her. The child, as she was and as she is, needs to be identified. Information about the normalcy of ambivalent feelings and the fear that other people may hurt her is important. Children need information about their bodies, about sexual reactions, and about masturbation. Based on adult male reports that fears related to homosexuality and becoming an abuser are common following childhood sexual abuse (Bruckner & Johnson, 1987; Mendel, 1995), these topics should be explored and accurate information given to boys. A therapist needs to be alert to play or conversation that expresses concerns related to illness, AIDS in particular, and for girls, pregnancy.

Engaging the child in the discussion helps involve the child in the information given. This involvement encourages integration of the information.

> Tell me what you were like as a 2-year-old. When do you notice that characteristic now?

> What is it like to love your father and to be angry or scared of him at the same time?

> Do you sometimes rub yourself between the legs? Lots of kids do, and it can feel really good. How does it feel for you?

Having the child visualize helps integrate information within the abuse-distorted sense of self that is held at a developmentally younger level.

> Why don't you picture the 2-year-old you in your mind. . . . What are you doing? . . . What do you notice about the way the 2-year-old is feeling? . . . What is scaring her? . . . What does she need to know? . . . Can the now you let her know that? . . . What is happening now?

Drawing can also help the child grasp the realities of the abuse situation.

> Let's see how big you were when you were two. . . . Draw a picture of you at that age. . . . Now, your father, how big would he have been? . . . When you draw him in the picture, where on the page will he come to or maybe I'll have to tape another piece to the top of the page so you can fit in all of him.

Practicing behavior. As children work through the feelings and the internalizations from the abuse, and as the level of trauma decreases, some children become more assertive and are able to state their opinions and wishes directly. Other children, still caught in a sense of powerlessness or perhaps more withdrawn by temperament, continue to be withdrawn and nonassertive. These children may have started to recognize what they want to say or do but are still unable to do so in a real situation. Practice at being assertive within the therapy setting can be helpful.

The therapist can encourage the child to say what she wants to the perpetrator while carrying out a physical activity.

> A 5-year-old throws the rubber ball at the door as hard as she can, while she first whispers, then says, and finally yells out, "Don't you touch me." "I hate you." "Get away."

Keeping the other objects in the room safe while a physical activity is going on is an important part of the experience. The child can learn that she and the people important to her are not hurt when she is assertive.

The therapist may also find it helpful, at times, to bring the parent into the session so the child can tell her about things that have happened, about feelings, and most particularly, about how angry the child is. This needs to be used carefully. The therapist needs to be sure the parent will be able to respond in a positive way. In addition, the therapist needs to be careful that talking to a parent in the therapy room does not take away the child's initiative to do the talking outside of therapy.

Using role or puppet play. Role playing and puppet play can provide practice for gaining control of situations—for example, telling about the abuse or becoming more assertive in social situations— thereby shifting the internalization of powerlessness.

> An 8-year-old worries that she will be touched sexually again. The therapist asks her what she knows now that she hadn't known last month when the abuse happened. Once the list is made, the therapist suggests that he, the therapist, play the "now her" while the child plays the "month-ago her." They act out the abuse scenario with the now child giving the month-ago child the information that the child had listed.
>
> The therapist and child then change roles, with the child playing the now child and the therapist playing the month-ago child. The child tells the therapist what to do.
>
> During the dyad sessions following the child's individual therapy, the child asks to redo the role play, with her mother playing the month-ago child as she plays the now child, and then they reverse roles. This is of particular significance in that the mother had been raped by the same individual.

Role and puppet play can also be used as a way to encourage internal communication within a child who dissociates. The now-self typically becomes angry at and blames the abused-self for not telling or for spending time with the abuser. The Gestalt chair technique (Perls, Hefferline, & Goodman, 1951) can help children clarify the experience at the time of the abuse.

> An 11-year-old talks about the abuse as being her fault because she had not told. As soon as she told, the abuse stopped, so she could have made it stop earlier. The therapist asks about some of the things that the child had done when the abuse first started. The child replies that she had peed in her pants and had misbehaved in many ways. The therapist comments that the little her had tried to tell, but no one had paid attention. The 11-year-old dismisses this as not important and continues to blame herself.
>
> The therapist suggests the child have a conversation between her 11-year-old self and 6-year-old self in which the 11-year-old could tell the 6-year-old how angry she is and the 6-year-old could tell the 11-year-old what she had tried to do. The child moves between chairs as she has this conversation. The 6-year-old explains that she had even peed down the heat registers and the whole house had stunk. She wonders why no one paid attention. The 11-year-old says she would have paid attention—and then realizes the 6-year-old was not at fault.

A child may also find it helpful to draw a picture of the different parts and then to do the conversation between the different pictured-parts.

Talking in the metaphor or telling stories. When a child is experiencing extremely high anxiety or fear, the child may have difficulty hearing and integrating direct interpretations or information. In these situations, the therapist may be of more help if she talks about what the dolls, the puppets, or animals are doing or feeling (Shirar, 1996). Allowing the situation to exist outside the child—that is, within the metaphor of the play—the child's anxiety is lowered and the child is better able to hear the therapist. The child is able, albeit indirectly, to begin working through abuse issues. With time, the child will be able to hear and recognize the links to her own experience without severe anxiety or dissociation occurring.

The reading or telling of stories can also help a child who is threatened by direct reference to the abuse. The therapeutic stories written by Davis (1990) are particularly helpful and can be used by a therapist or a parent. Reading *A Very Touching Book* by Jan Hindman (1985) together with a child can also be helpful.

Using art or craft activities. Because the child is at a concrete level of thinking, it is often difficult for the child to grasp and integrate the meaning behind a therapist's observation or interpretation. Encouraging the child to use art and craft materials to represent feelings and internalizations helps the child become involved in the process and experience the observation or interpretation.

> An 8-year-old sits listlessly at the play table. When the therapist notes the feeling of sadness, the child nods. The therapist asks the child to tell her about the sadness, but the child just shakes her head. The therapist comments that it seems that something inside didn't feel right. The child nods. When the therapist asks the child where inside the not-right feeling was, the child shrugs. The therapist then draws an outline of a body and asks the child to draw the not-right feeling in the body. The child took the black crayon and blacked in the top of the head.
> The therapist talks about the "not right" being the abuse, not the child. That the abuse belonged to mother's boyfriend, not the child. The therapist then asks the child what she wants to do with the not-right feeling. The child says that she wants to cut the feeling out, and the therapist encourages her to do that. The therapist then suggests that the child paste the body outline picture that now has a hole in it on top of another paper to fill up all of the child. The child pastes the paper and then colors the picture and draws features.
> The therapist asks what the child wants to do with the piece of blackened paper that she has cut out, the piece that belongs to mother's boyfriend. The child decides to put it in an envelope and mail it to the abuser.

Using imaging. Imaging can help a child work through negative situations and create new internal experiences (Wieland, 1996).

> A 6-year-old neglects her appearance and rips her clothing. As the therapist talks about how the baby part of the child, who had never

been cared for by mother, needs the child's special love and care, the therapist asks the child to see, in her head, the little baby her and to pick her up and rock her.

An 8-year-old tells about his nightmares in which the original abuse situation recurs. The therapist asks him who could help with that situation. At first, the child says no one but then, after further conversation, realizes that his foster parents are keeping him safe from his birth parents who had sexually abused him.

The therapist suggests that the child bring back the picture in the nightmare and, once it is there, take the foster parents into the picture. The child smiles and reports that not only were the foster parents there but that the therapist is up in the corner of the room. The child then describes the foster parents throwing the birth parents out of the dream and padlocking the door.

Imaging can also be used for practicing new situations and new behaviors, such as assertiveness. It can be used with children who dissociate for gathering parts together in one place so they can talk with each other. It is often helpful to have the child draw a picture of the image.

Reacting appropriately with the child. The child in his play is continually reenacting earlier situations as well as present internalizations. At times, this reenactment involves the therapist and the child's behavior with the therapist. The therapist needs to be careful she does not inadvertently fall into the inappropriate role the child has placed on her.

A 6-year-old takes the bear and buries her head, together with the bear, in the corner of the sofa.

The therapist waits, but the child stays in that position. The therapist feels tired; working with this child is always such an effort. Why not just let some of the session go by? Whatever the child is working out, just let it happen. Then there won't be as much wild time to handle.

Then the therapist realizes she is ignoring the child just like the child's mother ignored the child. This will reinforce the child's sense of abandonment. Quietly she starts to talk about what is happening.

If the child is quite fragile, a transference interpretation would be limited to talking about the relationship between the child and the therapist. If the child is stronger and able to look at the earlier relationship, the therapist could mention the parent in the interpretation.

> . . . just like mother ignored you when you were with her.

Being aware of a child's experiences, particularly attachment experiences (Friedrich, 1995), and abuse-related internalizations helps a therapist be aware of what a child's play is saying. A play sequence may, however, present several different themes at one time. What has happened previously in the session can help a therapist determine which theme is most pressing and, therefore, which intervention or activity is most appropriate. If the child does not react, a therapist needs to rethink what is occurring and may find it helpful to give an alternative interpretation. An alternative interpretation can even be given during the following session. The therapist's struggle with the issues often reflects a child's struggle, and the therapist's perseverance is important for the child's perseverance.

When the child denies something the therapist says, an alternative interpretation is not necessarily needed. Denial, or hands over the ears, sometimes means that an interpretation is correct but too threatening to deal with at that point.

> Debbie (a 7-year-old sexually abused at age 4 by her father and who had, despite positive medical findings, recanted her disclosure), in the second play session, takes the clothes off the dolls and says that they are going to a naked party.
>
> **Therapist:** [Realizes that Debbie is using the dolls to say what she has been unable to say.] It seems that you are thinking about a time your father had his clothes off or your clothes off.
>
> **Debbie:** No he didn't.
>
> **Therapist:** It was a long time ago and something you don't like remembering, but there was that time when your father touched you.
>
> **Debbie:** I let him.

Therapist: Children want to be close to their fathers and to be hugged by their fathers; that's not letting him touch you. Your father is responsible for all the touching.

It is also important for therapists to remember that every movement by the child does not need to be interpreted. Play presents a progression of thoughts. A therapist needs to attend to how the play develops to understand its meaning. An initial hypothesis may be disproven by what comes next in the play. The playing through of a theme without interpretation also allows a child a chance to think through and to do her own work.

Similarly, when a therapist has reflected hurt or anger or fear or grief, he should not move too quickly to have the child get rid of the negative feeling. A child needs to have these feelings validated and needs a chance to experience them. Moving a child too quickly toward resolving feelings can encourage repression. Abused children are masterful at doing things adults want them to do, even if it is not beneficial for themselves. Only after a feeling has had space to exist should the therapist encourage some resolution of the feeling.

As the therapist works with the child through any of the activities discussed, the child is helped to reexperience and broaden her world. This reexperiencing and broadening allows the sexual abuse to be integrated into the child's experience, thereby removing the trauma. The reexperiencing and broadening also provides a shift from abuse-related internalizations to a more positive internal sense of self and world. It will be through these more positive, as opposed to the abuse-related, internalizations that new events and new relationships can then be experienced.

❏ Summary

The child brings to the play therapy session his experiences, feelings, and internalizations. And these are expressed in his play. It is the therapist's job to observe and understand what it is that the child is playing. The Internalization Model and trauma theory form the base of psychodynamic trauma-focused play therapy. Within this model, the therapist observes, identifies, and verbalizes what the child is expressing through the play. In this way, the child is helped to recognize his experience of sexual abuse. The therapist then moves on to provide information or an activity that helps the child work through and shift his internal sense of himself and his world.

As therapy proceeds and abuse-related internalizations are addressed, the therapist will start to notice a relaxation within the child. Normal exploratory or representative play patterns start to appear. Parents report less tension and more socialization by the child at home. This shift in the child's behavior indicates a shift in the child's internal sense of himself and his world.

3

Recognizing and Addressing the Behavior: Adolescents

The child, through her play, crafts, and interaction with the therapist, presents to the therapist a view into her internal world. Her positive or negative sense of self and of the world are recreated in the therapy session. These issues can then be addressed by the therapist.

Although adolescents have moved away from the use of toys and crafts, many have not yet mastered the use of language as a means for expressing experiences and internalizations. Even for the adolescent who is at ease with verbal expression, the closeness in time to the abuse experience often creates such a sense of vulnerability that the adolescent's only wish is to discard the past—that is, "forget" or refuse to talk about past experiences—and move on with her life. Yet another adolescent coming to therapy may be able to express herself and may feel ready to look at past issues and present behavior, but because she is so involved with the tasks of adolescence (separating from her family, gaining a sense of self, moving on to new tasks and relationships), she rejects the part of herself that experienced past distress. Adolescents, with their limited ability to explain their world, their vulnerability in that world, and their appropriate movement away from the past, are indeed a challenge for therapists.

Despite this reluctance in therapy, adolescents constantly present material to the therapist. This material is occasionally presented by direct discussion but is more often presented indirectly through the adolescent's interaction with her world—that is, her behavior. Behavior within the home, the school, the peer group, and the therapy session reflects not only what is happening in the adolescent's world at that time but also the internalizations from past experiences— past attachments, past accomplishments, past losses, past traumas. And when the past was abusive, present behaviors reflect abuse-related internalizations. Adolescents repeat abuse-related behavior patterns, not because the adolescent necessarily wishes to, but because the behaviors are the reflection of the adolescent's internal world, the behaviors create situations congruent with the adolescent's understanding of the world (Littner, 1960), and the behaviors are familiar.

Repeating behaviors are particularly evident in relation to trauma experiences. Freud (1920/1955) used the term *repetition compulsion* to describe an individual "repeat[ing] the repressed material as a contemporary experience instead of . . . remembering it as something belonging to the past" (p. 18). Van der Kolk (1989), in his review of trauma, notes that the behavior of both animals and humans under stress returns to familiar patterns, thereby perpetuating early patterns. Terr (1990) refers to this as *psychophysiological reenactment* in which traumatized children, in both their thinking and their behavior, repeat patterns that occurred during the original trauma.

Observing an adolescent's behavior to understand her view of her world is particularly important when working with an adolescent who has been sexually abused. Adolescents, for the most part, do not want to talk about the abuse experience. It can be intrusive for a therapist to bring up the subject when the adolescent has not raised it. And because of the intrusive nature of sexual abuse, a therapist

needs to avoid intrusiveness as much as possible within the therapeutic relationship.

Repetition of behaviors allows the therapist to address the abuse-
related internalizations even when the adolescent herself does not
talk about the abuse directly. The adolescent presents, through her
behavior, that part of the past experience and the internalizations
from the experience that are encroaching on her—that is, that are
most relevant to her at that moment. Identifying the behavioral
patterns, recognizing the internalizations and feelings behind these
patterns, pinpointing where the internalizations come from, ac-
knowledging and giving space for the feelings, and providing new
experiences related to self and the world allows an adolescent to
process and work through the abuse. As the adolescent's behavior
patterns start to change, the therapist and the adolescent will know
that the trauma or distress from the abuse is being worked through.

As with children, many adolescents who have been sexually
abused have been emotionally, cognitively, and physiologically
overwhelmed (Terr, 1990). Herman (1992) refers to trauma as overwhelming the "ordinary systems of care that give [to the individual]
a sense of control, connection and meaning" (p. 33). The individual
reacts with hyperarousal, disconnection, and constriction. Herman
(1992) describes three necessary stages if the individual is to be able
to move back into caring for herself and thereby reducing, and
eventually eliminating, the trauma effect of the experience. First,
safety needs to be provided both inside and outside the therapy
session. Second, the affect, sensation, and knowledge of the experience need to be reconnected. Then, in the third stage, the individual
needs to explore new ways of interacting with herself and with
others. Through all of this, the individual needs to have a clear sense
of control.

The present chapter looks briefly at traditional therapy models for
working with adolescents and the advantages or disadvantages of
these approaches for working with adolescents who have been
sexually abused. Psychodynamic trauma-focused therapy based on
the Internalization Model (see Figure 1.2) and trauma work, as it applies to adolescents, is described. Psychodynamic trauma-focused
therapy has been found to be helpful for adolescents who have been
sexually abused, based on clinical observation and adolescent re-

port. Recognition of an adolescent's internalizations through the adolescent's conversation and behavior and the use of specific interventions are discussed.

❏ Adolescent Therapy Models

Whereas innumerable articles and books have been written about adolescents, adolescent behavior, and adolescent psychopathology, the discussion of therapy with adolescents is limited. Similarly, the behaviors of abused adolescents have been described in detail while little attention has been given to the therapeutic processes that are most helpful for this age group. Treatment literature tends to center on children or adults and includes only the occasional chapter on adolescents (e.g., Chaffin, Bonner, Worley, & Lawson, 1996; Meiselman, 1990). These chapters seldom address the specific difficulties of working with adolescents.

Psychoanalytic psychotherapy emphasizes the importance of an adolescent returning to early experiences and conflicts that were beyond the understanding and coping ability of the young child (Blos, 1967, 1983). These events need to be reexperienced with the adolescent's increased resourcefulness: that is, a greater knowledge of the world, an increased ability to take an objective perspective, and newly developed abstract thinking. As this occurs, the adolescent develops a healthier internal world and a more positive base for future development. Blos (1983) referred to this as "regression in the service of development" (p. 109).

The importance of addressing the adolescent's internal world as opposed to the objective reality is emphasized in psychoanalytic psychotherapy. The therapeutic relationship is viewed as a means whereby the adolescent can act out (transference) and reach a new resolution of distorted relationships from the past. The therapist's interpretations, by linking past experiences and conflicts with present behavior, help clarify the adolescent's experience (Lewis, 1991). The boundaries of therapy (time, setting, roles) are closely followed. As with psychoanalytic play therapy, this model, although important for its emphasis on the adolescent's internal experience and the therapeutic relationship, is too narrow for the treatment of adolescents who have been traumatized. Attention needs to be focused directly on the trauma and corrective information needs to be given.

Behavior therapy, similar to structured play therapy, focuses on observable behavior. Although feelings and thoughts are recognized as important in therapy, the treatment process is directed primarily toward observable behavior (Vitulano & Tebes, 1991). Assessment, development of a time-limited treatment plan, skills training, desensitization, and evaluation are important parts of the therapy process. Esther Deblinger's (1991, 1992) treatment program for children and adolescents who have been sexually abused has a behavioral format and content but also includes aspects of cognitive therapy. This three-module program includes: (a) discussion of abuse topics and training in coping skills, (b) exposure to abuse-related cues and identifying and changing statements attributing fault to the adolescent, and (c) education and training with regard to sexuality, abuse dynamics, and possible future abuse (Deblinger, 1991). Therapy with the nonoffending parent occurs concurrently, and therapy sessions are, at times, combined.

A behavior therapy plan, with its clear guidelines and objectives, helps the adolescent and his family view the abuse as an experience in the adolescent's life, rather than the adolescent's life. Inclusion of the parents in therapy is important. The structured nature of the therapy can, however, be problematic. Centering therapy around a therapist's agenda means that the adolescent and the adolescent's needs at a particular moment are not always validated, a situation that could parallel the abuse scenario. Given the types of defense mechanisms often used by adolescents who have been sexually abused (repression and dissociation), talking about the abuse before the individual is ready could strengthen dysfunctional defense systems. Following a treatment plan may also mean that the therapist misses the unique distress that a particular adolescent has experienced.

Cognitive therapies are based on the theory that "feelings and behavior are largely determined by how people structure situations or events in their own minds" (Petti, 1991). Personal schemata and coping mechanisms are developed early in life and evolve continuously, incorporating major events such as trauma. Cognitive therapy is based on a collaborative relationship between the therapist and the adolescent. The therapist is active in eliciting an adolescent's thoughts and beliefs, points out distortions in thought, provides accurate reality-based information and more positive experiences, encourages new strategies for processing information, and then encourages the adolescent to reevaluate both past and present situations, thereby developing new and more reality-based schemata (Petti, 1991). Emphasis is placed on the adolescent feeling in control of the flow of information (Bedrosian, 1981). Jan Hindman's (1991) proactive treatment strategies for working with children and adolescents who have been sexually abused fall under the purview of cognitive therapy.

Although cognitive therapies look at the messages an adolescent receives from the abuse experience and provide corrective information, they do not address the internalized and often unconscious sense of self and self in relation to others. Adolescents often say, "I know now it wasn't my fault, but I still feel at fault—the feeling is just there." Another concern that arises with cognitive therapy is the emphasis placed on the adolescent's cognitive distortions as the basis of problematic behaviors or situations. This can be misinterpreted by an adolescent to mean that he is responsible for present distress, and if he would just change his thinking, he would be fine. Although exercises (Hindman, 1991) can be helpful, particularly for a beginning therapist and for group therapy, there is a danger that therapy will be shaped to an exercise rather than the exercise being shaped to the therapy.

The psychodynamic trauma-focused model draws on each of these traditional models. The theory and techniques of psychodynamic trauma-focused therapy, discussed here as individual therapy, can also be used within group therapy and family therapy.

❏ Psychodynamic Trauma-Focused Therapy

The therapy model being proposed for adolescents who have been sexually abused is based on the Internalization Model and trauma theory. Central to the model is the psychoanalytic concept that early conflicts and traumas can be dealt with successfully only if the adolescent addresses the early internal experience (Blos, 1967). Work with adults who have been sexually abused has clearly indicated that although telling the story may be helpful, it does not, in and of itself, resolve the distress nor necessarily the trauma around the abuse (Briere, 1992; McCann & Pearlman, 1990). It is when the adolescent's perceptions and internalizations from the time of the abuse, the disclosure, and the present are addressed, understood, and shifted that an individual begins to feel relief.

RELATIONSHIP AND STRUCTURE

As with the other therapy models described earlier, the psychodynamic trauma-focused framework is respectful of the adolescent. Similar to that in psychoanalytic therapy, the relationship is not a friendship but is a working relationship in which the adolescent's dislike of therapy and of the therapist is accepted. The adolescent has a safe place for experiencing ambivalent and negative feelings toward others. In order that therapy be a time when the adolescent is safe and in control, the content of the therapeutic conversation, similar to that of psychoanalytic therapy, revolves around the issues raised directly or indirectly by the adolescent. Similar to that of cognitive therapy, the relationship is collaborative in that the adolescent and therapist agree to work on abuse issues as they arise in the therapy.

As with behavior therapy and cognitive therapy, an assessment occurs at the beginning of therapy (Wieland, 1996). Because this is a time of high anxiety for the adolescent, a short assessment is recommended, with further information being gathered as the therapy proceeds. Drawings and responses to questions about relationships, behavior, somatic responses, and the abuse provide information on the adolescent and the adolescent's processing of the abuse experience. With the adolescent's permission, the therapist would also interview the parent(s) with regard to developmental information, early experiences, home atmosphere, and changes in the home since disclosure. This information helps the therapist determine the components of a treatment plan—individual therapy, dyad therapy, group therapy, family therapy, consultation with the home, consultation with the school. The assessment can be reviewed periodically for key issues that need to be addressed and can provide a baseline for determining progress being made.

Similar to behavior therapy methods, a contract for a specific number of sessions is usually made. Time-limited therapy (8-12 sessions) helps an adolescent place the abuse in perspective—that it is not something that needs to take over the adolescent's life nor is it something that will dominate the adolescent's life forever. For an adolescent who is feeling particularly vulnerable, an initial shorter set of sessions may be easier to complete. For adolescents where abuse has dominated their experiences or high levels of dissociation are occurring, longer-term therapy will be needed. Children and adolescents with sexual concerns, posttraumatic stress, and dissociation have been found to need longer-term therapy (Lanktree & Briere, 1995).

When a therapy contract is made, the adolescent's and therapist's discussing and deciding on feasible objectives for that period of time can help an adolescent feel in control. Although some abuse-related internalizations may be included among an adolescent's objectives (getting rid of guilt feelings, stopping intrusive memories, learning to trust), others are unlikely to be listed. Internalizations become part of therapy as the therapist and adolescent together address the adolescent's issues. Nonabuse issues may also be listed as therapy objectives.

Subsequent contracts can be made with further discussion around specific as well as general objectives. Both the adolescent and the therapist need to appreciate that all the work around abuse issues does not need, however, to be done at one time. Often, it is easier for an adolescent to do bits at a time. Indeed, it can be helpful for adolescents who have experienced neglect or abandonment to have a break and then return to therapy. This can help an adolescent learn to trust others and to know that separations can be survived. Some adolescents will see a therapist two or three times a year for several years before they are at a point they can do more intensive therapy.

Adolescents in crisis (high levels of suicidal or other self-abusive behavior) will require more direct intervention within the adolescent's environment than that provided by psychodynamic trauma-focused therapy. Psychodynamic trauma-focused therapy can be used once the crisis is past. For adolescents with developmental delays, the trauma-focused play therapy approach can be used together with more verbal therapy. Conversation and therapy experiences need to be kept concrete. Psychodynamic trauma-focused therapy is not appropriate if the adolescent is continuing to live in an abusive setting.

Behavior therapy and cognitive therapy highlight the importance of working with parents. Children and adolescents who have received positive support from parent(s) experience fewer long-term negative effects (Gomez-Schwartz et al., 1990; Hindman, 1989; Johnson & Kenkel, 1991). Working with parents does not necessarily mean including them in the adolescent's therapy. In incest families, individual privacy and role boundaries are seldom observed. Thus, if an adolescent does not wish to meet with parents, this needs to be respected. In addition, parent(s) need their own time, separate from the adolescent, to work out their distress related to the adolescent's abuse. Dyad (parent-adolescent), family therapy, or both is important following an adolescent's individual therapy, if the adolescent is in agreement. Work with parents is discussed in Chapter 4.

PROCESS

As is the practice with psychoanalytic theory, the therapist does not initiate a topic at the beginning of a session but rather listens carefully to what the adolescent is reporting either about himself or others. This does not mean that the therapist sits and waits indefinitely for the adolescent to start. Abused individuals are often hypervigilant and feel unable to proceed until they know how the other person is going to behave. The therapist may comment on the difficulty of starting or may ask how the week has been. Because abuse issues and the abuse-related internalizations are reflected in an adolescent's present world, the topic of abuse does not need to overwhelm the therapy. Neither should the topic of abuse be avoided. Although the adolescent does not himself have to talk about the abuse until he is ready to do so, there does need to be an agreement that the therapist will refer to the abuse or the adolescent's internalizations from the abuse when she sees these dynamics reflected in the adolescent's life.

A therapist working with an adolescent listens and watches for behavior and thinking that reflects abuse-related internalizations. Once recognized, the therapist's intervention may be to inquire about what is happening, to help the adolescent clarify his own reacting or to provide the adolescent with a healthier response than that experienced in the past. At other times, the therapist's intervention will be more active—noting what has been said or done and how it relates to the abuse experience or internalizations. The therapist may address the adolescent's perception of the abuse, may recognize the emotions behind the behavior, may work with memories and flashbacks, or may consult with other adults in the adolescent's environment.

As is emphasized in trauma theory, it is important that the adolescent feels in control of what happens within the session. The therapist can talk with the adolescent about imaging, memory recall, or other activities that can be included in therapy. The adolescent, however, needs to be the one to determine what does or does not happen in the therapy. Unlike behavior therapy methods, an agenda is not set. The issues come from what the adolescent brings to the session—that is, content reflected in the adolescent's behavior and conversations. While several excellent activities are suggested in Jan Hindman's (1991) *Breaking the Mourning*, these should be used only when appropriate for the issue and for the adolescent. As an adolescent "re-views" the abuse scenario, understands his experience as a child or young adolescent, and processes it with the cognitive and emotional perspective of an adolescent, new attributional statements will evolve. New attributions should not be supplied by the therapist.

As proposed in behavior therapy and cognitive therapy, and in conjunction with trauma theory, information needs to be provided to the adolescent. This may include information about children's developmental needs for attention, affection, and a sense of control; child sexual responding and general sexual education; adult responsibility in both social and legal terms; and the limited options children have in abusive situations.

Based on psychoanalytic theory, but also highlighted in Deblinger's and Hindman's work, is the importance of accessing memories. More important than the memories themselves is the accessing of the feelings, sensations, and understanding (or rather, the lack of understanding) experienced during the abuse. The adolescent needs to re-view the abuse, not as seen now but as experienced then. The adolescent with new experiences, new support from the environment, and more developed cognitive abilities will be better able than the child or adolescent at the time of the abuse to integrate the feelings and the happenings from the abuse. The internalizations resulting from the abuse need to be addressed and shifted for the adolescent to experience a future not affected by the abuse.

❏ Working With the Adolescent

As discussed at the beginning of this chapter, adolescents often do not talk directly about the abuse and about their feelings related to the abuse. These can, however, be understood from the adolescent's behavior. The therapist needs to be alert to the adolescent's behaviors and to recognize the abuse-related internalizations behind behaviors. The therapist then intervenes—sometimes, by simply providing a new experience, and at other times, by highlighting the internalization and helping the adolescent work through the internalization in some way.

The following sections describe how an adolescent's experience and internalizations are expressed in present-day behavior and how specific abuse-related internalizations can be recognized. Therapist interventions and techniques for working through the abuse and abuse-related internalizations are discussed.

RECOGNIZING MEANING WITHIN THE ADOLESCENT'S BEHAVIOR

Behavior patterns, and the experiences and internalizations they reflect, become part of each therapy session through (a) the adolescent's interaction with the therapist (transference); (b) the adolescent's interaction with other people (environmental transference), which is reported either by the adolescent or another individual; and (c) the adolescent's coping responses, either observed or reported.

Transference. Although transference is an important dynamic within therapy, it often is difficult to recognize and may, therefore, be reacted to in a way that reinforces, rather than lessens, early negative interactions. Information on the adolescent's early history —in particular, the abuse history—and present relationships can alert the therapist to the types of interaction likely to be replayed in therapy. Recognition of one's own countertransference within a session can alert a therapist to the transference.

Information on early history can be obtained from the adolescent, parents, or social workers.

> Cleo (a 14-year-old abused by her mother's boyfriends, by uncles, and by a variety of other males over many years) had talked about putting her mother to bed when her mother was drunk. She told about her mother taking back the gifts that she had given Cindy. In therapy, Cindy is very accommodating and always checks on how the therapist is feeling. She assures the therapist that if sessions need to be switched to suit the therapist's schedule, that will not be a problem.
>
> The therapist, needing to alter her schedule, starts to call Cindy to ask her to change appointment times and then, recalling Cindy's early experiences, realizes that that would be confirming Cindy's internalization of herself as not deserving caring and attention and her experience that "gifts" are taken away. The therapist finds another way to alter her schedule.

An adolescent can be asked about early memories and what it was like at home when she was little. Having the adolescent bring in pictures of herself when younger, especially those taken during the time of the abuse, can be helpful in eliciting reactions and observations from that time. During the drawing of a genogram (McGoldrick & Gerson, 1985; Wieland, 1996), enquiries can be made as to the relationships between people.

Imaging can also be used to gather more information on the early relationships.

Curt (a 14-year-old sexually abused by his older half-brother and by a store keeper between ages 9 to 11) is talking with the therapist about his family.

Therapist: What were you like as a young child?

Curt: I don't know.

Therapist: Why don't you close your eyes and let your mind float back to when you were little, and let yourself see yourself as a little boy.

Curt: Whoa! I see Bart Simpson—but that's right, my father was a drunkard and my mother spent all her time with my sister and I was a hellion.

Therapist: [Notes that not being worth anyone's attention and being a hellion is part of Curt's self-perception and is likely to be repeated in the therapy relationship, with the therapist not noticing things about Curt until he creates trouble. The therapist increases her attention to small details and encourages Curt to talk about them.]

Information can also be gathered from parents' experiences: "What were the early years with their child like?" "What was happening for you at that time?" Review of disclosure statements or reports can alert therapists to relationship patterns that may recur in the therapy.

The second source of information for identifying transference patterns is current interactions and relationships.

Lynn (a 14-year-old sexually abused between ages 7 to 12 by her father and father's brothers as well as by several of mother's boyfriends) protests when her foster mother asks her to do something but then complies when pressured to do it.

The therapist recognizes from Lynn's present behavior the internalization of powerlessness and a pattern of helpless responding. He realizes that in therapy, Lynn is likely to do whatever he suggests even if she does not wish to do so, thus reinforcing her powerlessness. The therapist is very careful not to pressure Lynn even though this means that therapy is terminated before he thinks it should be.

The third source of information is the feelings the therapist experiences from the therapy sessions—countertransference. Some of the therapist's feelings may result from the therapist's own day-to-day concerns, and these reactions need to be understood and censored out. The other reactions, including those related to the therapist's issues that do not normally impinge on his thoughts, provide clues to the unconscious feelings and conflicts of the adolescent (Littner, 1960).

The therapist reactions are unconsciously and subtly evoked by the adolescent's attitude and behavior during therapy sessions. This does not happen because the adolescent wishes to provoke but rather as a result of the attitudes and behaviors the adolescent learned from past experience. The therapist, by attending to his own reactions (feeling ignored, being irritated, wishing to be rid of the adolescent, feeling cared for, wanting to tell the adolescent what to do, feeling threatened), can recognize the reactions of the early important figures in the adolescent's life to the adolescent or the reaction of the adolescent to these early important figures. The therapist, by being aware of the transference-countertransference relationships—uninvolved parent and unseen child, impulsive abuser and helpless victim, idealized rescuer and entitled child, seducer and the seduced—presented by Davies and Frawley (1994) and described in the final chapter, can be more alert to what is happening in therapy. The adolescent may, at different times, take different positions within any one of the relationships, thereby placing the therapist in the opposing position.

> Evelyn (a 17-year-old sexually abused by her father, an angry and threatening man, from age 10, when Evelyn's menstrual period started and Evelyn went to her father for assistance because her mother was out, continuing until age 14 when she left home) says to the therapist at the end of a session that she is not sure why, but that she feels the therapist is angry with her.

Therapist: [Feels that Evelyn is making progress in that this is the first time she has verbalized in the session that she feels the therapist is angry rather than writing her letters after the session or canceling sessions. The therapist chooses to respond to this openness with openness.] Angry? No, but I am feeling some frustration. Evelyn, you are handling so much on your own now yet still finding it difficult to realize this and still berating yourself.

Evelyn calls and cancels the next session saying that now that she knows the therapist is frustrated, she doesn't feel she should come back.

The therapist feels helplessly victimized. It feels as though her reacting in a straightforward manner has been used to manipulate her. She also feels enraged but knows that she cannot react with rage in the therapy relationship without destroying the relationship. Reviewing the dynamics of Evelyn's abuse in her own mind, she recalls that although Evelyn is able to say she is not to blame for the abuse, she continues to feel that it would not have started if she had not gone to her father that day when she started to bleed. She then recognizes a link between Evelyn's openness with her father, which was manipulated into abuse by her father, and her own openness with Evelyn that has led to a feeling of manipulation with Evelyn taking on the role of abuser, whereas she, the therapist, has become the helpless, impotently enraged victim (Davies & Frawley, 1994).

Environmental transference. Transference within the environment refers to the adolescent treating and reacting to people in her present environment as if they are the same as people in her early environment: for example, parents. When a child moves into a foster home or group home, she is likely to interrelate to the individuals in that home in a way similar to the way she interrelated with her own family members. If it was her father who abused her and this occurred within a pattern of closeness between father and daughter with a distancing of the two from mother, the adolescent will be likely to be attentive to the foster father and may be antagonistic to the foster mother. When interacting with child care workers, she is likely to act in such a way that the adults find themselves set up against each other. If it was her mother who abused her and this occurred within a pattern of being dependent on the mother, the adolescent in a foster or group home will be likely to move into a position close to the foster mother or group home leader and not associate with staff or peers in the home. If it was an older sibling who abused her and this occurred within a pattern of parental neglect, the adolescent is likely to align herself with the child in the home whom she perceives as most powerful while maintaining a distance from parents or child care workers. These are not chosen patterns; they are familiar and repeated patterns.

By noting behavior patterns of the adolescent with foster parents, group home workers, or friends, the therapist can further identify the adolescent's experiences and internalizations.

Joe (a 15-year-old sexually abused by his father between the ages of 7 to 10 and required by his father to watch his father abusing his sister and then to abuse his sister while his father watched) carefully watches his foster father complete chores and other activities and then does the chores for the foster father. Joe becomes interested in the activities that foster father has and then does the activities for approval from the foster father. Joe's attitude to the foster mother is quite different. He is dismissive and uses a domineering tone when he speaks to her.

Joe's foster parents are concerned that Joe does not take initiative in choosing his own activities but are pleased that he is so helpful. Although there is friction between Joe and his foster mother, the foster father has not intervened. He feels that it is important to maintain his positive relationship with Joe.

As the foster parents describe the situation at home, the therapist, knowing that these foster parents usually take a united position with regard to the adolescents in their home, realizes that earlier patterns are being reenacted.

Heather (a 17-year-old sexually abused by her step-brother between ages 5 to 10 when they were sent off to play together) reports that she is feeling a lot better and that things are generally going better. Yet she still never seems to have fun. Just as she starts to have fun with her friends, she suddenly becomes depressed.

Therapist: [Remembers that Heather's mother used to come into the playroom while Heather's stepbrother was abusing her inside the play house and then would leave saying, "Have fun."] I'm remembering how your mother used to tell you "have fun" at those very times that your stepbrother was abusing you. The thought of having fun may trigger that memory. No wonder you start feeling depressed. I'm wondering what new meaning "having fun" could have for you now?

At times, adolescents talk about situations where their own reactions and behavior upset them. They have reacted in a manner inconsistent with their normal behavior and more consistent with the behavior of a frightened child; for example, a normally assertive adolescent finds he is unable to reply in a situation that has upset him. Listening carefully to the adolescent's description of what has occurred just prior to this response, the therapist may notice something in the situation similar to the abuse scenario. This may have triggered the frightened-child feeling in the adolescent and led to the adolescent being unable to reply. From these triggers and responses, the therapist learns more about the adolescent's experience of abuse—the scenario itself and the aspects of that experience that continue to hold traumatic meaning for the adolescent.

> Tina (a 14-year-old sexually abused by her cousin, 6 years older than she, when she was between the ages of 6 to 9) comes in quite upset by a recent incident. She explains that she had sex with a boy whom she really does not like that much. But that wasn't the worst of it; the worst of it, she says, was that she had not made it clear that she didn't want to have sex.
>
> **Therapist:** [Thinks about how clear Tina has been, over the last year, about what is acceptable behavior from other people—even leaving her mother's house, if mother starts drinking—and wonders why there was a switch in normal behavior.] What was happening?
>
> **Tina:** Well, Ron and I were sitting in my room talking, and he suggested that we have a cuddle on the bed. I said I didn't want to, and we kept on talking. He raised it again, and I said, 'No' and then he said, 'Oh please.' And I don't know what happened except that I just didn't say anything else, and when he came over, we started hugging, and there you are.
>
> **Therapist:** [Remembers that Tina's cousin had always said, "Oh please," before he abused her.] I am remembering how your cousin used to always use that phrase, "Oh please." The 14-year-old you knew how to handle Ron, but it sounds as if that old phrase, "Oh please," triggered the 6-year-old you who felt she had to go along with what other people wanted. And a 6-year-old doesn't know how to handle situations like that.

Questions such as "Have you had sexual encounters that you did not wish to have?" "Are there times when you have behaved quite differently from how you wanted to behave?" can be particularly helpful in identifying situations or settings that trigger an adolescent back to the child she was at the time of the abuse.

A therapist may also learn about abuse-related dynamics and internalizations from behaviors reported by the adolescent's parents or group home workers. When behavior is reported to the therapist by someone other than the adolescent, it is important that the individual tell the adolescent he has spoken to the therapist. This allows the information to become part of the therapy session.

> Jim (a 14-year-old removed as an infant from his mother's care and later, when in a foster home, sexually abused by his older brother) uses a stick to stimulate his anus. The group home worker who discovered this calls the therapist to let her know about the activity.

Therapist: [Recalls that Jim was abused by his brother and also recalls that although there has been considerable sexual abuse in this family, this is the only reported instance of male-male abuse and that it is considered by the rest of the family as too awful to talk about. During the therapy session, when the therapist and Jim are talking about the week, the therapist comments as follows.] As you know, Lynn called me to tell me about the time during the week when you put a stick in your anus. Tell me what was happening.

Jim: Why don't you just butt out?

Therapist: Hard to talk about it, just as it has been hard to talk about the abuse. But it's all right to talk about the abuse, the abuse says nothing bad about you—something bad about Bill because he had no right to touch you—but nothing bad about you. And I know, from my work with young people who have been abused, that young people do sometimes end up sticking objects inside themselves. Sometimes, they do it to have a pleasurable physical sensation; sometimes, they do it to hurt themselves or maybe for another reason. Why do you think you did it?

Jim: Just butt out.

Therapist: Touching yourself is all right, but hurting yourself, as a stick could have done, isn't fair.

Jim: Seemed fair enough to Bill, and he's back at home and I'm not.

Therapist: Seems as if people are saying Bill did nothing wrong but that there is something wrong with you. I can see how it looks that way, feels that way. No, Bill was wrong, not you. If being home were decided by the abuse, you would be there and Bill would not. What do you think being home is decided by?

Adolescent's coping responses. Additional clues to the adolescent's experience of the abuse are the coping responses the adolescent demonstrates either during the session or in other situations. The adolescent will have developed ways of coping that reflect her temperament, the manner in which she coped with situations before the abuse, the degree of fright experienced during the abuse, the response of other people during and after the abuse, and the coping mechanisms she observed being used by people in her environment. The adolescent may intellectualize, minimize, deny, repress, or dissociate parts or all of an experience. A combination of coping styles may also be used. The type of coping response used by the child or adolescent during the abuse, as well as the present method of coping, can often be identified by observing the adolescent's responses when the topic of abuse is raised during a therapy session.

> Ann (a 14-year-old sexually abused by her mother's common-law partner between ages 8 to 10) begins to gaze sideways and her eyes take on a far-away look when the therapist refers to the abuse.

> **Therapist:** When I mentioned the abuse just now, you seem to have gone a long way away; where have you gone?

> **Ann:** Just away.

> **Therapist:** What is the going away like?

> **Ann:** There's a spot on the wall up there, and I stare at it and then I'm there.

> **Therapist:** I wonder if that's what you did during the abuse—took your mind away so that you would not need to experience the abuse. [Ann nods.] What a creative and skillful thing to do, and it makes sense that you would do it.

As the therapist recognizes the adolescent's distress both from early relationships and abuse experiences, she can address not only that distress but also the internalizations that underlie the distress.

RECOGNIZING THE ABUSE INTERNALIZATIONS

The Internalization Model (see Figure 1.2) provides the therapist with a framework for recognizing and understanding the sense of self and the world internalized by an adolescent who has been abused. A therapist is better able to recognize, from an adolescent's behavior, which internalization is paramount for the adolescent at a particular point. By addressing the internalization at that point, the therapist encourages a working through of the abuse without intrusion, without bringing up issues out of context.

I am damaged When an adolescent, by behavior or report of behavior, refers to self-abuse or to something being wrong with himself, he may be reflecting his internalization that he is altered or damaged in some way.

Bob (a 17-year-old sexually abused by his Cub Scout leader between ages 8 to 10) talks about the feeling he had as a kid that he was weird. The other boys had teased him a lot.

Therapist: [Realizes that Bob is talking not only about how others treated him but also about a feeling that something inside him is different or damaged.] Sounds as if the little Bob felt like he had become weird or been damaged in some way, perhaps by the abuse?

Bob: Was I ever!

Therapist: Mixed up, hurt, things out of control, a whole bunch of things— but not damaged. The Cub Scout leader touching you and getting you to touch him created all sorts of confused feelings. Anyone would be mixed up— being close to and hating at the same time, wanting the touching but not wanting it. But that's not damage, not weirdness, that's normal mixed-up feelings. And that's our work here—getting in touch with the feelings, sorting out the feelings. And we can do that here. What's great is that you are not damaged, that you are okay.

Bob: Yeah, but I get aroused when I see a pretty girl. I mean, this girl got on the bus and, well, I'm just a pervert.

Therapist: And adolescent boys do get aroused, have erections, when they see a girl who is attractive, when they think of something sexual, when they rub themselves or rub against something. That's being a normal adolescent. Do you realize that it is the same for other boys your age?

| I am powerless | Behavior that shows either helplessness or overcontrol indicates that the adolescent is feeling powerless.

> Mary (a 15-year-old sexually and emotionally abused by her stepfather over many years) comes in and sits without talking or replying to the therapist's comments. When the therapist comments on her not talking, Mary replies by saying, "If you say so."

Therapist: [Feels trapped and controlled and like giving up. Then she remembers that Mary's stepfather would tell Mary what she meant each time she said something or did something.] It may be feeling like I'm controlling what we talk about or do here, just like your stepfather controlled you. I'm wondering if your not talking is your way of trying to control what happens here.

Mary: I wondered when you would get it.

| I am guilty/bad/an object to be used | Self-deprecating behaviors or comments relating to the abuse or to situations in general can highlight for the therapist that an adolescent is seeing herself as an object, as bad, or as guilty and that this internalized view needs to be addressed.

> Beatrice (a 16-year-old sexually abused by a teacher at ages 11 and 12) was talking about the abuse, about how she never said "No" to Mr. Brown, how she would go and get help from him after school, even after the abuse started.

Therapist: Sounds as if you are feeling that the abuse was your fault.

Beatrice: Well, my mother says I should have known better.

Therapist: Sounds like your mother doesn't understand about the dynamics of abuse, about adolescents naturally wanting attention and closeness from someone they admire.

Beatrice: She says I should have known better.

Therapist: What do you think?

Beatrice: Yeah, I should have known better. I know it was his fault for starting the abuse, but I should have stopped it.

Therapist: Eleven-year-olds need a lot of support and closeness. And I remember you telling me that you had just moved, that you didn't have friends at school, and that you were never close with your parents. What do you suppose it was like for your 11-year-old self?

| I am responsible for . . . | When a therapist hears an adolescent become overly worried about what is happening to her family or about decisions, the therapist can recognize an internalized sense of responsibility for things beyond her control.

Jennifer (a 15-year-old sexually abused by her stepfather between ages 5 and 9) talks repeatedly about her mother's poor health and the problems her mother is having with the other children. She wants to do something about it but doesn't know what to do.

Therapist: [Realizes that Jennifer's worry about her mother's problems is far greater than that of most adolescents.] As I listen to you talk about your worry about your mother, it sounds to me as if you are feeling responsible for her.

Jennifer: Well, she wouldn't be in this spot if it were not for me.

Therapist: I don't understand; how is her health or her problems with your brother, and sisters related to you?

Jennifer: Well, if I hadn't told, she wouldn't be feeling this way, and the kids would have a father they could go and stay with. The abuse had stopped so I just shouldn't have told.

Therapist: It sounds as if you feel you made your mother ill. What did Gerry tell you would happen if you told about the abuse?

Jennifer: He said that she could never cope without him. And, you see, he was right.

Therapist: Yes, he said that to scare you and it does scare kids and makes them think that their job is to take care of Mom. But your mother's coping is her job. Her upset and feeling ill is one way she is working through the feelings she has about the things that have happened. Different mothers do it differently, and each one has a choice. You did your

job, which was to tell. Your telling gives people the chance to keep you
and your sisters and brothers safe.

| memories | When an adolescent reports disruptions to his
ongoing thinking and behaving (intrusive thoughts, flashbacks,
nightmares, triggered responses, dissociated incidents), the therapist can recognize that there are memories from the abuse that need
to be worked on. As each intrusion is thought about and discussed,
a small piece of memory work is done. (See later discussion of
memory work in this chapter.)

| I feel chaotic | When an adolescent describes himself as being
numb and without feelings, as having no negative feelings for the
abuser, or as experiencing extreme swings in emotions, the therapist
can recognize the chaotic feelings that occur for an adolescent who
is abused by someone he loves. For some adolescents, emotions
toward everyone and every activity constantly swing from love to
hate and back again. For other adolescents, positive and negative
feelings are split between people—one person is all wonderful and
another, all bad. Other adolescents cut off all feelings and are unable
to feel close to anyone.

Jody (a 14-year-old sexually abused by her adoptive father between
ages 12 to 14) talks about how unhappy her father is and how worried
she is about him. She talks about what a wonderful person he is and
how much he is trying to make everything right. She says that she
doesn't understand why she isn't mad at him and then says she
wishes he was dead.

Therapist: [Remembers that Jody's strongest attachment as she grew up
had been with her adoptive father.] Yes, there were many good times
with your dad and so there are many good feelings toward your dad.
And those you don't need to give up because they are a part of your time
with him. And then there was the abuse, and negative feelings come with
abuse. You would have been left with both love for your dad and
negative feelings for him. That can feel crazy.

Jody: It got all mixed up.

Therapist: What were some of the positive feelings, positive times and what were some of the negative feelings and negative times?

I am betrayed by people close to me When a trusted person abuses a child or young adolescent, the child or adolescent internalizes betrayal as part of an experience of closeness. This internalization can be recognized from the adolescent's conversation about present relationships.

Pat (a 17-year-old sexually abused by his aunt between ages 6 to 8) talks about girlfriends. He explains that he finds he likes a girl a lot until she starts to like him and then he stops liking her.

Therapist: [Recognizes that Pat's pulling away from someone as soon as there is some attachment—the girl liking him as well as his liking her—is a fear of being close or trusting someone.] Seems like it is really hard to trust a girl.

Pat: Yeah. I don't know what happens; just when we start having fun, I find I don't like her anymore. I like someone else, and then the same thing happens with the next girl.

Therapist: I'm thinking about the fact that it was your favorite aunt who abused you, the one you had the most fun with. So when you start to have fun with a girl, it gets scary, maybe scary that she might betray you like your aunt did. (Example is continued on page 142)

I have no boundaries Family dynamics around incestuous relationships vary considerably. In all cases, however, there are distorted family boundaries with the child or adolescent being placed in the position of having to take care of someone older. These distortions are internalized and become part of the young person's way of viewing and, therefore, interacting with others. The therapist may recognize this internalization in the relationship between herself and the adolescent or in the peer relationships the adolescent reports.

Lori (a 14-year-old sexually abused by her father between ages 5 to 10) talks about her siblings and her worries over how they are doing. She does not talk about doing things with her friends or herself.

Therapist: [Reflects on Lori paying all of her time and attention to her sisters and brothers and realizes that Lori has not had a chance to center on herself and to learn that she has a right to be cared for.] I'm thinking about how much care and attention you give to your sisters and brothers and how you have not had a chance to be taken care of yourself.

Lori: Well, what happens to me doesn't really matter.

Therapist: It felt that way in your family, but that wasn't as it should have been. What was some of the care-taking that the 5-year-old Lori needed?

| when I am sexual, good things happen | For young people who were abused extensively, sexual behavior may have brought them attention, physical pleasure, or both. This link between sexualized behaviors and positive experience is internalized and when, in the future, the adolescent wants to please someone, wants to get attention, or wants to have physical stimulation, he tends to behave in a sexual manner. For many young people, this is an unconscious response and, as a result, they become confused and distressed when other people then respond to them in sexual ways. Some adolescents may consciously use sexual behavior to attract friends or to feel physically better.

> Mable (a 13-year-old sexually abused by her father between ages 5 to 8) talks about sleeping with a lot of different boys. In reply to the therapist's question as to whether the sexual touching is enjoyable, Mable says no.

Therapist: [Recognizes that Mable has been deserted by her family and has been unable to make friends in the group home and wonders if Mable is using the sexual contact to have friends.] Because the sexual touching is not enjoyable for you, I am wondering why it is you are sleeping with so many boys?

Mable: Then they will be my friends.

Therapist: When you were little, your father taught you that sexual touching is a way of getting attention. And attention is really important, both for little kids and for 13-year-olds.

Mable: I asked for it.

Therapist: You asked for attention. What was it like, that needing attention in your family?

Mable: Lonely.

Therapist: And being sexual meant attention. I wonder what other ways there are for you to get friends? What do you notice other people doing?

sexuality means	$\left\{\begin{array}{l}\text{no feelings}\\\text{no control}\\\text{negative feelings}\end{array}\right.$

Another internalization that may occur when the abuse is extensive is sexuality as a negative experience. Because talking about sexuality when an adolescent is not thinking about it can be intrusive, the therapist needs to be alert for behaviors indicating sexual thoughts on some level, conscious or unconscious.

Amy (a 14-year-old sexually abused by mother's boyfriend, Ray, between ages 8 to 10 and again at age 13) talks about how childish Ray's behavior was. As she talks, she holds her mouth open and curls her tongue in. She then takes the bow of her sunglasses and rubs it back and forth on her lower lip.

Therapist: [Recognizes the oral stimulation occurring as Amy rubs the sunglasses on her lip and links this with Amy's discussion of Ray.] I was thinking about how confusing it must have been for the 8-year-old you, the 10-year-old you, the 13-year-old you—Ray being childish and his being sexual. I know from working with young people that one part that can be both nice and confusing is the tingling feeling that sometimes comes with touching.

Amy: [Pulling back in her chair] Yuck!

Therapist: Yes, yuck for the abuse, yuck for someone touching someone who is younger or someone who does not want to be touched, but not yuck for sexual feelings. Sexual feelings, that tingling, can be really nice. Do you get a sexual feeling when your boyfriend touches you or you touch him?

Amy: I couldn't care less—I mean, it's okay with me, I go along with it but I think it is all overrated. I wouldn't mind if I never had sex.

Therapist: What if you touch or rub yourself, what's that like?

Amy: Gross!

Therapist: Why "gross?"

Amy: You know, why touch yourself—it's all gross.

Therapist: Remember when we were talking about the time you were 3 or 4 and you and a little boy who lived nearby were showing each other your bums and your vagina and his penis, and we laughed over the curiosity of little kids and how that was normal and fun and how bodies are really neat. And one of the nice things about bodies is the good sexual feelings you can have. Girls often rub themselves between the legs to get a tingling feeling. Did you ever do that?

| what I am told ≠ what is meant | When the abuse has included distorted messages, the child or adolescent internalizes distortion as a quality of what people say. This distortion of meaning—the distortion now being done by the adolescent who distorts what others say to her—is best addressed when it occurs.

> Linda (a 13-year-old sexually abused by several of her mother's part-ners and emotionally abused by her mother who would constantly lie to her) reports getting into fist fights with her friends. She says that she thinks they have told stories on her. Her friends have denied the stories and said they know nothing about them, but Linda con-tinues to think stories have been told and is not going to "let anyone get away with this."

Therapist: [Recalls that stories were constantly told in Linda's family that not only had no truth to them but also had set up the abuse sce- narios. Linda would not expect people to say what was meant.] Seems like it felt scary for you to trust your friends when they said no stories had been told. It reminds me of how you were not told the truth at home and of how the stories that were told led to your being hurt, being abused. How are your friends now the same or different from your mother and other adults back then?

| I have { no emotions / no experience / no integrated self | The terror, stress, and pain around sexual abuse is often at a level that a child or adolescent is unable to integrate within his life. The experience has to be distorted in some

way for the child to be able to cope. "The abuse didn't matter"; "The abuse never happened"; "I never felt anything"; "I wasn't there." These perceptions are internalized and they are successful in keeping the distress away. As a therapist works with adolescents who distort reality in order to cope with their world, the distortions need to be addressed directly. The distortions need to be recognized as they occur, they need to be honored for the safety they provided to the adolescent at the time of the abuse, and new coping needs to be practiced.

> Shawn (a 12-year-old sexually abused by mother and father between ages 4 to 9) gazes far away as the therapist makes a reference to the abuse that had occurred.
>
> **Therapist:** [Recognizes that Shawn has dissociated in response to the topic of abuse being mentioned.] I'm noticing how far away you seem right now; where is it that you have gone?
>
> **Shawn:** Nowhere, I'm here, I'm sitting here, aren't I?
>
> **Therapist:** [Realizes that Shawn not only has used dissociation to cope but also has denied this experience.] Yes, you are here and I am here. And I noticed that when I mentioned the abuse, your eyes took on a far-away look, a look that usually means your thoughts have gone away from what I said—that is, from the abuse. As a child, maybe that is the way you protected yourself from the abuse by your mother. She was very special to you and her touching you sexually just could not fit into that specialness. By taking your thoughts away, you protected her specialness and you protected yourself.

Therapy with adolescents who have been sexually abused contains many issues and internalizations beyond those connected to the abuse. Early neglect, dysfunctional relationships within the family, and constant derogatory comments will have been part of the experience of many of these adolescents. For all adolescents, there are issues around others approving of them, dependence-independence, friction with parents, and sexuality. These issues need to be recognized and addressed along with the abuse. Therapy needs to be for the adolescent—for whom one or some experiences were sexual abuse—not just for sexual abuse.

THERAPIST INTERVENTIONS

Therapists always respond (countertransference) to an adolescent's behavior during therapy. The question that arises is whether the therapist's response reaffirms the abuse-related internalizations or helps the adolescent sort through and shift these internalizations. The response may be a relationship response: the therapist responding to the adolescent's behavior, or an intellectual response: the therapist talking with the adolescent about what has happened.

Relationship response. In a relationship response, the therapist reacts directly to the adolescent's behavior; there is not a formal intervention. If the therapist has not recognized and thought through what is happening (the adolescent's transference), he is likely to react directly to the adolescent's dynamics, a countertransference acting out (Klein, 1989). And if these dynamics developed within an early abusive relationship, they tend to evoke a response (countertransference) similar, in some way, to what occurred in the early abuse. This response from the therapist would reinforce the negative internalizations being acted out. If the therapist does recognize and think through what is happening, he can, with a monitored and therefore more appropriate response, provide a new relationship experience for the adolescent. As a new relationship is experienced, abuse-related internalizations are shifted.

> Sally (a 16-year-old sexually abused by stepfather between ages 8 to 12) starts the therapy session by saying that she feels that therapy just is not working; she is still feeling very depressed. She comments that the therapist has done so much, but she is afraid she just can't change the way she feels about things.
> The therapist feels impatient and exasperated and wishes Sally would just stop being so defeatist. Maybe they should take a break.

This is a relationship response to the dynamics of the transference, a reaction that would reinforce Sally's internalization that she is responsible for how things turn out and guilty for the abuse having gone on.

Therapist: [Recalls that mother had talked to Sally about sexual abuse while the abuse was going on but that Sally, not feeling safe, had not disclosed at that time. Sally had, throughout the therapy, been blaming herself for the abuse continuing. Sally seemed to be replaying her sense of being guilty.] It seems to me that therapy hasn't felt safe enough yet for you to be able to work through all the feelings from the abuse. And you know it is my job, not yours, to make therapy a safe place.

This is a relationship response that provides a new relationship experience.

Don (an 18-year-old sexually abused by his father between ages 4 to 8, had been moved, following his disclosure of the abuse at age 8, to a relative's home. Over the years, he continued to be moved from relative to relative when people became concerned about his not having enough nurturing or enough discipline. During the last year of high school, even as Don moved out on his own and made application to a university in another city, he continued to turn to his relatives and they continued to check on him and to remind him to do things) talks with his therapist about his worry that he would not be able to manage on his own, that he would forget to eat or start to drink.

The therapist becomes worried and decides to contact the counseling services of the university Don is going to attend and to meet with Don beyond their set termination date

This is a relationship response to the dynamics of the transference that would reinforce the internalization of helplessness.

Therapist: [Recalls that this is just what people have been doing all of these years, taking care of Don rather than trusting Don to care for himself.] Why don't I give you some information about the counseling service at the university and you can contact them for support, if you want to.

This is a relationship response that provides a new experience.

Intellectual response. In an intellectual response to the behavior, the therapist talks with the adolescent about the behavior and why that type of behavior may be happening. Working within the Inter-

nalization Model, the therapist identifies the abuse-related or other
negative internalization underlying the behavior. Based on trauma
theory, the therapist encourages the adolescent toward a new processing and reconnecting of the earlier experience. This new experience and the internalizations from the new experience can start to
shift the abuse-related internalizations.

(See the interchange with Sally presented earlier.)

Therapist: Sally, it seems like you are taking on responsibility for how the
therapy is going and blaming yourself that things aren't feeling better
quicker. It reminds me of when your mother was talking to you about
sexual abuse happening, yet she wasn't able to give you enough protection for you to feel safe to tell, so naturally enough, you didn't. I am
going to need to find a way for therapy to feel safer for you.

(See the interchange with Don presented earlier.)

Therapist: Don, I'm realizing that when you tell me how worried and helpless you feel as to whether you will be able to manage, I start to plan
ways to fix things for you. People have been doing that for years, yet as
I watch what you have done over the past year, I realize that you are
now planning and doing things for yourself. It seems as if that feeling
of helplessness that you felt with the abuse is still hanging around, even
though you have moved out of helplessness.

To do this processing, the therapist may (a) interpret the behavior
—linking present behavior to earlier experiences, to internalizations, or to defenses; (b) address the adolescent's perception of the
abuse—a perception resulting from the cognitive, emotional, and
physical level the child or younger adolescent was at when abused;
(c) recognize the emotions behind behavior; (d) work with the
memories and flashbacks; or (e) consult with the other adults in the
adolescent's environment. This section discusses each of these interventions. For the first three interventions, examples are given of a
therapist's response to the adolescent's behavior during the session
and of a therapist's response to the adolescent's description of
herself or of the abuse.

Interpreting. In an interpretation, a therapist links the adolescent's behavior to earlier experiences, internalizations, or defenses. By linking what is happening now back to the abuse, the therapist helps to clarify for the adolescent the experience of the abuse.

Responding to Behavior During the Session

Amanda (a 15-year-old sexually abused by her mother between ages 5 to 8) has become very engaged in therapy and expresses a genuine warmth toward the therapist. Then Amanda comes in exhibiting a cold and closed-off manner.

Therapist: [Feels hurt and discouraged and finds herself pulling back from Amanda, then realizes that Amanda may be acting out her fear that now that she feels close, the therapist will betray her, an abuse-related internalization.] I'm noticing how, after several weeks of our working really closely together, you seem to be distancing yourself from me. And it makes me think about how your mother was so close to you and then abused you. Does it seem that if I get too close, I might hurt you or betray you in some way?

Amanda: No, I know you won't, but I don't trust you. (See page 142.)

Responding to Adolescent's Report of Behavior

Amanda tells the therapist about having loaned some money to a friend who, Amanda says, is very unreliable with money and, indeed, has borrowed before without repaying. Amanda says that her friend knows that being repaid is really important to Amanda so asks what is wrong that the friend doesn't repay.

Therapist: [Recalls that even while the abuse was going on, Amanda would take on the job of staying with her mother, who was quite ill, when the rest of the family wanted to go out. She would try to be the perfect child, as she was now trying to be the perfect friend. Was she feeling that her friend was not trustworthy, her mother was not nurturing—because of Amanda not being good enough rather than because of themselves?] When I think about your loaning money even though you know your friend is unreliable with money, I am reminded about how you kept staying with and helping mother, wanting her to be a caring, protecting mother, even when she kept disappointing you, abusing you.

Amanda: I thought if I did enough, she wouldn't abuse me.

Therapist: [Recognizes that Amanda has internalized herself as the cause of the abuse, as not being good enough.] Seems as if you are blaming yourself for the abuse, like you are blaming yourself for your friend not repaying you. Your mother caused the abuse, and only she could have changed her behavior—you couldn't change that. And only your friend can change her behavior; her not paying you back is related to her inability with money, not to you.

Although interpretations can be an important therapeutic intervention, by themselves they may do little to help an adolescent. Anna Freud (1926/1974) noted that although interpretations may clarify the past and may help an adolescent deal with consequences of trauma, they do not, by themselves, undo the effect of early or adolescent trauma. The effect is altered when that earlier perception is altered, when the internalizations from the abuse are shifted. The interpretation is a first step that needs to be followed by the adolescent working through the situation in some way.

The therapist can encourage the adolescent to look at her recall of what happened in the past and to review this with her present level of understanding of abuse and abuse dynamics. The therapist and adolescent might draw the adolescent's genogram and list the messages, both overt and covert, that have been passed on through the family and that have reinforced the adolescent's abuse-related internalizations (Wieland, 1996). The therapist could encourage the adolescent to do some reality checking or problem solving. The therapist can encourage the adolescent to do some imaging in which the now-adolescent goes into the abuse image and comforts the younger child (Wieland, 1996).

Identifying defenses is particularly important if the adolescent is to learn new and nondistorting ways of coping with stress. As a link is made between the adolescent's behavior in the session and the coping used by the adolescent to avoid the reality of the abuse, the adolescent's understanding of her behavior increases, thus giving the adolescent more control over how she copes with stresses. This very process provides the adolescent with an alternative, and healthier, form of coping.

Briere (1992) has warned against the overuse of interpretations with individuals who have been abused. Because interpretations are often not exactly accurate, adolescents may experience a therapist who overinterprets as manipulative and nonvalidating. If the therapist uses phrases such as "reminds me of" rather than "it is like," the therapist not only does not sound as manipulative but also leaves more space for the adolescent to do her own thinking.

Addressing the adolescent's perception of the abuse. To address an adolescent's internalizations from the abuse, the therapist needs to recognize the level of cognitive, emotional, and physical functioning the child or younger adolescent was at when abused. It is within that level of functioning that the original experience was processed and the abuse-related internalizations were formed. The therapist can help the adolescent understand why that perception occurred, why she responded as she did, what was internalized, and where her present emotions and responses come from. The therapist can then help the adolescent re-view the past events with her present level of cognitive, emotional, and physical functioning. The therapist can help the adolescent comfort the younger part of herself through imaging, drawing, or talking.

Responding to Behavior During the Session

Katherine (a 16-year-old sexually abused by her uncle between ages 3 to 4) argues about everything the therapist brings up. Then she stops and looks directly at the therapist, commenting on how tired the therapist looks and apologizes for how she (Katherine) has again messed up the session.

Therapist: [Just as she is about to say that that is okay, some days just don't go well, the therapist realizes that Katherine was reacting from the abuse-related internalizations of being guilty for what happens as well as responsible for other people's reactions, internalizations resulting from the 4-year-old's perception of being to blame for the abuse and responsible for mother's distress around the abuse.] You seem to be blaming yourself and taking responsibility for my being tired. My being tired is not your fault and not your responsibility, it's mine. My being tired is a result of what I have been doing, not a result of you. This reminds me of how you felt while the abuse was going on and after you told, that time when your mother became so depressed. And you know, 4-year-olds do feel to blame and responsible and that is because a 4-year-old's thinking is only wide enough to see her own behavior. A 4-year-old's thinking is not wide enough to see what other people have done, and so a 4-year-old, the 4-year-old you, will think that things happen because of her.

Katherine: I know you tell me the abuse wasn't my fault, and I know that it wasn't, but it still feels that way.

Therapist: [Realizes that Katherine is talking about a feeling that comes from her 4-year-old perception and internalization of the abuse.] Why don't we take a look at that "being at fault" feeling, the feeling the 4-year-old you had. You could draw what the 4-year-old experienced, we could do some imaging, or we can talk about it.

Responding to Adolescent's Report of Behavior

Debbie (a 15-year-old sexually abused by her friend's father when she was 9) talks about the abuse and what she remembers of it. She goes on to say that what bothers her the most is that she hadn't just walked away. She doesn't remember any force, so why didn't she just leave?

Therapist: [Realizes that Debbie not only internalized a sense of herself as not walking away, as being guilty for the abuse, but is also judging her behavior when she was 9 in terms of her 16-year-old capabilities.] I wonder what it was like for the 9-year-old you when your friend's father told you to come with him. What had your parents taught you—to do what adults told you or to refuse to do what adults told you?

Debbie: To do what they told me, but he didn't tell me, he asked me—that's what I remember.

Therapist: And what is an adult question like for a 9-year-old, is it really a question or is it a statement, a directive? A 16-year-old can say no to things that a 9-year-old has a lot of trouble with.

Also, 9-year-olds are curious, curious as to what sex is all about. I don't know if you were, but that happens for a lot of 9-year-olds. You may have felt some arousal; a sexual tingling is a normal body response to being touched and that would feel good, so a 9-year-old would want to feel it again.

What do you suppose it was like for the 9-year-old you? If you want, why don't you let your mind float back to the 9-year-old, and when you start to see her, just nod your head to let me know. . . . Describe her.

Recognizing the emotions behind a behavior. As a therapist helps an adolescent recognize the emotions behind a behavior, the adolescent is able to reprocess earlier experiences.

Responding to Behavior During the Session

Matthew (a 16-year-old sexually abused by his father between ages 5 to 7) comes in with a scowl on his face and sits looking at the therapist in a defiant manner.

Therapist: [Realizes that she is feeling somewhat intimidated, even a bit frightened, and unsure as to how to proceed. The therapist recognizes that this might be the way Matthew felt as a little boy when his father was angry.] Angry? . . . Angry at coming, angry at needing to come?

Matthew: So!

Therapist: What's the anger like?

Matthew: Like anger!

Therapist: Some people feel anger in their stomachs, others feel it in their heads, others in their fists, others all over. Where do you feel your anger?

Matthew: In my fist.

Therapist: What shape does it have? . . . What size? . . . What color? . . . What feel if you touched it? . . . And as you look at that anger, what do you notice about it? [see Grove & Panzer, 1991]

Matthew: It's a fist, not mine, the hand is bigger, the veins are showing.

Therapist: Whose fist does it look like?

Matthew: It looks like my father's fist. He was so frightening when he was angry.

When discussing emotions, especially emotions based in childhood during the concrete stage of thinking, the use of concrete terminology can often help the adolescent access and understand the original feelings.

Responding to Adolescent's Report of Behavior

Jane (a 16-year-old sexually abused by mother's boyfriends between ages 4 to 12) comes in talking about spending the weekend on the streets again.

Therapist: [Notices a wide spectrum of feelings in Jane's rather brazen-sounding voice.] How are you feeling while you're telling me this now?

Jane: Fine, why shouldn't I, it was fun.

Therapist: I don't know, but I thought I heard something else in your voice, another feeling along with the "fine," the "having fun."

Jane: [pause] I'm angry, angry that that's what I have to do to have fun.

Therapist: Tell me about that anger. . . . What does it feel like? . . . [Also realizes that Jane's behavior is linked to her having internalized that sexual behavior is a way to get attention or to feel good, the therapist may go on to address this internalization.] As a child, you didn't have a chance to learn ways of having fun, of getting attention. How could you, the 16-year-old Jane, teach the 6-year-old Jane to have fun. . . . What does that fun feel like?

Working with memories and flashbacks. Adolescents differ considerably in the amount of memory work they want to do and, indeed, that they need to do. Whereas some want to tell about the experience or figure out exactly what did happen, more want to forget it and pretend it didn't happen. Although the "pretend it did not happen" approach must never be supported, the opposite approach—that all memories must be accessed—can be similarly distressing and nonproductive. Briere (1992) refers to working through accessible memories as having a generic effect—that is, a relationship to all painful memories. Forgetting, not denial, can serve as an adaptive strategy and should not be labeled as a pathological process (Briere, 1992). Thus, the question arises for the therapist working with adolescents—how much memory work should be done?

Memories that are available, whether they are visual, auditory, or body memories, should be worked through. Flashbacks as "symbolic manifestation[s] of a traumatic memory or a direct memory" (McCann & Pearlman, 1990, p. 30) should be looked at and worked through. Negative emotions or behaviors inconsistent with the adolescent's usual way of handling situations (trigger responses) should be traced, and if a memory is uncovered, it should be worked through. In addition, an adolescent's wish to remember more should be respected, discussed, and, when appropriate, gently pursued.

> Kim (a 16-year-old who became extremely upset by sexual comments from a teacher and then learned that she had been sexually abused on several occasions, around age 11, by her uncle) explains that all she knows about the abuse is a vague sense that something had taken place at her grandfather's house up in her uncle's room. She is wishing that she could remember more.

Therapist: What would the "remembering more" mean for you?

Kim: That it really happened, that I could tell without feeling so silly. And people wouldn't think I was making it up.

Therapist: What would you do with a memory once you had it?

Kim: I don't know what you mean.

Therapist: Sometimes, memories can be scary because all the feelings come back, and it may feel that it is happening now. Sometimes, memories can be helpful by letting you understand what it was like and where the feelings and fears you have now have come from. And sometimes it can be both. What do you think it would be like for you? . . . And sometimes, memories don't come back, and what would that mean for you?

If an adolescent has no memories but jhust a sense of something having happened, memories should not be pursued. If something happened and if the adolescent is at an appropriate point in her life for remembering, memories will come through the process of discussing feelings or early experiences.

Therapists need to be alert to memories that include events other than sexual abuse—for example, abandonment or extreme fright. Incidents of sexual abuse should not be expected or looked for in all memories. All the memories that come back, those including sexual abuse and those not including sexual abuse, need to be attended to and worked through.

McCann and Pearlman (1990) stress the importance of an individual having some ability to provide self-care and self-comfort before starting any memory work. It may be helpful for the adolescent to identify something about herself that represents the age she is now (a new ring, her leather jacket, a hair style) that she can touch to help her reorient to the present and to her present ability if the memory becomes distressing (Dolan, 1991). Comfort and trust in the therapy and the therapist's ability to keep the world safe is essential. For the therapist, this means being able to remain calm (neither panicking nor minimizing) and available to the adolescent, whatever is remembered.

The term *working through* refers to the adolescent (a) looking at whatever piece of memory exists; (b) expanding this piece by reconnecting content, sensations, and emotions; (c) feeling the confusion, terror, rage, or a combination of these and then the grief associated with the memory; and (d) adding to the memory some present resource. A memory is worked through when it can exist within the adolescent with the thought, the sensations, and the emotions connecting together without overwhelming the adolescent.

The therapist can encourage the adolescent to take the part of memory that does exist (auditory, visual, kinesthetic) and describe it in as much detail as possible. With gentle questioning, the therapist clarifies how old the child or adolescent is and what she, being that age, is thinking and feeling at that time. The therapist may then ask the adolescent to move on and describe what happens next or to stay with that moment and connect emotions to it. At some point during the memory work, the feelings and sensations related to the original abuse experience need to be recognized. If feelings are apparent from the adolescent's response, the therapist can comment on them; if the feelings are not apparent, the therapist can enquire about them.

If the emotions become too strong, the therapist can reorient the adolescent to the room and to herself as a competent adolescent. This can be done by reminding the adolescent of and having her touch the "now-item" chosen before (Dolan, 1991) or by asking the adolescent to take the now-her into the memory to be there, to comfort, and to help the younger self (Wieland, 1996). The adolescent's ability to dissociate can be used by suggesting that the adolescent step out of the memory (Dolan, 1991) or put the memory on a screen or a TV. The therapist should not, however, predefine memories as too distressing by having the adolescent immediately place them on a screen. If some distancing is done (stepping out of, placing on a screen), it will be important for the therapist to encourage the adolescent to take her now self into, or to the edge of, the scene to provide comforting and some reassociating before ending the memory work.

Encouraging the adolescent to do something for her younger part who experienced the abuse is an essential part of the memory work. Dolan (1991) suggests asking the part within the memory image, "What is it that you need that you are not getting?" If the therapist is working with the adolescent's now part in the image, the therapist might ask, "What does the now part want to do for the little child part (if the memory is coming from childhood) or the younger part (if the memory is coming from adolescence)?"

Time should always be left at the end of the session for the adolescent to talk about the experience of remembering, the experience of himself as the child in the memory, and the experience of himself now present in the room and with the therapist. The memory should be described as something that can be gone back to at another time if the adolescent wishes to do so. Distressing memories can be left in the therapist's room with the adolescent choosing an image for the container of the memory, perhaps a locked chest, a vault, the tissue box. Throughout the session, the adolescent needs to feel in control and to know that the therapist will respect her wish to stop or to change pace.

This process of working through available memories or vague memories allows the adolescent to understand what happened and to understand that she behaved like children or adolescents do behave, to experience the feelings and sensations—whether frightening or exciting—together with the happening, to recognize a sense of survival and "okayness" even with the memory there, and to provide self-comfort.

McCann and Pearlman (1990) point out that if memories or opportunities to talk about memories do not present themselves in the therapy sessions at some point, the therapist needs to take a look at the way he is responding to the individual. They point out that therapists who show distress (e.g., lean forward anxiously or have an expression of dismay or distress), become emotionally distant or numb, make premature statements as to how the child felt, quickly shift to other topics, prematurely tell an individual she was not guilty, or do not pursue the affective part of memories unknowingly discourage clients from dealing with memories in therapy. Even with good therapist support, there will be some adolescents who do not wish (i.e., feel too frightened) to look at memories. For these adolescents, the interventions discussed earlier will be more appropriate. Pressing an adolescent to do memory work can be intrusive and is unlikely to be successful. Instead, the therapist can support the adolescent in doing the therapeutic work she is ready to do. A supportive, nonintrusive experience in therapy may enable the adolescent to seek further therapy in the future.

Contacting other adults in an adolescent's environment. Because the adolescent's behavior occurs in many settings outside the therapy room, therapist contact with the other adults in an adolescent's environment can be an important intervention when working with adolescents. As transference, and therefore countertransference, occurs at home and at school, the adolescent's past negative experiences may be reinforced. A therapist can assist parents, foster parents, group home workers, and teachers to understand the types of dynamics that are likely to occur as a result of the adolescent's early experiences and as a result of the adolescent's internal sense of himself and of his world. If the parent figure is aware of the negative dynamics the adolescent is likely to play out, she is better able to respond in a new and more supportive manner to the adolescent.

> Keri (a 13-year-old sexually abused by her father for several years) is very attentive to her foster father. She quickly learns the types of TV shows he watches and likes those as well. She notes his habits in the evening and accommodates them. At the same time, Keri is irritable with the foster mother and refuses the foster mother's suggestions for doing things together. The foster mother, experiencing Keri's rejection and watching a bond form between Keri and her husband, is quite hurt. When she speaks critically of Keri to her husband, her husband does not understand how she can feel that way.
>
> The therapist reviews with the foster parents the types of interrelating patterns that had occurred in Keri's home and that, therefore, could be expected from Keri in the foster home. The foster parents note that they have fallen into those patterns. The foster parents

decide that father will make an effort to spend more time with mother, will refer requests from Keri back to the mother, and will explain to Keri that he is going to be distancing himself a bit from her so that she can have more opportunities to get to know her foster mother.

An adolescent needs to be told of any contact between the therapist and the home or school and of the general (or detailed, if the adolescent requests) subject of discussion. Content from therapy sessions would not be passed back to family or workers, and this needs to be made clear to the adolescent. If the adolescent requests no contact, this needs to be respected, with the exception, as explained to the adolescent, of situations where the adolescent or anyone else is in serious danger. Any change in approach by a family or group home should be explained, not just happen, to the adolescent.

Individual, couple, or group therapy for an adolescent's parents can often be helpful and would, if possible, occur with a therapist other than the adolescent's therapist. Dyad or family therapy that includes the adolescent could be done by the adolescent's therapist. This would need to be discussed carefully with the adolescent.

ASSISTING THE ADOLESCENT WITH WORKING THROUGH THE ABUSE

As the therapist responds to an adolescent's transference and report of behavior and memories, various techniques can be helpful. The present discussion includes (a) providing information, (b) normalizing the process, (c) problem solving, (d) reality checking, (e) using genograms and time lines, (f) imaging, (g) Socratic therapy, and (h) mirroring.

Providing information. Trauma occurs when an event (or events) overwhelms an individual's cognitive, emotional, or physiological system (Terr, 1990). The event is either so danger filled or so divergent from the child or adolescent's understanding of the world that it cannot be included within the child or adolescent's understanding (assimilation) or that understanding cannot be shifted to fit the event(s) (accommodation) (Piaget & Inhelder, 1969). By providing information about sexual abuse, the therapist helps the adolescent enlarge her world knowledge and, thereby, acquire schemata into which an experience of sexual abuse can fit. The sexual abuse obviously continues to exist, but the trauma connected to it starts to disappear.

The adolescent needs information on how children—at the age the adolescent was when the abuse happened—think to understand his feelings of guilt. Information on children's needs for attention and affection and adolescents' needs for control and approval enables an adolescent to be more patient with and to understand better how he behaved during the abuse.

Normal sexual responding of children and of adolescents needs to be explained so that the adolescent can recognize himself as normal. Indeed, most adolescents who have been sexually abused need considerable sexual education.

Mark (a 13-year-old sexually abused by his older brother between ages 5 to 8) talks about girlfriends and how they are always talking to him.

Therapist: [Remembers that the group home workers had told her that Mark avoids all girls and wonders about the present conversation. She then realizes that Mark may be thinking that the abuse from his brother means he is homosexual.] You seem really anxious that I know about you having girlfriends, and I am kind of wondering if there is a part of you that wonders if John abusing you means you are homosexual. What John did was not homosexuality. Homosexuality occurs between two adult males or two adult females who want to have a sexual relationship. An older male, like your brother, sexually touching a boy is sexual abuse, not homosexuality.

Mark: I don't know why you are making all this fuss.

Therapist: Some boys think that if they had an erection when they were touched by a male, that means they are homosexual or that they wanted the touching. Boys' penises become hard and erect when they are touched, that's simply the way penises are.

Mark: But I liked it.

Therapist: And that makes sense; touching and rubbing of the penis feels good. Of course you liked the good feeling and maybe the attention as well. All kids like attention and you didn't get much at home.

Adolescents need to know that sexual abuse is a happening and not them, that sexual abuse is an adult responsibility, and that children have limited ways of responding. Questioning can often help to clarify an adolescent's mistaken concept of responsibility: "How do you define sexual abuse?" "How big were you when you were 5 years old?" "What did your parents teach you about how to answer to adults?" "What would have happened if you had told?"

Normalizing the process. An extension of providing information is identifying for the adolescent the normalcy of the manner in which he is responding, given the experience he has had. The occurrence of flashbacks and intrusive thoughts, which can make an adolescent feel out of control and as if he is going crazy, is a normal response to having been severely frightened and can be explained as such to the adolescent. The fact that flashbacks and intrusive thoughts often increase after disclosure needs also to be explained. Adolescents count on their world improving following disclosure, and when this does not happen, they feel there is something wrong with them. Flashbacks and intrusive thoughts can be defined as part of the working through process and as valuable in letting both the adolescent and therapist know what work needs to be done.

The internalizations that feel so destructive (e.g., feeling damaged, loving and hating the same person) can be explained as feelings and reactions that normally occur with abuse experiences. Dissociative experiences (e.g., seeing things through a screen or from a distance, hearing voices inside the head) can be reframed as a creative process, whereby a child or adolescent is able to protect herself. Past behaviors, such as going to sit on a father's lap, can be labeled accurately as a child wanting attention. As processes are normalized and are seen within the perspective of normal child behavior or normal posttrauma behavior, the adolescent will feel more in control.

Problem solving. As discussed, interpretations need to be followed with active work that enables the adolescent to move away from repetition of the past. Problem solving engages the healthy side of the adolescent and encourages the adolescent to be in control of what is happening.

(Conversation with Amanda continued from 129)

Therapist: [Realizes that although not trusting protects Amanda from being hurt, applied indiscriminately, it prevents her from forming meaningful relationships.] Amanda, not trusting can be very wise at times, but at other times, it prevents you from forming friendships and close relationships with people who can be trusted. How could you identify who can be trusted and who can't be?

Amanda: I don't know.

Therapist: Are there some people who seem to you more trustworthy than others?

Amanda: Well, Tammy does, she's my friend. Don at the group home seems OK but the others, they always go back on what they say they will do. Sometimes you seem OK.

Therapist: What makes Don different from the others at the group home?

Reality checking. Reality checking can be used by a therapist to help the adolescent distinguish between then and now and to form a relationship with the world separate from abuse experiences.

(Conversation with Pat continued from 121)

Pat: Seems like I'll never have a normal relationship.

Therapist: It will take some work to straighten out what feelings belong where. But it can be worked through, and that's what you are already doing. Let's look at the distrust; does the distrust belong to your aunt or to all women and girls? What has your experience with girlfriends been like?

Pat: Well, like I said, I never stay with any one girl very long.

Therapist: While you did spend time with a girl, did she mislead you—let you think she liked you when she wanted something besides the liking and the fun of dating?

Pat: There was Ann. I dated her the beginning of this year, and I think she just wanted to make her old boyfriend jealous.

Therapist: And others?

Pat: Barb and Janet, they never did anything against me but they might have if I had kept on dating them.

Therapist: How was Ann different from Barb and Janet? What in her behavior could have let you know that it wasn't you she was interested in? . . . And Barb and Janet, how did they behave with you? . . . Who of the two do you think you could trust more? . . . What gave you that feeling?

Genograms and time lines. The distress from sexual abuse does not come from the abuse alone. Family interactions and the messages and myths passed down through the family affect an adolescent's understanding of the abuse and the adolescent's subsequent view of herself. For these to be addressed, a therapist needs to understand both the dynamics and the events that have occurred within the adolescent's family.

The construction of genograms (McGoldrick & Gerson, 1985) and time lines can help the therapist and the adolescent in understanding and sorting out the adolescent's experience (Wieland, 1996). These diagrams highlight patterns within the family and facilitate discussion about inappropriate messages and myths within the family, particularly those related to power and sexuality. Negative dynamics and inappropriate boundaries can be identified and questioned. The adolescent can be alerted to the new messages within his present environment and to the possibility of creating a new story for himself. As the information from the past is sorted out, the responsibility for the abuse can be placed more clearly where it belongs: with the perpetrator.

Imaging. Whereas learning information about abuse and thinking about abuse-related behaviors are important, this, by itself, is seldom enough working through for adolescents who have been sexually abused. Because the experiencing of abuse was a subjective experience and because it is held within the adolescent at the cognitive and emotional levels of the child at the time of the abuse, therapy needs to access internal feelings and the younger self.

Imaging, a process whereby the adolescent can focus inward and through this focusing can become aware of perceptions and feelings stored inside, provides this access (Wieland, 1996). Within imaging, an adolescent can use his present knowledge and resources for understanding the experience of the younger self and can provide for the younger self what he did not have at the time of the abuse. Imaging can provide a means for understanding and working on abuse-related internalizations.

> Jocelyn (a 15-year-old sexually abused between ages 7 to 11 by the next-door neighbor who was the father of her best friend) talks about being angry. She feels she has no right to be angry; after all, the abuse is not happening now. The anger feels so disconnected from her that she feels she cannot do anything about it.

Therapist: If it feels all right with you, let's look at that anger.

Jocelyn: But I can't. I don't understand it, it's not at anyone. I'm just angry all the time.

Therapist: What you can do is let yourself float back, inside your head, back to the first time you felt this anger, the first time you felt the anger that feels so disconnected. And if anything comes into your mind, if you start to see or feel anything, let me know.

Jocelyn: [pause] I see myself; I'm 9 years old.

Therapist: What do you notice about yourself? What do you have on?

Jocelyn: A white T-shirt, yellow shorts.

Therapist: Look around you for a moment. Where are you?

Jocelyn: There are bushes.

Therapist: Tell me about the bushes.

Jocelyn: They're the bushes between Steve's house and our house, and I have just come back through them.

Therapist: What else is happening?

Jocelyn: I can hear the car. My mother, father, and sister have just arrived back. My sister is running up to me, telling me that my parents are angry at me because I came back from Steve's before they called.

Therapist: You must have been angry. You had just gotten yourself out of an abusing situation—quite a task for a 9-year-old—and then you were being criticized for just that, for leaving Steve's house. . . . What's happening now?

Jocelyn: Nothing. I'm just sitting down on the steps. I don't feel anything.

Therapist: I'm thinking how scary it is as a child to be angry with parents, how scary to be angry at the people who are so important. How it is safer to feel nothing. But it makes sense that you were angry at them, and you can be angry and still love them.

Jocelyn: I'm scared, I don't like this. I'm all alone, why do they leave me alone?

Therapist: And while the 9-year-old Jocelyn is sitting on the steps, I want you to take the 15-year-old Jocelyn into the picture. And when she is there, nod your head to let me know. [Jocelyn nods.] Where is she?

Jocelyn: She is standing over by the bushes.

Therapist: Sounds as if the 15-year-old Jocelyn is disconnecting herself from the 9-year-old Jocelyn. [Therapist remembers that Jocelyn has blamed herself for the abuse, for going over to the neighbor's house.] Knowing that the 9-year-old had very few ways to cope back then, that as a 9-year-old, she could not stop the abuse, she could not change the way her parents behaved—see if the 15-year-old can go over and sit down next to the 9-year-old. The 9-year-old really needs someone to listen to her and be with her. No one did back then. Just watch, it may take a while, but if she is able to go over and sit on the steps, let me know. And if she can't go over, that's all right too, and just let me know.

Jocelyn: She's standing next to the steps.

Therapist: And, now have the 15-year-old Jocelyn tell the 9-year-old how brave and strong she was to leave Steve's house, that you realize how angry she is and that it makes sense that she would be angry. Tell her that you are here to listen to her and to help her work through all that happened to her—not just the touching that Steve did but also the fact that your parents did not believe you when you told. And when you have had a chance to tell the 9-year-old Jocelyn all that, let me know by nodding your head. . . . (Jocelyn nods.) What is happening now?

Jocelyn: The 15-year-old is sitting next to the 9-year-old.

Therapist: What would help the 9-year-old most now—a hug, giving her something, or just sitting quietly by her?

Jocelyn: A hug.

Therapist: All right, have the now-Jocelyn, the 15-year-old Jocelyn, hug the little Jocelyn, the 9-year-old Jocelyn. And when she hugs her, let me know by nodding your head. (Jocelyn nods.) What's happening now?

Jocelyn: The little Jocelyn is walking into the house.

Therapist: And now, while letting the little Jocelyn know that the 15-year-old Jocelyn is there to understand her and comfort her, start to come back to the 15-year-old Jocelyn here in the room.

Imaging needs always to be under the adolescent's control, with the therapist checking as to what is happening. Guided imagery runs the danger of putting the adolescent into a situation that may feel threatening or dangerous. In addition, guided imagery does not build up the adolescent's ability to self-care and self-comfort.

Although imaging can be helpful in identifying points of distress, exploring emotions, recalling experiences, communicating between ego-states or parts, reassuring oneself, and learning new skills, it also needs to be used with care. The adolescent should never be pushed to do something she does not want to do and should never be left in a scary situation. If the adolescent's imaging becomes frightening, the therapist needs to be able to stay with the situation, look at the fright that has come up, and develop a way the now self can help the younger self through that fright. It is suggested that a therapist not use imaging with adolescents, and particularly with adolescents who have been abused, until she has used it in other situations and feels comfortable with this technique.

Socratic therapy. Briere (1992) refers to Socratic therapy—"[the] gentle use of questions to facilitate the survivor's understanding" (p. 92)—as particularly helpful in encouraging an individual to discover his own reactions and his own capabilities. Questions involve the adolescent in his own therapy and encourage the adolescent to do his own thinking through of issues. Rather than making an interpretation that links the adolescent's critical self-statement back to something the parent might have said, the therapist might comment, "I am wondering who in your life that comment sounds like." Questions such as, "What would that have felt like for a 10-year-old?" "What do you think all of this means?" "What are you feeling right now?" help the adolescent look into, as opposed to moving away from, the abuse experience. Adopting a stance of curiosity as to why the adolescent sees a situation as he does allows the therapist to challenge the perspective the adolescent is taking without being critical or judgmental.

For many adolescents, the experience of being asked for their opinion and being listened to is a new one. For these adolescents and for adolescents who have difficulty verbalizing, it can be helpful if a therapist mentions several possible responses, as well as the possibility that the adolescent may have a different idea. The adolescent is less likely to feel put on the spot. At the same time, the therapist is giving the adolescent information about normal responding.

Mirroring. As an infant, then child, develops, the mother who is in tune with a child reflects back or mirrors for the child the child's own self (Winnicott, 1971a). This mirroring—which may be physical, as the parent copies or adapts to the child's pattern of movement, or emotional, as a parent experiences empathy for the child— helps the child develop a positive sense of self.

Abuse-related internalizations affect this sense of self. Mirroring within therapy (Kohut, 1977) provides for the adolescent a self-reflection separate from the abuse. Being in tune with what the adolescent is experiencing, respecting the adolescent's position, commenting on characteristics of the adolescent, and generally nurturing helps an adolescent gain a healthy sense of self. Noticing shifts in attitudes and feelings from week to week, even moment to moment, provides validation and a sense of internal existence. Negative as well as positive shifts should be noted, with attention being given to where these shifts came from. This mirroring enables the adolescent to have a greater sense of self and continuity.

❑ Summary

Working with adolescents who have been sexually abused presents a double challenge to a therapist. There is the challenge of working with individuals who not only have difficulty observing themselves but also, for the most part, have difficulty expressing verbally what is happening for them. In addition, there is the challenge of dealing with sexual abuse, an intrusive topic, without being intrusive.

Psychodynamic trauma-focused therapy provides a model based on the Internalization Model and trauma theory for working with adolescents. Abuse issues, and in particular abuse-related internalizations, can be recognized through an adolescent's behavior in and out of therapy sessions. These behaviors and discussion of the behaviors are responded to, interpreted, and worked through. As the adolescent's behavior shifts and her reports of how she is feeling become more positive, the therapist can recognize a shift in the abuse-related internalizations.

When working with adolescents, a therapist needs to respect the adolescent's stage in development. A therapist needs to give support and assistance and at the same time encourage independence. Ekstein (1983) has written, "In work with adults, we restore somewhat normal functioning. In work with adolescents, we clear the way for further development" (p. 145). Once the abuse-related internalizations are shifted, the adolescent will be able to experience her life separate from the abuse that occurred.

4

Identifying and Changing Messages: Families

How a child or adolescent[1] views himself as he grows up is determined to a great extent by how others in his environment view him and respond to him. Thus, the child who has been sexually abused will be affected not only by the abuse but also by the way his parents, and other people important to him, react to him. If a child is to perceive his world and respond to his world in a way not dictated by the abuse experience, not only must the internalizations from the abuse be recognized and changed but also any negative messages from the family at the time of the abuse and at present. Therapeutic work between the child and nonperpetrating parent(s) and between the child and perpetrator, if the perpetrator is someone important to her and someone who will be playing a role in her life, together with family therapy is an important part of the treatment plan for a child who has been sexually abused.

The occurrence of intrafamilial sexual abuse or the nonreporting of extrafamilial abuse indicates dysfunctional family interactions.

The level of safety and trust within the family has not allowed the child to be safe from intrusion or safe to report. Many of these children experience insecure attachments (Alexander, 1992; Friedrich, 1995) and there are, within the family, few supports for the child. The dysfunctional relationships and interactions within the family system need to be identified, addressed, and changed for the child to feel respected and safe within his world.

Dysfunctional family and attachment patterns, as well as negative responses to the child by others, will come up during the child's individual therapy as the issues of love and hate, trust and betrayal, distorted family boundaries, threats, and not having been protected are worked through. Although individual therapy can help the child understand these experiences and shift the resulting internalizations, it does not provide a setting for changing family patterns, attitudes, or responses. Neither does it provide a setting for the important people in the child's life to reaffirm the child. Individual therapy for other members of the family, dyad therapy involving the child and another family member, and family therapy provide opportunities for parents and siblings to sort out their reactions to the abuse and to the child and provide opportunities for the child and family to experience new and healthier interactions. Dyad therapy is particularly important for children with insecure attachment patterns. Whereas, ideally, dyad or family therapy (or both) would occur with the original family, for children living in foster families or group homes and unlikely to return home, dyad or family therapy can be carried out with the foster family or a primary group home worker.

In most situations, dyad therapy between the nonperpetrating parent and child would occur after significant progress has been made in their individual therapies. When, however, a child's level of fright is such that he is having difficulty connecting to the therapist's comments during individual therapy, the parent, foster parent, or group home worker could be included for the last 15 or 20 minutes of therapy to provide a time when the child can experience the therapist's comments within a safer setting and at more distance. The conversation between the parent and therapist can provide reflections on and information about abuse and how abuse causes confusion and distress for the child now. The child can be involved, together with the parent, in developing new experiences—experiences that contradict abuse internalizations.

Early dyad work is also important if the child feels he does not, or indeed does not, have permission to talk about the abuse (Friedrich, 1995). The therapist needs to meet with the nonperpetrating parent(s) and then with the parent(s) and child to discuss the importance of talking about the abuse and the effect talking may have on the family. The therapist needs to work toward establishing safety for the child from emotional as well as physical and sexual abuse.

Inclusion of dyad work together with the child's individual therapy can also be helpful when the parent (or parental figure) is having difficulty understanding that the child's behavior comes from his experiences—betrayal occurring with closeness, not being protected, needing to dissociate. This is only appropriate if the parent has been able to adjust enough to the disclosure that she is not blaming the child either for the abuse or for the distress brought on the family by the disclosure. These dyad sessions should be aimed at understanding, not controlling, behavior. The latter will occur if the former is accomplished.

Dyad and family therapy, following individual therapy for each family member, also provide opportunities for the family to talk together about the abuse, about their personal distress around the abuse, and about their concerns for the child who was abused. Family members need to take responsibility for the anger felt toward the child for disrupting the family's existence. Concerns for the family as a whole and for the future need to be discussed. It also provides an opportunity for a child to have his questions about the abuse answered. Some children are able to formulate and ask these questions, some children are only able to formulate them, and still others simply have a sense of unease. Dyad and family therapy, as follow-up to individual therapy, provide opportunities for questions to be formulated, asked, and, at least partially, answered.

If the perpetrator is an important family member and will be coming back into the family, dyad therapy with the child and the perpetrator and family therapy that includes the perpetrator is essential (James & Nasjleti, 1983; Trepper & Barrett, 1989). Therapy with the perpetrator would occur only after the perpetrator has reached the point of being able to assume responsibility not only for the abuse, but also for the effects of the abuse (see Trepper & Barrett, 1989). The perpetrator needs to have recognized the many different ways in which he abused the child and the family.

The following discussion looks briefly at the effects of sexual abuse on the nonperpetrating parent(s). Trauma theory and the Internalization Model (see Figure 1.2) are used as a framework for identifying the work that needs to be done with the nonperpetrating parent(s) and then the nonperpetrating parent(s) and the child. The importance of identifying and changing the messages given during the abuse are addressed in the section on dyad work with the perpetrator and child. Family therapy is discussed briefly.

❑ Dyad Therapy: Working With the Nonperpetrating Parent

Increased attention has been given in recent years to the effect of sexual abuse on the nonperpetrating parent(s).[2] Hooper (1992), in her study of mothers of children who had been sexually abused, refers to secondary victimization. Mothers experience not only guilt for what has happened but also major losses—loss of confidence in herself as a protective mother, loss of the perfect child, loss of trust in the world, loss of partner and stability in life (Hooper, 1992). Hooper (1992) observed that a mother was better able to define her child's experience as abusive if the mother had a sense of her personal capability as an adult. Unfortunately, the very experience for which a parent needs a strong sense of self to be helpful to her child erodes that sense and renders her less able to be supportive. Mothers of children abused within the extended family or outside the family, as well as those abused within the immediate family, experience significant psychological distress (Deblinger, Hathawa, Lippmann, & Steer, 1993; Williamson, Borduin, & Howe, 1991).

Because of her own traumatization, a mother may center on her own needs rather than on the needs of the child. She may become overly intrusive, asking multiple questions about the abuse, or she may withdraw and pretend that the abuse never happened. Similarly, she may become overly solicitous and protective of the child, or she may find that she has difficulty being close and affectionate with the child. A disclosure of abuse by a child may activate, in the mother, conscious or unconscious memories of her own childhood abuse. If the disclosure is related to a close family member, the mother will be left in a position of having to readjust her perception of and relationship with this individual.

When a mother is not able to believe her child's disclosure, individual therapy is important so that the mother has a place for processing what has happened. Therapist patience and ability to listen without judging is crucial (Lipovsky, 1991) for the mother not to feel pressured. Pressure is all too likely to lead to the mother becoming angry at the child for disclosing. Giarretto (1982), in his program in which mothers talk with another mother who has gone through a similar experience, found that this pairing was an invaluable support for mothers. Group therapy has also been found to be helpful (Damon & Waterman, 1986; Sgroi & Dana, 1982).

As with therapy for the child or adolescent, knowledge about trauma and abuse-related internalizations provides a therapist with a framework for working with a mother, whether individually or together with her child. Therapy related to a mother's own issues is not included in the present discussion.

RELIEVING THE TRAUMA

An individual is traumatized when her ordinary ways of adapting to life are overwhelmed, when she is left feeling helpless and has no sense of control in her world (Herman, 1992; Terr, 1990). The mother of a child who has been sexually abused experiences helplessness in that the event that she wishes never to happen has already happened. As she moves on from the moment of disclosure, the degree of trauma experienced depends on her ability to integrate—assimilate (Piaget & Inhelder, 1960)—the reality of what has happened into her understanding of her world. This integration allows a parent to regain some control with regard to her own response, her child's safety, and her family's future. This integration enables a parent to respond and cope with the result and the effect of the abuse rather than being overwhelmed by it. To help a mother integrate the abuse into her world, the mother's knowledge resources, emotional resources, and behavioral resources need to be expanded.

The mother needs information about abuse, how abuse happens, and why children tend not to report abuse. This starts to demystify the event and explain how it could occur despite the mother not wanting it to happen. Mothers need to know that most children do not report abuse immediately, and when children do report, it usually is not to mother (Gomez-Schwartz et al., 1990). This helps to relieve the stigma a mother feels from not having known. Information on recanting, when relevant, can be given (Gonzalez, Waterman, Kelly, McCord, & Oliveri, 1993). Mothers need information on the effects of the abuse on a child—the fright and confusion the child experiences and the abuse-related internalizations. Information on how the child is likely to behave takes away some of the unpredictability and "out-of-controlness" the mother experiences as she tries to help her child but finds her child acting out against her. Mothers need information on the normality of their own angry and distressed feelings.

The mother also needs very practical information (Sgroi & Dana, 1982)—the investigatory process, the difficulties that occur within the court system, and, if the perpetrator provided the financial base of the family, sources of financial support. She needs information about therapy: about the availability and appropriateness of therapy for her child and herself.

Information is only a part of the increase in resources needed for a mother to be able to assimilate the fact that her child was sexually abused. A mother's emotional resources need to increase as well. A mother needs a place where she can be acknowledged, listened to, and her fears accepted and even normalized. She needs a place where she is seen as someone not to blame but rather as someone who is in a position to make the world better for her child. Although therapy can be one place where this supportive experience occurs, it will be important that a therapist help the mother establish support systems for herself. For some mothers, the extended family may provide support, but for others, especially if the abuse is being denied in the family, support needs to be established outside the family.

Within therapy, as the mother's distress, guilt, sense of loss, and anger—at the child, at the perpetrator, at herself—is addressed and worked through, the mother's emotional resources increase. She becomes more resilient and better able to integrate events and information. Therapy related to mother's own personal issues and, in particular, childhood issues reactivated by the disclosure, can also free up emotional energy and resiliency.

An increase in a mother's behavioral resources comes as her knowledge and emotional resources increase. A mother learns new ways of working with and responding to her child. This expansion of resources—knowledge, emotional, behavioral—provides a larger world framework and one better able to integrate the fact of abuse, the experience of disclosure, and the stress of court. Indeed, for many mothers, as they start to find out when and how the abuse occurred, past observations and feelings begin to make sense.

To move on from the experiencing of trauma that ties one to the past, mothers need to distinguish between then and now. By identifying the characteristics within the family or within the larger system that allowed the abuse to occur when it did and to remain a secret at that time, a mother can identify what needs to be changed. As the relevant patterns and behaviors start to change, the mother can begin to identify how the family or larger system differs presently from the way it was in the past. Awareness of this difference helps establish the abuse as a happening in the past rather than as an overwhelming presence, or trauma, in the now.

CHANGING THE CHILD'S ABUSE-RELATED INTERNALIZATIONS

As a mother moves through her own understanding of what has happened, she needs to address her perception of herself, her perception of her child, and her child's perceptions of himself. The Internalization Model (see Figure 1.2) provides the therapist with a framework for the work that needs to be done with the mother and then between the mother and child if the child's abuse-related internalizations are to change. Given the heavy demand on services as well as the heavy demand of each abuse case, therapists often move too quickly over the work that needs to be done with a mother or with a mother and child. By describing abuse-related internalizations—internalizations that often occur for the mother as well—the Internalization Model highlights areas that need to be addressed.

I am damaged   On learning about the abuse, some nonperpetrating parents experience their child as different or damaged, talk about their child as different or damaged, and treat their child as different or damaged. This response is reinforced by the messages presented in the media, by general conversation about abuse, and indeed, by some therapists as they talk about the long-term and severe effects that can occur from abuse. Unfortunately, a distinction is seldom made between actual damage and a child's feelings of hurt, confusion, anger, loss, and sense of damage. Whereas a sense of damage certainly occurs and, in some cases, physical damage occurs to the vaginal or rectal areas, the child himself—with his potential to continue growing and developing as the trauma and distress is worked through—continues to exist. The parent needs to be helped by the therapist to recognize that the child after the abuse is the same as the child before the abuse. Giving parents information on the resiliency of children who experience a supportive family setting can help parents see their child as moving on from abuse rather than as synonymous with abuse (Kiser, Pugh, McColgan, Pruitt, & Edwards, 1991).

Parents sometimes feel that a child who has been abused needs to be treated differently from other children. Realizing that their child is distressed, they may discipline the child less than they did before. Although the child does need more reassurance of love and protection than other children and more patience with his mood or behavior changes, the child also needs consistent and firm limits (Kiser et al., 1991). The child needs the same limits, if those limits were appropriate, as those imposed before the disclosure. When a parent lets a child get away with unacceptable behavior or starts expecting different behaviors, the child's internalization that there is something altered about her is reinforced.

> Cynthia (a 17-year-old sexually abused by her mother between ages 6 to 8) reports that her father has, since she disclosed the abuse last spring, started talking to her about sex. He keeps warning her against "sleeping around" to be popular.

Overprotection gives the message that the child has no ability to protect herself and thus leads to increased vulnerability.

> Janet (an 18-year-old sexually abused by her uncle between ages 4 to 8) says that she has to wait for one of her parents or a friend to drive her if she is to go somewhere in the evening. She notes that after she told about the abuse at age 8, her parents alerted the minister, her teacher and principal, the neighbors, every adult around to keep an eye on her and keep her safe. Somehow, it seems as if she still needs them. She watches her friends take buses or drive themselves places and wonders how they do it.

Discussion of behavior, discipline, and protection is appropriate in both individual and dyad sessions.

For some parents, the child has become a sexual person and no longer is viewed as a child. When the child displays sexualized behaviors, the parent may see this as confirmation rather than recognizing that the child is trying to please or get attention, a true childlike response to his world. If a mother sees her child as sexual, she is likely to respond to him as a sexual being, either avoiding touching him or being sensual in her touch with him. This behavior reinforces the child's negative internalization about himself.

Often, the parent who sees her child as sexual was herself abused during childhood and has not worked though the meaning and effects for herself of her own abuse. In other cases, the parent may have rigid and negative views related to sexuality. These issues will need to be addressed in the parent's own therapy and the responsibility for dealing with them placed with the parent during dyad therapy.

A mother's view of her child can be accessed by questions such as, "How do you see what has happened to your child?" and "How do you find yourself responding to your child?" Questions such as, "Do you think your mother responds to you any differently now than she did before?" during a dyad session can bring attitude changes out in the open. It is better to have a negative attitude verbalized where the child can experience the therapist's opposing view than to let it remain unspoken and, thereby, unwittingly supported. Circular questioning encourages exploration of the differ-

ences and similarities between the mother and child and the assumed or felt effect of each on the other are explored (Penn, 1982).
Curiosity about family patterns and how issues are seen by different
people in the family creates space for new attitudes and patterns to
develop (Cecchin, 1987).

| I am powerless | A disclosure of sexual abuse heightens a
mother's awareness of her inability to keep her child's world safe.
If the mother's support system, in or out of therapy, does not
provide her with a place to process the feelings of powerlessness,
the mother may respond, much as the child has done, by becoming
helpless and, therefore, being unavailable to her child or by becoming overcontrolling and, therefore, allowing little space to the child
for his processing. In the case of father-child abuse, the mother's role
in the marital or past marital relationship needs to be talked about.
For mothers who stayed in a relationship because of a sense of
powerlessness or who used keeping the family intact as their source
of power, there will need to be time to review past choices and
decide on new behaviors.

In situations of extrafamilial abuse or abuse from the extended
family, the parental couple needs an opportunity to discuss feelings
of powerlessness—how this is experienced and how it is expressed
by each parent. Without this discussion, parents may start to blame
each other, and the increased tension within the couple places added
stress not only on the family but also on the child for disclosing the
abuse (Kiser et al., 1991).

The parent whose world has been turned upside down often has
difficulty recognizing that the child is feeling powerless. The very
act of disclosure is often experienced by a mother as the child taking
over control in the family. This is particularly true when the child
reacts to his own sense of powerlessness by becoming overcontrolling. As the child orders the other members of the family around
and acts out in a variety of negative ways, the parent feels increasingly powerless, and feelings of resentment may block her feelings
of concern.

The meaning of a child's acting-out behavior, including the child's
anger at the nonperpetrating parent, can be discussed in mother's

individual therapy. Further discussion of the controlling behavior, the child's fright, and the sense of powerlessness that underlies that behavior can be discussed in the dyad therapy.

> Joe (a 13-year-old sexually abused by his grandparents between ages 4 to 9) has been ordering his mother and brothers and sisters around at home. Mother says, as she has so often in the past, that she can no longer handle him and will have to place him outside the family.

> **Therapist:** [Thinks about Joe's behavior and wonders what part of it reflects the sense of powerlessness that Joe not only experienced during the abuse but may be experiencing now when his mother talks about sending him away.] Joe may be letting you know how frightening it was not to be able to control what went on in his world. Joe, what was it like when you could not stop what your grandparents did? . . . Mom, what is it like for you when Joe starts ordering everyone around? . . . It gives me, it gives you, a small sense of what the world must have been like for Joe. How is it going to be possible for Joe to start to know that he can have some control? . . . I'm not sure that Joe is going to be able to take control of his behavior until he first knows that he is in control. What are the things, not related to behaving well or behaving poorly, that Joe can decide? . . . Which of those things do you like deciding most, Joe? . . . Let's start with something small where Mom will feel comfortable with whatever decision Joe does make.

Helpless behavior by a child can similarly be discussed. By involving the child in the discussion, the child can start to feel some control.

Children who have been abused often find themselves in sexual-type situations without knowing how to extricate themselves. Within the abuse scenario, the child responded in some way to the sexual advances of the perpetrator—silliness, paralysis, sexual behavior. If new ways of responding are not taught, the child, all too often, will respond in future situations in the same way as he did in the past. Because mothers of children who have been sexually abused often do not, themselves, have assertive skills, their children have difficulty learning to be assertive. Dyad therapy can provide a setting in which a parent can be encouraged to be assertive on behalf of her child.

Diane (mother of Aggie, a 4-year-old sexually abused by her father at age 3) talks about her concern over a situation that occurs at church when a particular man starts to tickle Aggie. She explains that Aggie starts acting silly and then in a flirting manner.

Therapist: [Notices Aggie drawing back as she listens to her mother.] I'm thinking about the fact that Aggie has not had a chance to know that she does not need to go along with things adults do. She has not had a chance to learn how to tell adults if she does not like things they do. Because this is something that is bothering you, Diane, perhaps you could speak to the man. By watching you, Aggie would start to learn how to speak up when she is bothered by something. . . . Why don't you and Aggie practice with the dolls, having the man start to tickle Aggie and you speaking to the man.

Opportunities for a child to be assertive with his mother can also be provided in dyad therapy, thus helping to establish the child as an independent and resourceful person.

I am guilty/bad/an object to be used   Feelings of guilt and shame occur for the mother as well as the child (Hooper, 1992). For some mothers, these feelings block her ability to report a disclosure to legal authorities or, in cases where it is reported, her ability to be available to the child. A mother may be afraid to face other members of the family or friends and colleagues. These issues need to be discussed within the mother's own therapy. Although responsibility for the abuse is placed with the abuser, the mother does need to be encouraged to look at what was going on for her at the time of the abuse. Recognizing, accepting responsibility for, and grieving the things she had not done are important stages in a mother working through her own sense of guilt.

As a mother works through her guilt, she will be less likely to blame her child either for what happened or for not telling. She will be better able to place total responsibility for the abuse outside of the child. Trepper and Barrett (1989) include in their treatment model an apology from the mother to the child for "those problems in her relationship with [the child] that prevented the child from coming to her mother when the abuse began" (p. 139). The therapist can talk with the mother and then help the mother talk with her child about how the family or social system should have been safer and how she will work to make it safer now. Apology also needs to be made by the mother for not noticing what was happening and for not noticing the child's nonverbal ways of telling. Acknowledgment of the child's nonverbal telling is extremely important for the child. A therapist needs to realize that if the mother has not been treated with respect and as someone who deserves love, comfort, and protection, she may be unable to respond in a supportive and respectful way with her child (Leifer, Shapiro, & Kassem, 1993). Demanding a response from mother that she is unable to give does not create that response. It may, instead, increase mother's sense of discouragement and depression. Alternatively, developing support systems, including therapy, for the mother can be the most effective way of creating a support system for the child.

Within some families, negative feelings toward the child were there before the abuse, and the abuse is used by the mother as confirmation that her child is "bad." Friedrich (1995) has noted the lack of maternal support for sons, particularly among mothers abused by a male. Friedrich stresses the importance of helping mothers see their sons as different from the father or grandfather and more like themselves.

A child's sense of badness and self-blame can also be discussed in dyad therapy. Behaviors such as destroying clothing or toys can be explained, and then the reasons why children often blame themselves can be discussed with the child and mother. A mother can learn to respond to a child ripping or hiding new clothes by reflecting on how awful the child feels he is and restating that the child is separate from the abuse. This response, in contrast to condemning the child's treatment of the clothing—a response that reconfirms for the child that he is bad—provides a new internalization for the child.

I am responsible for . . .   As responsibility for the abuse is placed with the perpetrator and responsibility for not being aware of the abuse is placed with the nonperpetrating parent, so responsibility for each person's response following the disclosure needs to be placed with that person. If a father goes to jail, this is a result of his behavior and is his responsibility; if the parents separate, this is a result of friction between them—and the child needs to know that although the abuse forms part of that friction, it is by no means all of it—and is their responsibility; if the mother becomes distraught or depressed, this is a result of her not having a support system and resources and is her responsibility.

Parents are seldom aware, and there are certainly many other issues demanding their attention at that point, of the extent to which children blame themselves for what happens following disclosure. A therapist can highlight this. A discussion, during dyad therapy, of what happened following the child's disclosure allows the mother to take responsibility for her own reaction, or if she continues to blame the child, allows the therapist to redirect the responsibility back to the parent.

| memories | Just as the child is dealing with memories of the abuse, either on the conscious or the unconscious level, so also is the nonperpetrating parent dealing with memories of that period. Although a mother may find it possible to push these memories out of awareness because they are not traumatic, it is often helpful, both for the child and the mother, if she reviews her memories of that time, at least briefly. If the mother is able to give an accurate description, this can provide validation for the child.

For some nonperpetrating parents, sexual abuse of their child reactivates memories from their own childhood and, in particular, abuse memories. These memories need to be addressed in the parent's own therapy and the distinction between their personal abuse and the child's abuse carefully and clearly made. A parent telling her child about her own abuse without carefully distinguishing between the two can cause further distress for the child.

> Shelly (a 13-year-old sexually abused at age 6 by an older neighbor boy each time she went to his tree fort to play) talks about the abuse. Mother tells Shelly about a time when she was little when she had gone to a neighbor's house and the neighbor had abused her. Mother says that she never went back to the neighbor's after that.
>
> Therapist: [Realizes that mother, in her conversation with Shelly and, indeed, in her own thinking, has not seemed to recognize the difference between a tree fort and an adult neighbor's house, the difference be-

tween an unimportant adult and an important older child. Mother has
not acknowledged the normal wish, and indeed right, of a child to go to
an intriguing place to play without being hurt. The comparison to
mother's experience may make Shelly feel guilty for going back to the
tree fort.] I am thinking about how different your two experiences
were—yours, Mom, and yours, Shelly. Your abuse, Mom, happened at a
neighbor's house, not a place that was fun to be at. Your abuse, Shelly,
happened at a tree fort, a place that is a lot of fun for a child, and a place
that a child has a right to play in without being hurt. Although you may
wish, Mom, that you had known about the abuse so that you could have
found another intriguing but safe place for Shelly to play, Shelly's going
back to the tree house makes sense.

If the child is experiencing nightmares, flashbacks, intrusive thoughts,
or trigger responses, the therapist can help the mother and child
develop a way the mother can be supportive without being intrusive. Because nightmares can be retraumatizing, parents should
wake a child. A parent can encourage the child to talk about or draw
the nightmare, and then they can work together to decide how the
nightmare can be changed. Replays of the abuse that occurred
should not be deleted from the nightmare. This is the child's reality,
and to delete it would require the child to distort his world. Comforting the child, putting in protection, and changing scenarios of
future abusive or frightening situations can be done.

Flashbacks and intrusive thoughts can be talked about or written
down. The mother should listen carefully—neither minimizing nor
dramatizing—but should not provide extra attention or favors following these discussions. Reinforcements can encourage con-
tinuation of flashbacks beyond the needed working through.

| I feel chaotic | A parent who is angry at the perpetrator has a
hard time accepting a child's positive feelings toward the perpetrator. Even more difficult for nonperpetrating parents is accepting the
child's negative feelings toward themselves—after all, they did not
hurt the child, and they are trying hard now to help the child. A
therapist can help parents understand the child's ambivalent feelings and, thereby, enable parents to listen to and validate the child's
feelings.

A mother may, herself, have ambivalent feelings both toward the perpetrator and toward the child. If the parent is unable to tolerate these feelings, she is likely to swing between supporting the child and supporting the perpetrator and, in some cases, swing between believing the child and believing the perpetrator. She, herself, experiences an internal chaos.

For the parent who is having difficulty believing her child, a therapist can ask why the child would feel the need to report abuse (Giarretto, 1982). Questions about what was happening in the home that contributed to the disclosure, true or false, can direct criticism away from the child and focus attention more on dysfunctional family dynamics. In individual therapy, a mother can explore what believing her child would mean for her as a mother and what not believing her child would mean. Dyad therapy between mother and child is usually not appropriate if the mother is unable to believe her child.

Mothers often believe their child yet find themselves becoming angry at and recoiling from the child. This can be normalized, and the therapist can describe mother's individual therapy as an appropriate place for venting this anger. Discussing the abuser's responsibility for the abuse before the mother's anger at her child is recognized may affect the mother's rational responding but will not help her emotional responding.

| I am betrayed by people close to me | In cases of incest, both the child and the nonperpetrating parent have been betrayed (Sgroi & Dana, 1982). Thus, both are left struggling with trust issues. The mother has had her trust in a particular individual, or in society in general, betrayed. In addition, her trust in her ability to choose someone trustworthy or to know when to trust or not trust the world around her is destroyed (Hooper, 1992). This needs to be discussed in mother's individual therapy.

Between mother and child, the question of trust becomes crucial (Mitchell & Gardner, 1991). A child will, at times, tell a parent about abuse and ask the parent not to tell anyone. If the parent does not tell, the child feels betrayed in that nothing is done. In such situations, the child's behavior generally deteriorates. If the parent does tell, and in particular, if the parent tells people undiscriminatingly or tells people the child has specifically asked not to be told, the child feels betrayed. A parent needs to let a child know that telling is a protection issue and, therefore, certain people (police, child protection agency, other parent, anyone at risk of being abused, therapist) need to know.

In addition, the parent needs to have someone with whom she can talk. This helps to relieve the parent's sense of isolation[3] and to work through her losses. The mother's need for someone to talk with should be explained to the child and can be used to model the use of talking as a way of coping with stress. A mother should not choose individuals the child has asked her not to talk to and should not talk indiscriminately about the abuse.

Some parents find it difficult to be consistent in their parenting because of their own past and, thus, place their children in the position of being disappointed repeatedly. Enabling the child to talk about this with the parent within therapy may not necessarily change the parent's behavior. Talking about it can, however, help the child place the parent's behavior in context: that is, the parent's behavior reflects the parent's own experiences and is not caused by the child. Discussion of how to know whom to trust and when to trust can be helpful in dyad therapy.

| I have no boundaries | The nonperpetrating parent(s)' individual therapy provides an opportunity for the parent(s) to begin to become aware of the distorted roles and inadequate boundaries within the family system. A child who has been abused by someone within the family has been placed in a caretaking position—meeting sexual and, in some cases, companionship and comforting needs— with someone older than he (James & Nasjleti, 1983; Sgroi & Dana, 1982). This role does not disappear with disclosure of abuse. Indeed, in some situations, the role is reinforced with the child now taking care of the nonperpetrating parent who is experiencing distress. Within families where the mother was herself sexually abused as a child, children are more likely to be placed in the position of providing emotional support and general parenting for the mother (Burkett, 1991). This distortion of roles will need to be addressed in

the mother's individual therapy, mother-child dyad therapy, and family therapy.

Moving a child out of a parentified role and into a more appropriate child role often means placing new rules on the child (Lipovsky, 1991). A child may find this restrictive and often resents these shifts. Parents will need considerable support while the family readjusts (Lipovsky, 1991).

In some situations, a mother and daughter may have been in competitive positions and may, therefore, be relating like jealous siblings (Sgroi & Dana, 1982). These dynamics need to be examined. A mother can work through her feelings in relation to her daughter in individual therapy and then, in dyad therapy, start to form a new way of relating to her daughter.

In families where sibling abuse occurred, the boundaries between siblings are too porous, whereas the boundary between the children and the parents is too impenetrable. The older or stronger child has used his or her position and the power of that position in an abusive manner. The younger or weaker child's right to privacy and respect has been invaded. The parent will need to look at the spoken or unspoken messages within the family with regard to gender roles, sexuality, and respect. Family therapy, which has consistently been reported as the most important step in resolving the effects of sibling abuse (Loredo, 1982), will be needed.

Any sexualization of relationships within the family needs to be identified. A mother may be unaware of the inappropriateness of some of her behavior and language patterns, particularly in interactions with sons. These patterns need to be identified and the mother helped to find new ways of being close to her child (Friedrich, 1995).

Attention needs to be given to issues of privacy (who goes into whose rooms, who takes whose things) and boundaries (who is placed in which roles, who imposes on whom). A mother who grew up in a family with inadequate privacy and distorted boundaries may not have had an opportunity to learn these concepts. Mother's relationship with a therapist can provide an opportunity for mother to experience boundaries. Discussion during therapy can clarify behaviors by mother that are intrusive to others or that allow too much intrusion from others.

| when I am sexual, good things happen | Within the abuse scenario, the sexual touching would have meant attention and, in some cases, pleasant body feelings for the child. A mother needs to understand this dynamic and to recognize that for the child, behaving in a sexual manner often is not a conscious decision. A child may engage in sexualized behavior, not because the child wishes to be sexual but because he, like any child, needs attention and enjoys pleasure.

The parent who understands this dynamic is less likely to react negatively toward the child (getting angry or withdrawing) when sexual behaviors occur. When a mother feels she can do something about the behavior—for example, talking to the child about having learned the behavior and providing alternative attentions and pleasures—she does not feel as helpless.

A mother often needs direction from a therapist as to how to talk to her child about sexualized behavior. The behavior should be discussed when it happens or, if this is going to be embarrassing, as soon afterwards as possible. The behavior needs to be clearly named. All too often, parents tell a child to stop "that," and the child does not know what the parent means. The parent should label the behavior as something taught by the abuser, thereby shifting guilt away from the child. The parent can then state that the behavior is not what other adults or children and, in particular, the individual with whom the child was interacting, want to do with the child. The child should then have an appropriate behavior or activity suggested to him and a chance to practice the activity. Practicing the activity allows the child to start experiencing positive attention for more appropriate behavior.

Unfortunately, changing a child's behavior seldom is a simple one-step process. Both the child and the mother need considerable support as old habits are dropped and new habits learned.

Tara (mother of Annie, a 9-year-old sexually abused by stepfather between ages 5 to 7) reports in the dyad session that she had been embarrassed and furious over the weekend when her new male friend came over for dinner and Annie climbed on his lap and rubbed her bum against his genitals.

Therapist: I am thinking about how Annie's stepfather taught her to rub against him and that she would have been praised or rewarded in some way when she did it.

Mother: I know all that. But I've told Annie that she mustn't do it anymore, and here it is happening all over again.

Therapist: Yes, it is really hard when you've talked about something and you know that Annie knows in her head what she is to do or not do but still has a taught habit that she falls into without thinking.

And how confusing for you, Annie—your stepfather having taught you to sit with your bum against his genitals, and yet, this is not the way to sit; it is not the way your mother's friend wants you to sit. Touching genitals can feel really good and that is why it is saved for people to do by themselves or, when they are older, with someone they love.

Mom, could you teach Annie a new way of sitting? Could you teach her things for 9-year-olds to do with boys or men?

Within the dyad work, sexual messages given during the abuse and sexual self-labeling by the child can be explored. The mother's attitude regarding masturbation can be explored during mother's individual therapy and then, if appropriate, discussed during dyad sessions (Deblinger, 1992).

Encouraging discussion between mother and child sets a pattern of the child receiving attention for a positive behavior—talking—and provides a way in which the topic of sexuality can be explored. Discussion within the family of inappropriate sexual activity—for example, date rape—can also be encouraged by introducing this topic during dyad or family sessions.[4]

> my sexuality means { no feelings / no control / negative feelings }

Although attitudes on sexuality are constantly presented in our society through TV, magazines, and family behaviors, little discussion regarding it tends to occur within families. Many nonperpetrating, as well as perpetrating, parents will have come from homes with dysfunctional sexual attitudes (adults, males have a right to use others to meet their sexual needs, sexuality is gross, sexual activity is an obligation) and behaviors (blatant promiscuity, sexuality with violence). If a mother's attitudes are not explored and she is not given an opportunity, in her own therapy, to discuss sexual attitudes, negative sexual messages will continue to be passed on to the child.

Dyad therapy can provide an opportunity for discussion of sexuality. This is not a time for a mother to talk about her sexual experiences; indeed, privacy of sexual experiences is an important boundary that may need to be introduced for some families. Similarly, questions from a mother about an adolescent's sexual activity would be inappropriate. It is a time when the difference between sexuality and sexual abuse can be clearly stated, and the possibility of positive sexual experiences for the child can be introduced. Respect for the child's emerging sexuality is important and can be modeled by the therapist. Although some mothers will be unable to verbalize such an attitude, they can be part of listening to someone else verbalize it. Some mothers find that reading books written for children on sexuality, either by themselves or with their child, is helpful.

| What I am told ≠ what is meant | Double messages exist in families in which sexual abuse occurs, both in connection to the abuse—"Your father is a good man" and father abuses—and to behaviors in the family—"Everyone must be responsible" and older brother is not punished for hitting his sister. With severe abuse, contradictions between messages and reality are extreme. Awareness of these messages, both from the past and present, is important if the mother is to change her pattern of relating to her child and help her child be able to trust what others say to him.

Dyad therapy provides a setting for exploring the meaning behind something a parent says and how it does or does not fit what she does. The therapist, by verbalizing some of the unspoken messages that may have occurred in the home, is able to bring issues out into the open. The therapist can model the use of direct query as a way of sorting out double messages.

| I have { no emotions / no experience / no integrated self | Nonperpetrating parents often go through a period of denial following disclosure of abuse. This may

be complete denial by actively disbelieving the child's report[5] or emotional denial by blocking awareness that the abuse has happened even though the parents believe the child's disclosure. When awareness is blocked, the mother is unable to take proactive steps to report the abuse or to help the child. Whether the denial is active disbelief or emotional disbelief, the child's reality is not validated. The child's own denial or dissociation is strengthened.

The wish to deny is best addressed in mother's individual therapy. Dyad therapy is usually contraindicated in such a situation. If the mother who is denying the abuse maintains contact with the child, the therapist may decide to discuss this dilemma and its effect on the child in a dyad session. Where the indicators of abuse are such that the therapist is able to support the child's statement, this can be discussed in the dyad session. Mother's inability to support the child in this area can be defined as an issue that belongs to mother and not to the child.

A mother intellectualizing or explaining away the abuse as something that happened at one point but will not happen again may be mother's effort to keep her family together. This should be addressed in both individual and dyad therapy. A parent's use of the statement, "It won't happen again," as a defense against looking at family dynamics can be addressed by asking the parent what she would have said, if, before the abuse occurred, she had been asked whether abuse would occur.

If a child is using dissociation as a coping mechanism, it is important for the parents to learn about this process. They need to understand what is occurring when the child "goes off in space" or abruptly changes character. They can learn ways of helping the child reorient and become aware of internal switches. Parents of a child who shows signs of dissociation need to be reassured that a supportive and comforting environment can protect a child from developing multiple personalities (Kluft, 1984b). Peterson (as cited in O'Neill & Chu, 1994) noted that if the parent herself experiences high dissociation or multiple personalities, contracting for one part of the parent to do the parenting will be an important part of the parent's individual therapy.

The use of coping mechanisms can be discussed by the parent and child together: how each of them copes with stress, which coping mechanisms they want to keep, which coping mechanisms they want to change. Dyad therapy, by encouraging talking about distressing events and feelings, provides a model for healthier coping.

❑ Dyad Therapy: Working With the Perpetrator

Dyad therapy between the child and the perpetrator is quite different from dyad therapy with the child and a nonperpetrating parent. It is the perpetrator's[6] messages, by behavior and words, that have caused the child's trauma and abuse-related internalizations. Dyad therapy with the child and father would only occur after the father had received therapy related to his abusive behavior and then therapy in which he looked at the overt and covert messages he had given and may still be giving to his child. Dyad therapy would provide an opportunity for the father to take back the distorted messages that had led to the child's abuse-related internalizations. Addressing internalizations without first removing the messages would be like giving a child an antibiotic while leaving the child in a germ-infested environment.

A review of the literature on dyad therapy with individuals who have been sexually abused and the abuser indicates that dyad work has concentrated on apology-clarification sessions by the offender and confrontation sessions by the individual abused. Relevant to the present discussion are apology-clarification sessions. Yokley and McGuire (1990), in a compilation of victim-offender communication programs, note that although careful experimental studies have not been done, no negative effects from apology-clarification sessions have been observed, and both adolescents and adults have reported positive effects. Within the work of the present author, children as well as adolescents have benefited from such sessions.

The following discussion assumes that the father has admitted guilt and accepted responsibility for the effect of the abuse (see Trepper & Barrett, 1989); has received individual therapy, group therapy, or both with regard to his sexually abusive behavior; and wishes to make reparation for the abuse. When reference is made in the following discussion to individual work with the father, this does not refer to therapy related to father's own issues but to the individual work with father in preparation for dyad sessions with the child. Therapy related to father's issues should be done by a different therapist from the child's therapist. Therapy in preparation for dyad sessions may be done by the father's therapist working closely with the child's therapist—an understanding of the child's experience helps the therapist recognize hidden messages within the father's language—or by the child's therapist with the child's knowledge.

If this work is done by the child's therapist, the position of the therapist must always be that of working on behalf of the child. This must be clear for the father, the child, and the therapist so that the dangers inherent in dual relationships be avoided.

The second assumption is that the child's therapist has talked with the child about the possibility of meeting with the father. The child would be told that a therapist is presently meeting with father because father has expressed a wish to help the child with her understanding of his abusive behavior. She would also be told that if it is appropriate *and* if she wishes, sessions together with the father would be held after the father and the therapist have done their work together. If the father is working with a therapist other than the child's therapist, the child's therapist would also be at the dyad sessions. The therapy related to father looking at the messages he has and is giving to the child is important whether or not dyad therapy with the father and child occurs.

In addition, it is assumed that the therapist is able to work with the father in a positive but confronting relationship. This may be difficult because of anger or revulsion experienced by the therapist or because of the therapist's discomfort with the role of confronting and pressuring. McElroy and McElroy (1991), in their discussion of countertransference issues with incest families, point out the danger of a therapist feeling more positive and forgiving toward the perpetrator as the perpetrator shows regret and expresses thanks to the therapist for her support. The "ability of the offender to successfully manipulate and beguile the therapist [is] a clear enactment of his control over the child victim" (McElroy & McElroy, 1991, p. 52). A therapist must be able to retain a clear perspective of the acts of abuse and that the responsibility for the abuse must be assumed by the father.

The following discussion describes the initial work with the perpetrator and then, briefly, the work with the child and the perpetrator.

INITIAL WORK WITH
THE PERPETRATOR

The therapeutic relationship between the therapist and the father
needs to coexist with a clear statement that what the father did,
whatever were the circumstances in his life that led him in that
direction, was unacceptable and must not happen again either sexually or emotionally. The father has a responsibility to help his child
as she tries to make sense of her world. In addition, the father has a
responsibility to figure out why his abusive thinking and behavior
occurred *and* to resolve those conflicts and insecurities. Within this
framework, the therapist can align herself with the father in assisting
his child, his family, and himself. The therapist needs always, when
doing the dyad work, to have a clear sense of her primary objectives:
helping the child and making sure that abuse, in any form, will not
occur again.

Identifying Messages

Working together with a therapist who is knowledgeable regarding the internal dynamics that occur for a child when abused, a
father needs to identify the abusive messages he gave his child.
These messages would include those that occur in all abuse situations, those given in situations where the abuse is by someone close
to the child, and the messages unique to the relationship between
this particular father and child. The unique messages can be identified by examining the story of the abuse, as written out by the father
and as known from the child, and by noticing the manner in which
father talks and relates during the individual sessions.

Father's written story of the abuse. Writing out the abuse scenarios
is often part of an offender treatment program. Whether the father
has done this previously or not, he would be asked to write out what
happened as part of preparing for meeting with his child. Included
in the description should be (a) how an abuse scenario started: what
happened and what was said by whom; (b) how and when each new

sexual activity was initiated; and (c) threats—physical, verbal, situational—that were used. Details of what the father said, how he did or did not describe what he was doing to his child, and the type of pressure used need to be included. Some perpetrators feel that they used no pressure. A therapist may need to help the father identify pressures: for example, the importance of a father to the child and the difference in size. Ways in which a father placed the child in a special role in the family and created divisions or alliances in the family should also be included.

For a father who has had limited previous therapy, there may need to be considerable discussion about the abuse, about father's world at that time, and about father's present world before the father does the written assignment. The written form is recommended for several reasons. In writing out what happened, the father is forced to give more thought to what he did. If the description overlooks the father's subtle behaviors, these can be added at the appropriate points. In addition, a written format makes it easier for the father and therapist to examine together the detail of the father's thought structure, the father's interaction with the child, and the child's experience.

As the therapist and the father review what he has written, the therapist can point out the manner in which the father may have implicated the child in the activity.

> Alfred (father of Shirley, a 16-year-old sexually abused between ages 10 to 14 by Alfred) writes the following: Shirley would come into my room when my wife was at work and suggest that we have sex.

> Sam (father of Jane, a 10-year-old sexually abused between ages 5 to 6 by Sam) writes in his description: Jane approached me and asked me if I wanted to play our special game. She would ask me to tickle her in that special way and say how much she liked it.

The therapist needs to point out that it was the father *who taught* the child an activity, *who put* the child in the position of choosing or experiencing inappropriate activities, and *who created* the chaotic world that the child then tried to control. A child will do what she has been taught pleases someone, will be curious about things she does not know, will want pleasant sensations, and, in an effort to

control what happens when, will plan activities. Each of these behaviors are normal child responses. They did not cause the abuse
and do not implicate the child in the abuse. Any description or use
of language that appears to implicate the child needs to be chal-
lenged directly by the therapist. The reality of the role of the father—
initiating, failing to protect, teaching inappropriate activities, controlling, threatening—and the role of the child—wishing to please,
wishing to have attention, following what she was taught, trying to
keep some control in her world, trying to survive—needs to be
clearly phrased by the father.

The terms a father uses to describe or talk about the sexual activity
with the child also need to be examined.

> John (father of Tammy, a 12-year-old sexually abused at ages 10 and
> 11 by John) writes this: I told Tammy I was teaching her what she
> needed to know for when she was older and spent time with boys.
> She told me she didn't like it, but I assured her that it would get easier
> and then it would be okay for her with boys.

> Ivan (father of Edith, a 14-year-old sexually abused at age 13 by Ivan)
> writes this: When I would go in to say good night to Edith, I would
> ask her if I could lie down on the bed with her, and she would say no.
> But then I would say, "Oh please, you let me before." If she didn't
> say yes, I would sit there very depressed, and I guess she would start
> to feel sorry for me and would say "Okay, but don't touch me."
>   Then I would climb under the covers—of course, I would keep my
> clothes on—and curl up next to her. After a time, I would start to
> stroke her and ask her to rub my penis. If she said no, I would say,
> "But you did it last time, so it won't do any harm for you to do it
> again." She would tell me that I should be doing this with her mother.
> I would agree but say that I was so sad that I needed her to make me
> feel better.
>   If she wouldn't masturbate me, I would become depressed and for
> the next few days, I wouldn't talk to anyone. If she did, then I would
> feel better and the next few days, I would be more cheerful with the
> other people in the family.

The therapist needs to emphasize to the father that he is forming
how the child looks at and experiences her world. The therapist can
then help the father recognize the message he has given his child:

John's message to Tammy: You cannot learn things by yourself.

Ivan's message to Edith: You have a responsibility to make other people feel better even if it makes you feel worse.

Although fathers often are not consciously aware of all the messages they give their children, children certainly pick up the messages, at least at an unconscious level.

The father's interaction. Father's way of talking and relating with the therapist is a further resource for understanding the messages a father may have given his child.

Alfred (see page 174) talks about the abuse and says that he realized at the time that it should not be happening. He would tell his daughter that he should not be having sex with her but that he was sick and just as soon as he could, he would stop.

In his conversation with the therapist, Alfred refers to himself as someone who is addicted to sex and, therefore, could not control what he was doing. He becomes angry with the therapist, feeling that she does not appreciate the awful situation he was in. He states that he feels he is being judged and looked down on rather than considered as someone who is unhappy and should be helped. As he leaves the office, Alfred says to the therapist, "Don't give up on me. I really am a nice guy."

The therapist notes that despite the fact that the session had been described to father as a time to focus on helping his daughter, Alfred has focused on himself and the importance of people taking care of him. In his abusive interactions with his daughter, Alfred would have given the message that his daughter needed to focus on and care for males. There would have been the message that she should stick by someone no matter what he does. In addition, father was giving the message that if someone is addicted to something, they are not responsible.

Sam (see page 174), on leaving the first session with his daughter's therapist, puts his hand on the therapist's shoulder and then his head on his hand.

The therapist reflects on Sam's lack of awareness of appropriate boundaries between people as well as his wish to have others feel sorry for him and take care of him. His daughter would have been given that message; perhaps that was why she could not remember the abuse.

Messages can also be recognized from the way a father talks about his child.

Alfred talks about his daughter as needing to control her behavior— that was her responsibility and had nothing to do with him.

Sam describes himself and his child as a "team."

These messages (Alfred: Shirley should have stopped the abuse; Sam: Jane is an extension of me) need to be clearly verbalized and addressed if a father is to change the manner in which he interrelates with his child and with his family. When the father has his own therapist, these perceptions of the abuse and the child should be discussed with the father's therapist. When the father is not in individual therapy, the dyad therapist will need to address these issues and also work toward father recognizing the need for therapy for himself. Connecting the father with his own therapist, a therapist who can address father's individual issues rather than just perpetrator behavior, can be an important step in helping the child.

Retracting the Messages

As messages are identified, father's distorted cognitions can be recognized, worked through, and shifted. Father then rewrites his explanation of the abuse, taking responsibility not only for the abusive activities but also for pressures placed on the child. In this explanation, the father labels and takes back the messages he gave. He then can move on—to talk about positive times that he has enjoyed with his child in the past. This description of good times is included to provide a base for a future healthy father-child relationship.

The rewriting of the abuse story is not only a concrete goal but also a vehicle by which the therapist can help a father recognize how he both overtly and subtly used his child, and undoubtedly other people as well, to serve his own purposes. A father's explanation of the approach he used needs to be specific. Any activity by the child within the abuse—for example, asking to play "the special game"— should be mentioned and placed within the context of the child wanting attention—an appropriate child reaction. The father needs to take responsibility for placing his child in the position of having to participate in abuse to have attention. If these activities are not discussed, the child may retain her original perception of the activity: that is, her initiating or eliciting a sexual activity.

The rewritten story needs to establish the child as a special person who has a right to attention, love, and caretaking and a right to privacy of the body. When appropriate, the father should recognize the specialness of bodies and sexual feelings.

> Sam (see pages 174-176) and the therapist talk about his having called the abuse *the special game* and giving Jane the message that this was what made her important to him. By doing this, he had set up the two of them as a team against Mom and taught Jane that that was what family interactions were suppose to be like.
>
> Sam writes to Jane: I taught you to touch and rub my penis. Like all children, you wanted to please me because I was your father and so you would, to please me, suggest that we play the special game. Also, I touched you on your vulva in a way that would have felt good because that is the way bodies are made to feel when they are touched. And so, naturally, you would want to feel that feeling again.
>
> I never should have started those things, I never should have taught you those things, touching you or your touching me. I should not have started what I named as "the special game," which taught you to ask for the special game. It was my responsibility as an adult, and as your father, to teach you games that did not have to do with body touching. Your body is yours for you to decide about as you get older and not for anyone else to decide about.
>
> You and Mom and I should have done things together, that is what families are about, not split into parts.
>
> The therapist makes a note that she will need to address the dysfunctional divisions and ganging up in the family during family therapy.
>
> John (see page 175) and the therapist talk about how John gave Tammy the message that she could learn things only if they were taught to her.

Therapist recalls in her mind that Tammy had, in her therapy, shown the therapist over and over again what she had learned in school. She seldom created anything on her own. The therapist would need to address this in Tammy's individual sessions as well as helping father retract his message.

Therapist: I am thinking about how this will limit Tammy as she grows up, the message that she cannot learn on her own, and particularly that she is dependent on a male with regard to learning about her own body. Is this what you want for your daughter?

John writes to Tammy: I told you I was teaching you things—that was an excuse I made up. You can teach yourself about your body. You can teach yourself a lot of things. Sure, there are things I can teach you, like swimming or how to play monopoly. But about yourself, no! Your body is private, just like everyone's body is private, for you to teach yourself about and learn about. What I taught you—that adults can touch children, that people can touch people who don't want to be touched—was wrong. I had a lot of things mixed up and I am now learning to respect other people, other people's things and other people's bodies.

Ivan (see page 175) and the therapist talk about how Ivan changed his behavior, being depressed or being cheerful, depending on whether the abuse did not occur or did occur. The therapist notes how Ivan had made Edith responsible for how he felt rather than his being responsible. When depressed, he needed to talk with his wife or friends or to see a therapist, not abuse his child. Why did he think he had chosen the abusing?

Ivan writes to Edith: I made you feel that it was your job to make me feel better. I was wrong, it is my job to make me feel better. You were so right when you told me that I should have been with Mom. I am sorry for touching you and making you touch me. I am sorry I didn't take care of myself and for making you feel you had to take care of me. I am learning now to take care of myself.

The unspoken but implicit messages given by father also need to be addressed in father's story. After these messages are made explicit by the therapist, the father can start to review and, most importantly, shift his perceptions that underlie the implicit messages. Then, and only then, can the father not only take responsibility for the messages but also start to give new messages.

Sam (see pages 174, 176, 178) and the therapist talk about how Sam talks about Jane as if she is part of him rather than a separate person. Sam talks about how lonely he has always been but that after Jane was born and he could play with her, he felt okay. He had wanted Jane there all the time and dependent on him. The therapist asks about the loneliness and then about what Sam can do by himself or with other adults to fill that loneliness. Does he want Jane to feel empty like he has, or does he want her to have a full sense of herself as a person?

Sam writes to Jane: I treated you as if you were mine, but you were you, and you are you. Yes, we were a good team, a good team when we went fishing and I threw the line and you held the pole and watched for the fish. And we are a good team, a team of two separate people who have fun together.

As Sam plans activities for himself and his daughter, he makes sure that they play two distinct roles even as they do something together. When she defers a decision to him, he helps her figure out what she wants, separate from his wishes. Sam also makes sure he does activities on his own and develops his own self-reliance.

Many children are afraid that their fathers will be angry at them for the disclosure. They feel they have let their fathers down by letting other people find out what happened. This fear needs to be addressed in father's story. A father can congratulate a child on having the courage to tell and let her know that, however hard, it has helped him start to learn new behavior.

In a final section of the story, the father can talk about the appropriate things that he and his child have enjoyed together over the years, if they did indeed occur. He should *not* mention activities that were used as bribes or rewards during the abuse. Many children have positive feelings for their fathers, and this part of the story allows those feelings to be confirmed. Talking about the good times allows the child to maintain the important attachment that she has. It allows her to look forward to future positive times together.

The work between the father and therapist is not complete until the father's implicit messages have not only been acknowledged and retracted within the story but also no longer exist in father's interactions with people and with his child in particular. This is, obviously, not something that changes quickly and, thus, will need to be monitored as the therapist works with the father in dyad sessions and then in family sessions.

WORK WITH THE PERPETRATOR AND THE CHILD

As the father and therapist work together, the therapist evaluates whether the father will be able to behave appropriately in a joint session with the child. The father needs to be able to tell or read the abuse story and also to be able to listen to the child. The conversation during the session, whether about the abuse or other topics, should be such that the child feels validated as a separate person and as someone important to father. The father must be able to refrain from putting pressure on the child to feel sorry for him, take care of him, or forgive him.

Once the decision is made to have a dyad session, the therapist meets with the child and the child's therapist, if he has not been the therapist working with the father, to determine whether she wants to meet with the father and to set up guidelines that will help the child feel safe. It is important that the child feel some control over the meeting. Even if the child is already in contact with the father, this meeting will be different from other times with him, and the child needs a way to stop the session if she wishes to do so.

Betsy (a 9-year-old sexually abused by her father between ages 5 to 8), during the session prior to meeting with her father, goes over to the therapist's desk and starts making pretend phone calls. Betsy phones for someone to come and get a sick student from school.

Therapist: [Notes Betsy's theme of needing someone to take a child who wasn't feeling well out of a situation.] You may be worried about who will come and help you if you start to feel upset during the session with Dad. (Betsy nods.) We can set up a signal that you can give if you start to feel nervous or for any reason want to stop the session. I would then let your father know that the session had been long enough and ask him to leave. You and I would then have time to talk about it, if you wanted to. And, if you wanted, there could be another meeting, at another time, with Dad.

A child usually has questions that she wants to ask her father. Sometimes, the child is able to formulate these questions before the initial dyad session; sometimes, they will be formulated after that session and can become the basis of a second session. Some children are ready to confront their father with their memories or with their feelings. Others are unable to do so and should not be pressured into doing it. A therapist who pressures the child into confronting a father before the child is ready repeats the abuse dynamics of having the child meet an adult's, in this case the therapist's, needs.

If this is the first time the child has seen the father in several years, the child is often more at ease if she can bring something that she has made for him. It gives her something to do when she first sees him and, thus, lets her feel more in control.

During the session, the therapist is there to support both the father and the child. She continues, however, to have the child's welfare as her primary objective. If the father, by his manner or language, becomes offensive in any way, places any blame or responsibility on the child, or pressures the child for forgiveness, the therapist must correct him immediately. For the therapist to overlook these messages, however subtle, would be similar to the time of the abuse when the nonperpetrating parent overlooked clues. If the father does not correct himself after the therapist's intervention, then the therapist needs to terminate the session. Although a therapist may feel that this is a negative outcome, it can be positive for the child.

Bert (father of Edith, a 7-year-old sexually abused by Bert between ages 4 to 6) is meeting with Edith and the therapist. Bert explains to Edith that he never should have touched her. He has prayed to God and God has forgiven him so now she can forgive him.

Therapist: No, Bert. Edith does not need to forgive you. How she thinks and what she does is for her to decide. She had to take care of you in the past, that was part of the abuse, but she does not need to take care of you now. She does not need to forgive you.

Bert: The Lord said people are to be forgiven.

Therapist (standing up): It seems, Edith, that Dad is still really confused about the fact that you have a right to decide about yourself. And when adults are confused, they need to talk with another adult. It is not a child's job to take care of adults.

I am going to take you back out to the waiting room where Mom is. Then your Dad and I will have some time to talk about his needing to learn that you have a right to decide what you do.

When the therapist and Edith arrive in the waiting room, Edith runs to her mother with a huge grin on her face and says, "Sandra told Daddy I don't have to forgive him."

Terminating a session that becomes inappropriate reinforces for the child that inappropriate behavior by the adult is not acceptable.

Another reason for interrupting the flow of a session or a session itself would be any inappropriate physical touching or proximity between the father and child.

David (father of Alice, a 4-year-old sexually abused at age 3 by her father) is sitting on the floor with his legs stretched out in front of him watching Alice play. David asks Alice to come and sit with him while he talks to her. Alice comes over and stretches out on her stomach on top of his legs. This places her face at his crotch.

Therapist: [Notes that although there is nothing erotic about either Alice's movements or father's movements, this is probably a position learned from the abuse.] I'm noticing how Alice is stretched out on top of your legs, David, with her head at your crotch. This may be one of the behaviors you taught her during the abuse. It is unfair that Alice had to learn this behavior. Fathers and daughters can sit side by side and be really close. It is going to be your job, David, to teach Alice a new way of sitting with you and a new way of being close with you.

Most often, the dyad session goes smoothly. After the father has gone through his story (some will want to read it, whereas others will want to tell the story) and the retraction of messages, some children want to talk about what happened or how they feel. Others want to talk about school or what is happening at home. The child should have control of the conversation. Although talking about nonabuse-related topics can be labeled as avoidance, it provides an appropriate interaction between father and child and allows the child to gain approval from her father for appropriate activities.

Following the session, completed or not, the therapist should meet again with the child to check out how she felt during the session. The possibility of the child having questions about the abuse or about her father should be raised.

> Jane (see Sam, pages 174, 176, 178, 180) says, when discussing how she felt during the dyad session, that she had just wanted the session to be over.

Therapist: [Notes the similarity between this and the way Jane has described the abuse.] That's rather like how you felt during the abuse and how you feel now in wanting the therapy to be over. That makes sense, but I'm also thinking about the fact that children have lots of questions. Some children have questions come into their minds while abuse is going on or after it is over, others have questions come into their minds while they are talking to their fathers or after they have talked to their fathers. I'm wondering about questions you might have.

Jane: Why did it happen? Why did it have to happen to me? Why did he have to do it? Will he get angry at me? Can I get angry at him?

Talking about angry feelings at father is particularly important. If the child denies angry feelings, the therapist can ask how the child thinks her father would respond if she were angry at him. The therapist can ask the child what she may want to say to her father at some point in the future. Imaging can be used as a way of helping the child practice being assertive with her father.

The therapist would then meet with the father alone to go over the questions and for the father to write out answers. This enables the therapist to address, once again, any distorted thinking on the part of a father. Further dyad sessions would then be scheduled.

The number of dyad sessions that should be held will vary depending on the situation. If the father is going to be, or has already, returned to the home, family therapy is an appropriate setting for further exploration of the abuse dynamics and abuse-related messages.

Hindman (1989) recommends that the father give a copy of the written story to the child so that it can be available to her if she wishes, in the future, to do further work related to the abuse. The present author has found that some children and their families prefer to have the therapist keep this copy. This requires the therapist to inform these children if she moves or when she retires. If the child is then an adult and so wishes, the copy would be sent to her.

In some cases, a father is never able to reach a point in his own processing and his interaction with others that a dyad session would be appropriate (for example, see Alfred, pages 174, 176). The therapist, with the father's knowledge, can meet with the child to explain that the father still is confused as to appropriate roles for parents and children. If the father gives his permission, the therapist can talk with the child about the false messages her father has realized he gave her during the abuse. If the father does not give his permission, the therapist would not refer to content from the sessions with father but is in a better position for recognizing—within the child's conversation or behavior—messages given by the father. As the therapist recognizes these messages, she can verbalize them and, in this way, help the child sort through the abuse messages.

❏ Family Therapy— Intrafamilial Abuse

After a decade in which the role of family therapy within the treatment of sexual abuse, and incest in particular, has been debated, it is now recognized as an important therapeutic modality (Barrett, Trepper, & Fish, 1990). Concerns had been raised that a family therapy approach would lead to the system rather than the perpetrator being held responsible for what had happened. There was also concern that even if the perpetrator were held responsible, attention might be diverted away from the abuse to family system problems (Conte, 1986). Family therapists are now recognizing that in situations of abuse, therapists should not take a neutral stance and should be active in directing the discussion (Conte, 1986; Orenchuk-Tomiuk, Matthey, & Christensen, 1990; Trepper & Barrett, 1989; Wheeler, 1990).

Family therapy is most often conceptualized as a part, and usually the last part, of a total treatment program (Giarretto, 1982; James & Nasjleti, 1983; Orenchuk-Tomiuk et al., 1990; Trepper & Barrett, 1989). Within these treatment models, the child, the nonperpetrating parent, and the perpetrator have received individual treatment and may have participated in dyad therapies.

Family therapy is particularly important for establishing appropriate boundaries and roles within the family (Furniss, 1983; James & Nasjleti, 1983; Lipovsky, 1991; Sgroi, 1982; Trepper & Barrett, 1989). Barrett et al. (1990) have emphasized the need for attention to messages related to power and gender.

Cohesion, as distinct from enmeshment, and open expression have been found to be significantly lower in families where abuse has occurred (Alexander & Lupfer, 1987; Dadds, Smith, & Webber, 1991). It has also been found that when cohesion and open expression is high, less distress is exhibited by children following disclosure (Friedrich, 1988). Family therapy provides a setting for learning more effective ways of communicating and encouraging empathic understanding (Sgroi, 1982; Trepper & Barrett, 1989).

Attention should be given to the attachment patterns within the family. When there is an insecure attachment, as occurs in most families where maltreatment occurs (Crittenden & Ainsworth, 1989; Karen, 1994), family therapy should work toward creating more consistent, positive engagement between the parent and child (Friedrich, 1995).

Because the therapist cannot be in a neutral position with the incestuous family as she is with most families in family therapy, she needs to think through carefully how to approach these families. Gelinas (1988) talks about the importance of the therapist recognizing the family's efforts to function despite the fact that these efforts have taken a dysfunctional form. By recognizing the family's sense of loyalty, the father's search for relatedness, and the mother's wish to care for and protect her children, the therapist is able to align with the parents and thereby help them find positive ways of achieving these objectives (Gelinas, 1988). Depending on the resistance level of the family, both direct and indirect interventions are needed (Trepper & Barrett, 1989). Wheeler (1990) refers to the kick-stroke method in which there is direct confrontation related to the abuse and then encouragement for any movement the family has made away from the abusive pattern. Friedrich (1995) suggests a variety of family therapy techniques—creating a new story, positive reframing, externalizing the problem, family of origin work—for working with these families.

Most therapists include an apology-confrontation session involving the nonperpetrating parent as well as the perpetrating parent (Giaretto, 1982; James & Nasjleti, 1983; Trepper & Barrett, 1989). Trepper and Barrett (1989) include a discussion of what the family was like in the past and what it is like now. Each individual in the family can be asked what they want to say to the other people in the family about the past and about the future (Bentovim & Davenport, 1992). This needs to be done carefully so that the child is never put in a position of apologizing for behaviors that occurred because of the abuse. A child may wish that she had not chosen a particular way of behaving, and the family can take a look at why those particular behaviors occurred—breaking doors as a way of trying to get Mom to notice what was happening; prostituting as a way of letting others know how badly she felt about herself. The responsibility for these abuse effects, however, needs to remain with the abuser.

Working within the present model, the therapist will want to clarify the messages that both the father's and the mother's behavior would have given to the children in the family. The messages to the children who were not abused (such as "You are not important") as well as the messages to the children who were abused need to be elicited and discussed. Parents need to be asked what they want to do about those messages and how healthier messages can be given in the future.

Attention should also be given to the strengths of the family and their willingness to work through all that has happened. The abuse needs to be treated as something that must never happen again but not as something that has irretrievably damaged the family. The family will retain memories, but these memories do not need to intrude into daily life.

Ways to express feelings, both positive and negative, need to be talked about and reinforced. How each person in the family will decide about trusting others, both within and outside the family, needs to be considered. Appropriate boundaries and roles need to be observed. Appropriate ways of gaining attention and pleasure can be discussed and encouraged. Sexuality as a special dimension of the self can be discussed. The many messages given by society and the media with regard to sexuality can be discussed with a view as to what each member of the family, as an individual, accepts or does not accept. Throughout the work with the family, emphasis would be placed not only on people saying what they mean but also on people dealing directly with the situations and behaviors that distress them.

❏ Family Therapy—Extrafamilial Abuse

Family therapy is also important when working with children who were abused outside the family. As with intrafamilial abuse, the family's view of itself—capable of protecting, able to judge others accurately, able to work things out—and of itself in relation to society—safety, trust, support—is severely affected (Kiser et al., 1991; Van Scoyk, Gray, & Jones, 1988). If the child did not disclose at the time of the abuse or the family did not respond immediately, these dynamics need to be explored. The potential of the family for supporting the child can be highlighted.

The child's reaction and behavior in response to the abuse needs to be normalized and to be understood by the family as the child's way of expressing her experience (Kiser et al., 1991). Her ability to work through the distress and to continue with healthy development needs to be emphasized. It is important that the parents and the child discuss together the times in the child's life when feelings from the abuse may again intrude so that they can help each other recognize those times and respond in a supportive manner.

As discussed in the section on working with the nonperpetrating parent, the parents' own issues around the abuse of their child and their own secondary traumatization should be addressed initially in individual or couples therapy. Fathers tend to react initially with fury and then wish to forget what happened (Jonker & Jonker-Bakker, 1991). Mothers tend to be sad and remain concerned about what this will mean for the child growing up. A couple may experience difficulty around their own sexual relationship and understanding each other's reactions (Jonker & Jonker-Bakker, 1991).

After the parents work through their personal reactions, these reactions can be discussed in family sessions with the responsibility for the parents' reaction remaining with the parents. Other children in the family should be included, and their worries both for the sibling and for themselves can be explored. Open discussion of feelings and of the trauma allows the family to integrate what has happened and to move forward in a way that provides safety yet encourages exploration.

❏ **Summary**

Sexual abuse, intrafamilial or extrafamilial, affects the entire family. Nonperpetrating parents may experience secondary traumatization, and if they are to be available to and supportive of their child, this traumatization and feelings related to the abuse need to be addressed. These issues are appropriate for a nonperpetrating parent(s)' own therapy. Issues related to responsibility, communication, family roles, child behavior, and expression of feelings need to be addressed within dyad and family therapy. Dysfunctional relationship patterns between mother and child need to be identified and opportunities created for more positive relating.

Therapy with the perpetrator needs to identify the mistaken messages given by the perpetrator to the child. The perpetrator's present relating as well as past relating to the child needs to be examined. The perpetrator, in dyad therapy with the child, needs to take responsibility for the abuse and needs to retract and change abuse-related messages.

Family therapy, both in situations of intrafamilial and extrafamilial abuse, is being increasingly recognized as essential to the treatment process. The child receives support for her role in the disclosure process and is provided with a safe and supportive setting for working through the trauma. Most important, family therapy provides a space for members of the family to practice new ways of relating, communicating, and supporting each other.

Notes

1. To simplify structure, *child* will be used in this chapter to refer to both adolescent and child.

2. Because mothers are most often the nonperpetrating parent, *mother* will be used interchangeably with *nonperpetrating parent* in the following discussion. To clarify grammatical reference, the male pronoun will be used consistently when referring to the child.

3. Nonperpetrating mothers' perception of loneliness has been found to correlate significantly with psychological distress (Deblinger et al., 1993).

4. The book, *No Is Not Enough* (Adams, Fay, & Loreen-Martin, 1984), is particularly helpful in providing a basis for a discussion of date rape for adolescents and their parents.

5. Research has indicated that 16% (Pierce & Pierce, 1985) to 29% (Leifer et al., 1993) of parents do not believe children when sexual abuse is first disclosed.

6. Although child sexual abuse by females is being increasingly recognized (Mendel, 1995), the majority of perpetrators are male. For this reason, the male pronoun will be used in the present discussion. Dyad and family work is more likely to be carried out when the perpetrator is a member of the close family. The term *father* will be used in the following discussion. *Mother* can be substituted for father in situations of abuse by mother. To clarify grammatical reference, the female pronoun will be used consistently when referring to the child.

5

Hearing Oneself:
The Therapist's Experience

The preceding chapters have looked at the child, the child's internalizations, and the child's behavior. The therapist has, in most situations, been presented as the ideal therapist—attending to the child, understanding the child, and responding to the child. Unfortunately, we as individuals seldom become the ideal. We bring to each session our knowledge of developmental and trauma dynamics and our wish to understand and support the child. We also bring our own childhood experiences and our personal responses to trauma and distress. Then, within the session, we experience our reactions to the child and the child's experience. To understand and support a child, we need to understand therapy relationships. We need to understand and support ourselves.

Therapists' reactions are typically discussed in the last chapter of books on treatment, as it is in this book, almost as if these reactions were an addendum to therapy rather than a central part of therapy. Perhaps they are discussed last because we are taught as students and academics that we need an understanding of the issues being addressed, and we are taught as caretakers that our first concern must be for the individual with whom we are working. If a book could be written in three dimensions, the conceptual model; the client's responses through play, behavior, and words; and our reactions as therapists and individuals would all be discussed at the same time. Given the single dimensional nature of books, the present and last chapter looks at the therapist's experience.

This experience, referred to in psychoanalytic and psychodynamic literature as *countertransference* and in behavioral and cognitive literature as *therapist response,* includes the reaction of the therapist as she works with the issues of sexual abuse and her reaction as she works with each particular child or adolescent who comes to therapy. The therapist's experience is affected by her knowledge and understanding of abuse and trauma dynamics and of child development and by her knowledge and understanding of the therapeutic process. The therapist's experience is also affected by her own experiences as a child and in particular, experiences of sexual abuse, other forms of child maltreatment, sexuality, interpersonal patterns, and the extent to which she has recognized and worked through those experiences. The therapist's experience is also affected by ongoing pressures, both personal issues and her present level of fatigue and stress. These three areas (knowledge, experience, pressure) interact to determine the therapist's capacity within a therapy session. This capacity is also affected by the way in which each particular child expresses his needs and the child's particular abuse experience. And, perhaps most important, the therapist's experience is affected by how she as a person processes the experience in the therapy room.

The preceding chapters have discussed abuse and trauma dynamics and child development as related to sexual abuse issues. The Internalization Model and psychodynamic trauma-focused therapy have been described. The present chapter discusses briefly the relevance of the therapist's own experiences. The chapter examines how a particular child's pattern of interacting may interact with a therapist's experience. The interaction in the session between the child's content and behavior presentation (transference) and the therapist's noticing, recognizing, and responding (countertransference) is described.

❏ The Therapist

Sexual abuse has been recognized as eliciting strong responses in therapists (Briere, 1992; Davies & Frawley, 1994; Herman, 1992; McCann & Colletti, 1994). These responses and the effect of the responses on a therapy session depend on a number of factors. Figure 5.1 presents a schematic view of what the therapist (left side) and the child (right side) bring to a therapy session (midsection) and how each imposes on and affects the other.

KNOWLEDGE BACKGROUND

The therapist brings to each therapy session his knowledge of abuse and trauma dynamics, of child development, and of therapeutic processes. Unfortunately, this knowledge does not include all of the reading, discussions, and experience that the therapist has accumulated. Only that part that has been thought and rethought, and in particular the thinking related to the child being seen, forms the therapist's knowledge base. Conceptual frameworks, such as the Internalization Model, are important in making this knowledge usable.

If the therapist has little knowledge of sexual abuse and the internal dynamics (that is, internalizations) that occur with abuse, she may, in an effort to preserve a nonabusive world view, deny the reality of what the child is playing or reporting (Wilson, Lindy, & Raphael, 1994). Wilson et al. (1994) describe the therapist in such situations as experiencing an empathic withdrawal. The therapist may intellectualize, may take the position of "therapist as a blank screen," or may misperceive dynamics.

If the therapist is knowledgeable and is able to use that knowledge for understanding the child's activity within a session, however, the therapist will notice and recognize what is happening for the child. If the therapist understands the effect of a child's developmental

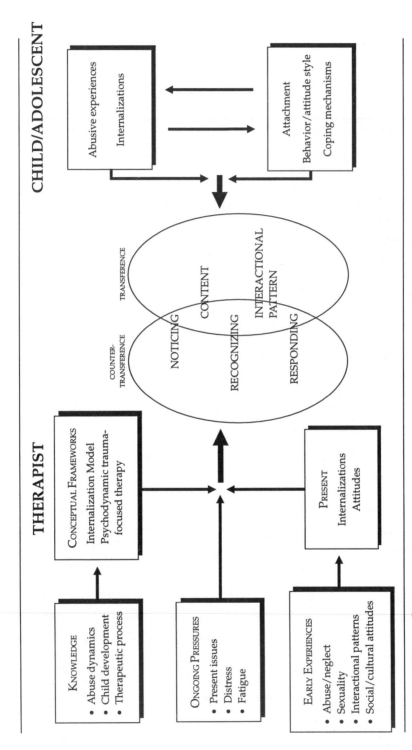

Figure 5.1. Therapy Session

level on the child's experience of abuse, the therapist's understanding of the child will be more accurate. If the therapist has an appreciation of the interdynamics between transference and countertransference, the therapist's grasp of what is happening in a session and ability to respond therapeutically increases.

EARLY EXPERIENCES

The therapist also brings to the therapy session her own personal internalizations resulting from her experiences when growing up and her processing and reprocessing of these experiences. Of particular relevance to therapy with children and adolescents who have been sexually abused are the therapist's experiences with abuse and neglect, with sexuality, with negative emotions, and with interactional patterns.

There has been considerable discussion of the effect of having been sexually abused on an individual's ability as a therapist (Briere, 1992; Dolan, 1991; Friedrich, 1990).[1] More important than the fact of sexual abuse is the therapist's processing of abuse experiences. The internalizations of damage, of blame, of responsibility, and of memories together perhaps with internalizations of emotional chaos, of betrayal, of inappropriate boundaries, and of sexualized behaviors being positive, of sexuality being negative, of people not meaning what they say, and of negation of oneself and one's experiences were part of the therapists' early internal world. As the future therapist or practicing therapist addresses these abuse-related internalizations, recognizes the reality of her world back then, acknowledges her child perception of the abuse and the emotions that were too scary to have then, and comforts herself, these abuse-related internalizations shift. It is the therapist's *present* experiencing of the early abuse and the therapist's present sense of self and the world—that is, her present internalizations—that are with the child in the therapy session.

If a therapist has not worked through her own abuse-related internalizations, however, the therapist is likely to see the child she works with as damaged. She may have difficulty recognizing the child's emotions and, in particular, the swings of emotion. She may have difficulty maintaining adequate boundaries and indeed, even recognizing boundaries that are needed: *time* (the beginning and ending of sessions, the number of consultations related to a child), *structure* (objects from the therapy room or objects made during therapy not being taken out of the room, confidentiality being respected), *roles* (interactions centering around the child's, not the therapist's, needs), and *content* (the child, not the therapist, determining the content of the session, interventions not moving beyond what the child is ready for). Of particular danger when working with children is becoming overly protective and wanting only positive experiences for the child or becoming angry and judgmental toward the parents or the social-legal system. Without adequate personal boundaries, the therapist may depend on a child improving for personal reassurance. This would place the child, once again, in the role of caring for the adult.

> Billy (a 9-year-old sexually abused and neglected by both parents until age 7) folds up the picture he has made and puts it in his pocket. The therapist reminds him that what is done during the session stays in his box and will be here for him next week. Billy replies that he needs the picture to make himself feel better. The therapist agrees to let Billy take the picture.
>
> When discussing the situation in supervision, the therapist points out that Billy has experienced so much neglect and having others not hear his wishes that it was important for her to respond to his wish to feel better.
>
> The supervisor wonders why the therapist chose to shift therapeutic boundaries rather than interpreting Billy's sense that he was unable to feel better—an internalization of damage—and by maintaining boundaries, assert her belief that he was able within himself to hold a better feeling. Why did the therapist, who usually kept these boundaries, feel unable to do so in this situation?

In addition, the therapist who has not addressed and shifted her own abuse-related internalizations is likely to have difficulty (a) recognizing the manner in which the child distorts reality, (b) talking about the child's abuse experience, and (c) talking about sexuality. The therapist's reaction or countertransference during therapy sessions is likely to reflect the therapist's own issues rather than the child's issues.

Wilson et al. (1994) describe the therapist who has not worked through her own trauma-related issues as responding with either empathic repression or empathic enmeshment when working with individuals who have been traumatized. In an effort to protect herself from her own distress, the therapist may withdraw, deny, or distance herself from the child's feelings and issues.

> Lydia (a 7-year-old girl emotionally abandoned by mother and sexually abused for several years by her older brother who was left to baby-sit) clears a space on the table for playing by pushing all of the animals to one side. She then takes the adult animals and has them prancing around in a circle.
>
> The therapist notes the gaiety of the adult animals and feels that Lydia is simply enjoying playing. He quietly gives her time in which to play.
>
> When the therapist talks about the play in supervision, his supervisor wonders what else is going on and asks the therapist to describe what happened right before the animals started prancing. The therapist notes that no play had happened; Lydia had simply pushed the other animals aside to clear a place on the table. The supervisor notes that being pushed aside was Lydia's experience as a little child, especially when her mother partied. The supervisor notes that the idea of children being abandoned, like the idea of children being abused, destroys our belief in the world as a caring place and, thus, is hard to see. She also wonders if being abandoned echoed any of the therapist's experience, because that might be part of the reason why the therapist did not notice it.

"On the other hand, when the therapist has not totally processed her own experience, she may interpret the child's experience through her own." Another therapist, who is able to keep her own and the child's experiences separate, may still, as a result of the internal emotions triggered, become so engaged with the child that, as noted earlier, boundaries blur and a reciprocal dependency starts to occur between the therapist and the individual (Wilson et al., 1994).

A therapist who has been sexually abused needs to have processed her own experiences of abuse and neglect to a point where her internal sense of self and the world—that is, her present internalizations—are not distorted by the abuse experience. This does not mean that her own abuse issues are never triggered. Abuse issues will be triggered when a therapist works with a child of the same age or in the same situation that she was when she was abused. Abuse issues will be triggered when something in the therapist's life parallels her abuse experience— for example, when the therapist's own child is the same age she was when the abuse occurred.

Adequate processing of abuse issues means that when issues are triggered, they are recognized by the therapist as being her own and are tucked away for later processing. Dolan (1991) notes that being distracted during a session by one's own memories, not just having the memories come and go, being extremely emotional during or after a session, and being overly invested in a client taking a particular step or resolving a particular issue are indications that personal issues are intruding. Dolan suggests that therapists be open to this and not self-blaming. A therapist self-blaming, even after realizing that this is part of the process, would indicate that the abuse-related internalizations of damage, guilt, or responsibility remain active and need to be addressed further. Triggers can provide a therapist with a new opportunity to review and reprocess the past, an opportunity to address any abuse-related internalizations still within.

For this therapist, the personal experience of sexual abuse increases her awareness during a session. The therapist brings an internal knowledge of the links between abuse and later behavior and an internal knowledge that abuse-related internalizations can be shifted. This perceptivity and hopefulness increase the therapist's ability to respond therapeutically to the child. Briere (1992) refers to the "extraordinary psychotherapist—one who has directly experienced both childhood injury and adult growth and integration" (p. 162). The therapist's present internalizations include ones of no damage (a sense of pain and lost time but not damage), of not being bad (regrets but not guilt or shame), of not being responsible for other adults, and of memories that are there but do not distort one's functioning. The therapist's present internalizations recognize that love and hate can go together; that if one person betrays, all people do not; that she has her own emotional, cognitive, and physical space that she can choose to share or not share; that there are many ways to gain attention and physical pleasure; that sexuality is positive and special and that sexual abuse is not sexuality; that most people mean what they say; and that she can deal with what is happening as it happens.

For the therapist who did not experience abuse, listening and learning from the individuals with whom she works, from her colleagues whose experiences were different, and from her own personal struggles similarly can bring perceptivity and hopefulness. Whereas many therapists have not been sexually abused, all therapists have had experiences related to sexuality, abuse, or neglect at some level, and to interpersonal relating.

Each of us has issues around sexuality, issues coming both from childhood and adult experiences. Early learning about sexuality comes from our family's mores and taboos, from our sexual play experiences and other people's responses to these, from the sexual experiences we had as we grew up, and from any abuse experiences. Although some of this may be consciously recalled by the therapist and can be thought through in personal therapy or personal introspection, much of it is unconscious and springs out at the therapist when least expected.

Linda (a 7-year-old girl sexually abused at various times over the years by father and by several boarders in the home) takes the scissors out of her box and then looks through the box for one of the large crayons that has not yet been cut up.

Therapist: [Recognizes this sequence and recalls the number of times before when Linda has cut off ends of crayons, and she has commented on Linda's wish to cut off her father's penis. Linda has, in the past, thoroughly enjoyed the activity.]

Linda: [Picking up the scissors and crayon] Talk to me about what I'm doing.

Therapist: [Freezes inside and finds she is unable to say anything for what seems like an interminable amount of time. What is happening? Linda has played this out before, and she has given words to what she was doing. Why this panic—there is no other way to describe it— now? Linda told her to talk about cutting penises. Is that it, had she been told as a kid not to talk about penises? Interpreting was all right, no childhood lectures there. But talking about sexual things, that wasn't allowed.]

If the therapist's awareness of her own sexuality as she grew up was positive, she may have difficulty realizing the degree of fear or numbing occurring for the child. On the other hand, if the therapist's experiences around sexuality were negative even though not abusive, the therapist may assume that her wariness or disinterest in sexuality as a child and adolescent was normal and may use that as a base for understanding the responses of the children with whom she works. She may fail to value and, therefore, to help the child value normal developing sensations and curiosity.

All therapists working with children who have been sexually abused need to think through their own sexual experiences, both positive and negative. They need to read about normal developmental stages in sexual awareness. They need to be aware of their own attitudes, positive and negative, with regard to sexual activity and sexuality and to be able to hold these attitudes and any judgments that come from these attitudes separate from the children with whom they work.

Therapists' clothes and the way they sit or move, as with any individual, expresses their sexuality and their comfort with who they are and with their bodies. If a therapist's clothing or behavior has a sexual quality or could be interpreted in a sexual way, the child is likely to reexperience the contradictory messages given at the time of the abuse. A therapist needs to be alert to her own dressing and behavior patterns and to be aware whether these shift when she is seeing a particular child or adolescent.

> Lin (a 16-year-old sexually abused by her older brothers between age 6 to 10) talks about her experiences with boys at school. As she does, she tosses her head to keep her hair out of her eyes.
>
> The therapist reflects on how attractive Lin is and how appealing the gesture is. She then becomes aware that she has crossed her legs and is swinging her leg, not something she usually does. What's happening? She had always wanted to be attractive, appealing. Was she competing with Lin? What was happening that brought out this competition? What part of this reflects her questions about herself, and what part reflects Lin's dynamics? She will need to think about this after the session. For now, her leg is still, and she is centering better on what Lin is saying.

The therapist needs to be at ease with sexual topics to be able to discuss sexuality and sexual activities, both abusive and nonabusive, easily with the child. Lack of ease certainly should not discourage a therapist from working in this area; rather, it should prompt the therapist to think back through her own experiences, to educate herself about sexuality, and to find opportunities to talk with colleagues or friends about sex and sexuality.

Therapists' experiences of neglect and abuse when growing up vary in type, in intensity, and in frequency. But they do, in some form, occur for each of us. They may occur inside the family or outside the family. What was it like, what did we internalize, what did we feel about ourselves and others, how has this shifted over the years, how have our reactions changed? How is this different from the experience of the child with whom we are working? How may it be the same? How will that affect us—the differences and the similarities—as we work with the child?

Early experiences around expressing feelings, confronting negative situations or people, and talking about hurtful topics also need to be considered. These experiences, if not thought through, can shape the way in which we respond within a therapy session.

Sam (a 6-year-old sexually abused by mother at ages 4 and 5) pushes the baby doll off the table and then pounds the doll with his foot.

Therapist: [Feels pleased that the play is so clear] Seems like you are showing me what it was like for you when your mother touched you.

Sam: [Continues to push at the baby doll and then dumps the box of toys on top of the doll.]

Later, when the therapist is thinking back over the session and feeling pleased with her interpretation, she starts to worry as to why she felt so pleased with herself. That feeling did not fit what was going on in the play. The interpretation fitted what she had read in the textbooks, but maybe something more was happening. In fact, the angry quality of the play had continued. Was anger there? Is Sam angry at himself for the abuse? That certainly fitted what came next in the play. Why, if anger was there, had she jumped in with such a stereotypic response? She thinks about how hard she finds it to talk about anger; in her family, people were not supposed to show anger.

Is this standing in the way of her recognizing and talking about anger in therapy sessions?

Many of us were taught as children not to stare or ask questions about people's scars or strange-seeming behaviors; this was not polite. It could get us into situations we might not be able to handle, and it could be embarrassing for us as well as the other person. We were taught not to bring up disagreeable topics that could make people feel uncomfortable. Now, as therapists, we need to label the scars and examine the behavior, we need to risk the child becoming angry and distressed, and we need to be with the child as he faces what he may not want to face. Talking about a child's painful reality goes counter to so much of our early learning but is necessary if the child's past and present experience is to be validated (Sinason, 1991).

Our experiences growing up have also formed personal biases and social and political attitudes. Each of us needs to be aware of how particular habits or attitudes of a child (ways of dressing, attending or not attending sessions, sense of responsibility) may affect us so that these reactions do not alter our respect for (and therefore, availability to) the child. Some therapists do considerable work on their family of origin dynamics; however, this is seldom a part of formal clinical training. Such work is particularly important when practicing in the area of sexual abuse. Examination of one's own genogram, the role one played in one's family, the attitudes and messages passed down, and subsequent efforts to establish one's own outlook on the world is important if one is to be open to a child's or family's experience. This processing helps the therapist move her own reacting out of a therapy session. She is better able to be aware of the child and respond therapeutically to the child.

ONGOING PRESSURES

Therapists also need to be aware of their levels of energy and distress as well as any ongoing personal issues that may impinge on their availability to a child during a session. Increasing attention has been given recently to the stress and fatigue experienced by therapists who work with individuals who have been traumatized and to the need for therapists to take care of themselves (Dolan, 1991; Pearlman & Saakvitne, 1995; Yassen, 1995).

Wilson et al. (1994) discuss the empathic disequilibrium a therapist may experience when the distress of the individual a therapist is working with overwhelms the therapist. If this distress intrudes on the therapist outside the therapy room, the therapist has no break from tension and distress. Centering on a child's strength (and each child who makes it to the therapy room has strength, or she would not be there), centering on the child's continued effort to be heard and on any positive shifts that do occur can help a therapist not be overwhelmed. Having variety within one's caseload—seeing children who have already worked through part of their distress as well as children who are just starting to explore the distress, seeing children who experienced limited abuse as well as children who experienced extreme abuse, can decrease the therapist's stress. Seeing individuals of several different ages can help to balance a caseload. Supervision or peervision provides an opportunity to talk about cases and, thus can alleviate the distress created by difficult therapy cases. Recreational activities and attention to one's own personal relationships helps a therapist maintain her energy level.

Similar empathic disequilibrium can occur when a therapist's personal issues start to intrude on the therapist while inside the therapy room. All therapists go through times of personal distress. These need to be acknowledged by the therapist. The therapist needs to provide ways of working through this distress for herself, whether it be formal therapy, conversation with friends, or personal reflection. Having colleagues who are available to listen and support—not to do therapy—can be important at these times. Taking time for oneself is essential.

A therapist enters the therapy session with her conceptual frameworks and with his present internalizations and attitudes. Separating out personal, ongoing issues or distresses then enables the therapist to be available to the child: to notice what is happening, to recognize the child's experiences and internalizations, and to respond to the child.

❏ **The Therapist's Reaction to the Child**

The child comes to therapy not only with a history of sexual abuse and the internalizations resulting from this abuse but also with a pattern of interrelating to other people. This pattern of interrelating is shaped by the child's early attachment relationship, his behavioral and attitude style built up over the years, and his particular style of coping. And each of these in turn shapes the interaction the child has with the therapist within the therapy session.

Considerable research has been carried out on early attachment patterns and the effect of that pattern on a child's relationships as he grows up (Main et al., 1985). This pattern is affected by the abuse experience when the child is abused by someone close to him (Alexander, 1992; Friedrich, 1995). The pattern is affected by the manner in which the parent(s) react to the disclosure of the abuse, intrafamilial or extrafamilial, and to the child following the disclosure. Some children, having experienced early secure attachments are able, despite their distress, to establish a secure relationship with the therapist and to use this as a base for working through the abuse experiences and internalizations. Children who experienced an insecure early attachment (avoidant, ambivalent-resistant, or disorganized) (Main et al., 1985), transfer those dynamics to the therapeutic relationship (Santostefano & Calicchia, 1992).

Along with attachment pattern, a child will have a particular style of behaving and attitudes. Some children are active in the expression of feelings, whereas others are more introverted. Attitudes are formed in part by messages, both overt and covert, passed down through the family and in part by the child's experiences. These attitudes may relate to the society as a whole, the family in particular, or the child specifically. An additional factor affecting the child's pattern of interacting in the therapy room is the method of coping— the defense mechanisms—that the child has developed over the years.

The therapist is going to be affected by each factor. When a child is avoidant, one therapist may be able to observe this, allow it to occur, and, when appropriate, address it and the fear the child has of people hurting or rejecting him. Another therapist, however, because of lack of knowledge of attachment patterns, past experiences that are still emotionally binding, or present fatigue, may feel rejected by the child's behavior and react by being more emotionally closed during the therapy sessions. When the child is clingy but resistant or disorganized in his reaction to the therapist, some therapists—again, because of their knowledge, their pasts, and their present—may remain observant (see Friedrich, 1995, for a discussion of adapting therapist approach to attachment style). Others may either feel so needed that they become overly close and protective or may feel threatened and therefore, in subtle ways, push the child away. For this therapist, the capacity to notice, recognize, and respond to the child decreases.

Therapist reactions to a child's behavior and attitude style vary considerably. For a therapist who comes from a family in which attitudes and feelings were expressed openly, in which yelling or confronting someone directly was part of daily life, a child acting out in a therapy session is not threatening. For the therapist whose family and subsequent relationships revolved around quiet discussion or no discussion, a child acting out can be frightening, and the therapist may find it difficult to think clearly when this happens. The first therapist may not notice the intensity of the feelings of a child whose behavioral style is less expressive, however, whereas the second therapist may be more alert to those feelings.

A therapist who comes from a background in which responsibility and active solutions were stressed may have a difficult time working with an adolescent who does not accept responsibility and waits for others to solve his problems. When a therapist is aware of her biases, she is better able to monitor her judgmental reactions and, therefore, to respond more therapeutically. Therapists with a laissez-faire approach may have difficulty understanding the internal pressures experienced by adolescents who are overresponsible. A therapist needs to remember that she is there to hear and respond to the child's internalizations, not to impose her view of the world.

The child's coping pattern also affects his interacting in the therapy session. He may deny, intellectualize, minimize, attack the therapist, dissociate, or discuss what is going on for him. For the therapist who is knowledgeable and feels comfortable working with each style of coping, the child's pattern may not seriously affect the therapeutic relationship. For therapists who become overly involved in therapy as a solution rather than a process and in their role within therapy, denial, intellectualizing, minimizing, or attacking is all too likely to be labeled as resistance rather than recognized as protection. A therapist, feeling unappreciated, may become angry or dismissive of the child. When a child dissociates and the therapist does not recognize it, the therapist is likely to feel confused and, depending on the dissociated presentation, overly encouraged or rejected by the child.

Each therapist will find some children easier to work with than others (Friedrich, 1990). This is to be expected. If, however, a therapist finds herself consistently closing down or becoming overly anxious with a particular child or type of child, she needs to spend more time examining her own patterns of interacting—How could these be affecting her reaction to the child? She needs to examine the early dynamics that occurred for the child, the child's internalizations, and how these may be playing themselves out within the therapeutic process. She needs to find time for a walk around the block or just a few moments to close her eyes and rest before seeing the child.

Anxious or negative reactions by the therapist, even very minor ones, not only narrow the therapist's capacity to notice and respond in the therapy session but also affect the child and restrict what the child presents in the session.

❑ The Session

The therapist's reactions discussed to this point are those resulting from the therapist's own self and from the therapist's experience of the child. If the therapist is aware of these reactions and able to separate them from her interaction with the child, he will be better able to notice and recognize the content the child brings to the therapy session. Even when these reactions do intrude into the session as they are bound to do at times, if the therapist can recognize them and consciously tuck them away, they will not block his capacity to notice, recognize, and respond to the child and the child's issues.

> Emily (a 16-year-old sexually abused by her father at age 13 when she went on weekend visits) tells the therapist how excited she is since she found out she is pregnant. She talks about the babies she has seen recently, how they hold on to their mothers, and how much fun they are.

Therapist: [Cringes inside as he thinks about how young Emily is and how she has not yet had time to hold onto a mother and to have fun. How can she adequately mother a child? There must be some alternative. He starts to ask Emily about alternatives and then realizes that he is reacting from his own value judgment regarding teenage mothers. Taking a deep breath, he carefully moves back the judgmental part of himself—he can think about that later—and focuses on the way Emily is telling about looking at babies.] It sounds as if that "holding on to" feels really important to you. Maybe you are wishing you could have held on to your mother like that? . . . How would that have made things different? . . . Who are you going to hold on to now?

Into each therapy session (the intersecting ovals of Figure 5.1), the child (right hand oval) brings content—play and discussion—and her interactional pattern. Both the content and the interactional pattern reflect a transference of earlier experiences and internalizations onto the present therapeutic experience. The therapist (left-hand oval) reacts to both. This reaction may be a *countertransference acting out* (Klein, 1989) in which the therapist reacts directly to the child's transference and, therefore, may be behaving in a way similar to the context of the child's past experience. Or the reaction may be a *monitored countertransference* in which the therapist, being aware of the child's issues and of therapeutic dynamics, reacts from a healthier context. When the therapist has difficulty separating out his own issues, past or present, his capacity to be aware of the child and of the dynamics occurring within the session decreases. The overlap between the therapist's oval and the child's oval decreases. As the therapist monitors his reaction, remains cognizant of abuse and therapeutic dynamics, recalls the child's experience, and attends to the child's reactions within the session, his awareness of the child and the dynamics within the session increases. The overlap between the therapist and the child increases. The therapist is better able to notice and recognize the child's internalizations.

The therapist notices a child who lies on the floor pressing her ear to the floor and looking up at the therapist. The therapist notices an adolescent who repetitively states that no one listens to her. The therapist also notices within himself a feeling of not knowing. This feeling of not knowing could reflect the child-adolescent not knowing what will happen, the child-adolescent not having known what would happen, the parent having not known what was happening, or indeed, the therapist being confused and not knowing. The therapist knows that he is rested and is attending well; he knows that he has worked through his own experiences of not being heard, both in the past and the present. This feeling of not knowing seems to come from the child's experience, not his.

As the therapist thinks about the child's ear on the floor or the adolescent's feeling of not being listened to along with the feeling of not knowing, the therapist recalls that no one knew about the abuse until long after it had happened. Using the internalization framework, the therapist recognizes the child-adolescent's memory of no one coming, no one hearing—not being protected.

From this point, the therapist responds. This may be an inquiry within the transference interaction: "What would you like me to hear, to know?" It may be an interpretation linking the transference to the abuse experience: "It may feel as though I am not listening-hearing, just as your mother didn't when the abuse was going on." It may be an inquiry linking back to the abuse experience: "What did you want others to hear, to know, back then when the abuse was happening?" It may be addressing the internalization: "What was the not being heard, not being protected like?" It may be further attending to the child-adolescent: "What do you hear?" It may be providing for the child what she did not have previously: further listening.

From the responding, either verbal or behavioral, the therapist moves back to noticing, then again to recognizing what is going on for the child. Each time, the therapist filters out reactions that relate only to himself and keeps the reactions that reflect what is going on in the session. He reviews the content and reactions in terms of his knowledge of the child, of abuse-related internalizations, and of therapeutic dynamics. Based on his knowledge of trauma-focused therapy, the therapist then responds.

Within the session, it is important for us as therapists to trust the child to bring the issues and to trust ourselves to pick up the issues. And then, perhaps, it is wise to trust the child to bring the issue again if we miss it the first time. That gives us time to think back over a session, pick out the strands, sort through our reactions, and start to see some order in the puzzle. That gives us a chance to be clearer the next time as to what is happening and how we can respond to the child.

❏ Conclusion

The therapy session is affected not only by the child's experiences and internalizations but also by the therapist's experiences and internalizations. A therapist working with children and adolescents who have been sexually abused needs to process her own early experiences of abuse, neglect, sexuality, and interactive patterns and her early internalizations from those experiences. She needs to be aware of and attend to her present sense of self and the world and her present attitudes and biases. The therapist needs also to attend to pressures in her present life.

The therapist needs a conceptual framework that enables her to understand the dynamics of sexual abuse, the child's processing of the abuse experience, and how abuse-related internalizations are expressed by children. She needs a model of therapy in which not only the experience of abuse but also the internalizations from the abuse are addressed.

In addition, the therapist needs to be aware of how this particular child and his way of interacting with others is affecting her. As the therapist thinks this through, whether by personal reflection, supervision, or consultation, she becomes better able to notice the content, the interaction, and most of all, the child. Working within the Internalization Model and psychodynamic trauma-focused therapy, the therapist can recognize the meaning within the content and the interaction and can respond therapeutically.

The Internalization Model has been presented as a conceptual framework for understanding what the child internalizes from an experience of sexual abuse. All children who are sexually abused experience some sense of being yuck or damaged; being powerless; being bad, guilty, or an object to be used; being responsible for others; and having memories of abuse and no protection. Those children who are abused by someone close to them or who are severely abused experience additional internalizations. For the child abused by someone close, a sense of emotional chaos, an expectation of betrayal, and inappropriate boundaries become part of his internal world. The child who experienced severe abuse internalizes sexualized behaviors as positive yet sexuality as negative, people as not meaning what they say, and himself as having limited emotions, experiences, or self. Each of these internalizations forms part of the filter through which the child experiences future events and relationships, thereby leaving the child unable to experience himself or the world separate from the abuse dynamics. For the child to be able to experience the future separate from the abuse, the abuse-related internalizations need to be identified and addressed.

Psychodynamic trauma-focused therapy provides a model for observing, within the child's play and behavior and the adolescent's conversation and behavior, the abuse-related internalizations. As these internalizations are addressed, the child-adolescent gains new understanding and new experiencing of the abuse. The child starts to assimilate the happening of the abuse, thereby relieving the trauma. The child starts to shift the abuse-related internalizations, thereby creating a healthier filter through which to experience the future.

Therapy with a child or adolescent who has been sexually abused is demanding and rewarding. The strength of these children, as it is recognized by the therapist, provides strength to the therapist. The growth of these children provides growth for the therapist.

Note

1. Studies have found a higher percentage of childhood sexual abuse among therapists working with individuals who were sexually abused or individuals with high dissociation than in the general population (Elliott as cited in Briere, 1992; Perry, 1993).

References

Adams, C., Fay, J., & Loreen-Martin, J. (1984). *No is not enough: Helping teenagers avoid sexual assault*. San Luis Obispo, CA: Impact.

Adams-Tucker, C. (1982). Proximate effects of sexual abuse in childhood: A report on 28 children. *American Journal of Psychiatry, 139,* 1252-1256.

Alexander, P. (1985). A systems theory conceptualization of incest. *Family Process, 24,* 79-88.

Alexander, P. (1992). Application of attachment theory to the study of sexual abuse. *Journal of Consulting and Clinical Psychology, 60,* 185-195.

Alexander, P., & Lupfer, S. (1987). Family characteristics and long-term consequences associated with sexual abuse. *Archives of Sexual Behavior, 16,* 235-245.

American Psychiatric Association. (1994). *Diagnostic and statistical manual of mental disorders* (4th ed.). Washington DC: American Psychiatric Association.

Axline, V. (1947). *Play Therapy.* New York: Ballantine.

Bandura, A. (1977). *Social learning theory.* Englewood Cliffs, NJ: Prentice Hall.

Barrett, M., Trepper, T., & Fish, L. (1990). Feminist-informed family therapy for the treatment of intrafamily child sexual abuse. *Journal of Family Psychology, 4,* 151-166.

Bedrosian, R. C. (1981). The application of cognitive therapy techniques with adolescents. In G. Emery, S. D. Hollon, & R. C. Bedrosian (Eds.), *New directions in cognitive therapy: A casebook.* New York: Guilford.

Beitchman, J. H., Zucker, K. J., Hood, J. E., daCosta, G. A., & Akman, D. (1991). A review of the short-term effects of child sexual abuse. *Child Abuse and Neglect, 15,* 537-556.

213

Beitchman, J. H., Zucker, K. J., Hood, J. E., daCosta, G. A., Akman, D., & Cassavia, E. (1992). A review of the long-term effects of child sexual abuse. *Child Abuse & Neglect, 16,* 101-118.

Bentovim, A., & Davenport, M. (1992). Resolving the trauma organized system of sexual abuse by confronting the abuser. *Journal of Family Therapy, 14,* 29-50.

Blos, P. (1967). The second individuation process of adolescence. *Psychoanalytic Study of the Child, 22,* 162-186.

Blos, P. (1983). The contribution of psychoanalysis to the psychotherapy of adolescents. *Adolescent Psychiatry, 11,* 104-124.

Bowlby, J. (1971). *Attachment and loss: Vol. 1. Attachment.* London: Pelican.

Bowlby, J. (1973). *Attachment and loss: Vol. 2. Separation.* London: Pelican.

Briere, J. (1992). *Child abuse trauma: Theory and treatment of the lasting effects.* Newbury Park, CA: Sage.

Briere, J. (1996). A self-trauma model for treating adult survivors of severe child abuse. In J. Briere, L. Berliner, J. Bulkley, C. Jenny, & T. Reid (Eds.), *The APSAC handbook on child maltreatment.* Thousand Oaks, CA: Sage.

Briere, J., & Conte, J. (1993). Self-reported amnesia for abuse in adults molested as children. *Journal of Traumatic Stress, 6,* 21-31.

Bruckner, D., & Johnson, P. (1987). Treatment for adult male victims of childhood sexual abuse. *Social Casework, 68,* 81-87.

Burgess, A. W., Hartman, C. R., McCausland, M. P., & Powers, P. (1984). Response patterns in children and adolescents exploited through sex rings and pornography. *American Journal of Psychiatry, 141,* 656-662.

Burkett, L. P. (1991). Parenting behaviors of women who were sexually abused as children in their families of origin. *Family Process, 30,* 421-434.

Carson, D. K., Council, J. R., & Volk, M. A. (1989). Temperament as a predictor of psychological adjustment in female adult incest victims. *Journal of Clinical Psychology, 45,* 330-335.

Cecchin, G. (1987). Hypothesizing, circularity, and neutrality revisited: An invitation to curiosity. *Family Process, 26,* 405-413.

Chaffin, M., Bonner, B., Worley, K., & Lawson, L. (1996). Treating abused adolescents. In J. Briere, L. Berliner, J. Bulkley, C. Jenny, & T. Reid (Eds.), *The APSAC handbook on child maltreatment.* Thousand Oaks, CA: Sage.

Conte, J. R. (1986). Sexual abuse and the family: A critical analysis. In T. S. Trepper & M. J. Barrett (Eds.), *Treating incest: A multiple systems perspective.* New York: Hayworth.

Courtois, C. A. (1988). *Healing the incest wound: Adult survivors in therapy.* New York: Norton.

Crittenden, P. M., & Ainsworth, M. D. S. (1989). Child maltreatment and attachment theory. In D. Cicchetti & V. Carlson (Eds.), *Child maltreatment.* Cambridge, UK: Cambridge University Press.

Dadds, M., Smith, M., Webber, Y., & Robinson, A. (1991). An exploration of family and individual profiles following father-daughter incest. *Child Abuse & Neglect, 15,* 575-586.

Damon, L., & Waterman, J. (1986). Parallel group treatment of children and their mothers. In K. MacFarlane & J. Waterman (Eds.), *Sexual abuse of young children.* New York: Guilford.

Davies, J. M., & Frawley, M. G. (1994). *Treating the adult survivor of childhood sexual abuse: A psychoanalytic perspective.* New York: Basic Books.

Davis, N. (1990). *Once upon a time . . . Therapeutic stories to heal abused children.* Oxon Hill, MD: Psychological Associates of Oxon Hill.

Deblinger, E. (1991). *Cognitive behavioral interventions for treating sexually abused children suffering post-traumatic stress: Preliminary treatment manual.* Stratford, NJ: Center for Children's Support.

Deblinger, E. (1992, October). *Cognitive behavioral interventions for treating sexually abused children.* Workshop presentation, Ottawa, Canada.

Deblinger, E., Hathawa, C. R., Lippmann, J., & Steer, R. (1993). Psychosocial characteristics and correlates of symptom distress in nonoffending mothers of sexually abused children. *Journal of Interpersonal Violence, 8,* 155-168.

deYoung, M. (1986). A conceptual model for judging the truthfulness of a young child's allegation of sexual abuse. *American Journal of Orthopsychiatry, 56,* 550-559.

Dolan, Y. (1991). *Resolving sexual abuse: Solution-focused therapy and Ericksonian hypnosis for adult survivors.* New York: Norton.

Drell, M. J., Siegel, C. H., & Gaensbauer, T. J. (1993). Post-traumatic stress disorder. In C. H. Zeanah (Ed.), *Handbook of infant mental health.* New York: Guilford.

Ekstein, R. (1983). The adolescent self during the phase of termination of treatment: Termination, interruption, or intermission. *Adolescent Psychiatry, 11,* 125-146.

Elwell, M. E., & Ephross, P. H. (1987). Initial reactions of sexually abused children. *Social Casework, 68,* 109-116.

Femina, D. D., Yeager, C. A., & Lewis, D. O. (1990). Child abuse: Adolescent records vs. adult recall. *Journal of Child Abuse and Neglect, 14,* 227-231.

Finkel, K. C. (1987). Sexual abuse of children: An update. *Canadian Medical Association Journal, 136,* 245-252.

Finkelhor, D. (1979). *Sexually victimized children.* New York: Free Press.

Finkelhor, D. (1987). The trauma of child sexual abuse: Two models. *Journal of Interpersonal Violence, 2,* 348-366.

Finkelhor, D., & Browne, A. (1985). The traumatic impact of child sexual abuse: A conceptualization. *American Journal of Orthopsychiatry, 55,* 530-541.

Fossum, M., & Mason, M. (1986). *Facing shame: Families in recovery.* New York: Norton.

Fraiberg, S. (1980). *Psychoanalytic study of the child: The first years of life.* New York: Basic Books.

Freud, A. (1946). *The psychoanalytic treatment of children.* New York: International Universities Press.

Freud, A. (1966). The ego and the mechanism of defense. In *The writings of Anna Freud* (Vol. 2, rev. ed.). New York: International Universities Press. (originally published in 1936)

Freud, A. (1974). Four lectures on child analysis. In *The writings of Anna Freud* (Vol. 1). New York: International Universities Press. (Originally published in 1926)

Freud, S. (1955). Beyond the pleasure principle. In *The standard edition* (Vol. 18). London: Hogarth. (originally published in 1920)

Friedrich, W. (1988). Behavior problems in sexually abused children: An adaptive perspective. In G. E. Wyatt & G. P. Powell (Eds.), *Lasting effect of child sexual abuse.* Beverly Hills, CA: Sage.

Friedrich, W. N. (1990). *Psychotherapy of sexually abused children and their families.* New York: Norton.

Friedrich, W. N. (1995). *Psychotherapy with sexually abused boys: An integrated approach.* Thousand Oaks, CA: Sage.

Friedrich, W. N., Gramsch, P., Damon, L., Koverola, C., Wolfe, V., Hewitt, S., Lang, R., & Broughton, D. (1992). Child sexual behavior inventory: Normative and clinical comparisons. *Psychological Assessment, 4,* 303-311.

Friedrich, W. N., Urquiza, A. J., & Beilke, R. L. (1986). Behavior problems in sexually abused young children. *Journal of Pediatric Psychology, 11,* 47-57.

Furniss, T. (1983). Family process in the treatment of intrafamilial child sexual abuse. *Journal of Family Therapy, 5,* 263-278.

Gelinas, D. J. (1983). The persisting negative effects of incest. *Psychiatry, 46,* 313-332.

Gelinas, D. J. (1988). Unexpected resources in treating incest families. In M. Karpel (Ed.), *Family resources: The hidden partner in family therapy.* New York: Guilford.

Giarretto, H. (1982). *Integrated treatment of child sexual abuse: A treatment and training manual.* Palo Alto, CA: Science and Behavior Books.

Gil, E. (1991). *The healing power of play: Working with abused children.* New York: Guilford.

Gold, E. R. (1986). Long-term effects of sexual victimization in childhood: An attributional approach. *Journal of Consulting and Clinical Psychology, 54,* 471-475.

Goldston, D. B., Turnquist, D. C., & Knutson, J. F. (1989). Presenting problems of sexually abused girls receiving psychiatric services. *Journal of Abnormal Psychology 98,* 314-317.

Gomez-Schwartz, B., Horowitz, J. M., & Cardarelli, A. P. (1990). *Child sexual abuse: The initial effects.* Newbury Park, CA: Sage.

Gonzalez, L. Waterman, J., Kelly, R., McCord, J., & Oliveri, M. K. (1993). Children's patterns of disclosures and recantations of sexual and ritualistic abuse allegations in psychotherapy. *Child Abuse and Neglect, 17,* 281-289.

Grove, D. J., & Panzer, B. I. (1991). *Resolving traumatic memories: Metaphors and symbols in psychotherapy.* New York: Irvington.

Harlow, H. F., & Zimmerman, R. R. (1959). Affectionate responses in the infant monkey. *Science, 130,* 431-432.

Harter, S. (1983). Developmental perspectives on the self-system. In E. M. Hetherington (Ed.), *Handbook of child psychology: Socialization, personality, and social development* (4th ed.). New York: John Wiley.

Hartman, C. R., & Burgess, A. W. (1988). Information processing of trauma: Case application of a model. *Journal of Interpersonal Violence, 3,* 443-457.

Hartman, C. R., & Burgess, A. W. (1993). Information processing of trauma. *Child Abuse & Neglect, 17,* 47-58.

Herman, J. L. (1992). *Trauma and recovery: The aftermath of violence—From domestic abuse to political terror.* New York: Basic Books.

Herman, J. L., & Schatzow, E. (1987). Recovery and verification of memories of childhood sexual trauma. *Psychoanalytic Psychology, 4,* 1-14.

Hindman, J. (1985). *A very touching book: For little people and for big people.* Ontario, OR: Alexandria.

Hindman, J. (1989). *Just before the dawn.* Boise, ID: Northwest.

Hindman, J. (1991). *The mourning breaks: 101 "proactive" treatment strategies breaking the trauma bonds of sexual abuse.* Ontario, OR: AlexAndria.

Hooper, C. (1992). *Mothers surviving child sexual abuse.* London: Tavistock/Routledge.

James, B. (1989). *Treating traumatized children: New insights and creative interventions.* Toronto: Lexington.

James, B., & Nasjleti, M. (1983). *Treating sexually abused children and their families.* Palo Alto, CA: Consulting Psychologists Press.

Johnson, B., & Kenkel, M. B. (1991). Stress, coping, and adjustment in female adolescent incest victims. *Child Abuse & Neglect, 15,* 293-305.

Johnston, M. S. K., (1979). The sexually mistreated child: Diagnostic evaluation. *Child Abuse & Neglect, 3,* 943-951.

Jones, D. P. (1986). Individual psychotherapy for the sexually abused child. *Child Abuse & Neglect, 10,* 377-385.

Jonker, F., & Jonker-Bakker, P. (1991). Experiences with ritualist child sexual abuse: A case study from the Netherlands. *Child Abuse & Neglect, 15,* 191-196.

Karen, R. (1994). *Becoming attached.* New York: Warner.

Kiser, L. J., Pugh, R. L., McColgan, E. B., Pruitt, D. B., & Edwards, N. B. (1991). Treatment strategies for victims of extrafamilial child sexual abuse. *Journal of Family Psychotherapy, 2,* 27-39.

Klein, M. (1965). A contribution to the theory of intellectual inhibitions. In *Contributions to psychoanalysis: 1921-1945.* London: Hogarth. (Originally published in 1931)

Klein, M. (1975a). Envy and gratitude. In *The writings of Melanie Klein* (Vol. 3). London: Hogarth.

Klein, M. (1975b). The psycho-analysis of children. In *The writings of Melanie Klein* (Vol. 2). London: Hogarth. (Originally published in 1932)

Klein, R. (1989). Countertransference with the borderline patient. In J. Masterson & R. Klein (Eds.), *Psychotherapy of the disorders of the self: The Masterson approach.* New York: Brunner/Mazel.

Kluft, R. P. (1984a). An introduction to multiple personality disorder. *Psychiatric Annals, 14,* 19-24.

Kluft, R. P. (1984b). Multiple personality in childhood. *Psychiatric Clinics of North America, 7,* 121-146.

Kohut, H. (1977). *The restoration of the self.* New York: International Universities Press.

Lanktree, C., & Briere, J. (1995). Outcome of therapy for sexually abused children: A repeated measures study. *Child Abuse and Neglect, 19,* 1145-1156.

Laplanche, J., & Pontalis, J. B. (1973). *The language of psycho-analysis.* London: Hogarth.

LeDoux, J. (1994). Emotion, memory and the brain. *Scientific American, 270,* 50-57.

Leifer, M., Shapiro, J., & Kassem, L. (1993). The impact of maternal history and behavior upon foster placement and adjustment in sexually abused girls. *Child Abuse & Neglect, 17,* 755-766.

Lewis, M. (1991). Intensive individual psychodynamic psychotherapy: The therapeutic relationship and the technique of interpretation. In M. Lewis (Ed.), *Child and adolescent psychiatry: A comprehensive textbook.* Baltimore: Williams & Watkins.

Lipovsky, J. (1991). Disclosure of father-child sexual abuse: Dilemmas for families and therapists. *Contemporary Family Therapy, 13,* 85-101.

Littner, N. (1960). The child's need to repeat his past: Some implications for placement. *Social Service Review, 34,* 128-148.

Loredo, C. M. (1982). Sibling incest. In S. M. Sgroi (Ed.), *Handbook of clinical intervention in child sexual abuse.* Lexington, MA: Lexington Books.

Lusk, R., & Waterman, J. (1986). Effects of sexual abuse on children. In K. MacFarland & J. Waterman (Eds.), *Sexual abuse of young children.* New York: Guilford.

Main, M., Kaplan, N., & Cassidy, J. (1985). Security in infancy, childhood, and adulthood: A move to the level of representation. *Monographs of the Society for Research in Child Development, 50,* 66-104.

Mandler, J. M. (1983). Representation. In J. H. Flavell & E. M. Markman (Eds.), *Handbook of child psychology: Vol. 3. Cognitive development* (4th ed.). New York: Wiley.

Mannarino, A. P., Cohen, J. A., & Berman, S. R. (1994). The Children's Attributions and Perceptions Scale: A new measure of sexual abuse-related factors. *Journal of Clinical Child Psychology, 23,* 204-211.

McCann, L., & Colletti, J. (1994). The dance of empathy: A hermeneutic formulation of countertransference, empathy, and understanding in the treatment of individuals who have experienced early childhood trauma. In J. Wilson & J. Lindy (Eds.), *Countertransference in the treatment of PTSD.* New York: Guilford.

McCann, I. L., & Pearlman, L. A. (1990). *Psychological trauma and the adult survivor: Theory, therapy, and transformation.* New York: Brunner/Mazel.

McElroy, L. P., & McElroy, R. A. (1991). Countertransference issues in the treatment of incest families. *Psychotherapy, 28,* 48-54.

McGoldrick, M., & Gerson, R. (1985). *Genograms in family assessment.* New York: Norton.

McIntyre, J., Manion, I., Ensom, R., Wells, G., & Firestone, P. (in press). Traumatization in mothers follow.ing disclosures of extrafamilial sexual abuse: Relationship to maternal sexual abuse history. *Journal of Traumatic Stress.*

McLeer, S. V., Deblinger, E., Atkins, M. S., Foa, E. B., & Ralphe, D. L. (1988). Post-traumatic stress disorder in sexually abused children. *American Academy of Child and Adolescent Psychiatry, 27,* 650-654.

Meiselman, K. (1990). *Resolving the trauma of incest: Reintegration therapy with survivors.* San Francisco: Jossey-Bass.

Mendel, M. P. (1995). *The male survivor: The impact of sexual abuse.* Thousand Oaks, CA: Sage.

Minuchin, S. (1967). *Families of the slums: An exploration of their structure and treatment.* New York: Basic Books.

Minuchin, S. (1974). *Families and family therapy.* Cambridge, MA: Harvard University Press.

Mitchell, J. T., & Gardner, S. (1991). Treating sexual victimization: Developing trust-based relating in the mother-daughter dyad. *Psychotherapy, 28,* 333-338.

Nilsson, L., & Archer, T. (1992). Biological aspects of memory and emotion: Affect and cognition. In S. Christianson (Ed.), *The handbook of emotion and memory: Research and theory.* Hillsdale, NJ: Lawrence Erlbaum.

Offer, D., & Boxer, A. M. (1991). Normal adolescent development: Empirical research findings. In M. Lewis (Ed.), *Child and adolescent psychiatry: A comprehensive textbook.* Baltimore: Williams & Wilkins.

O'Neill, R., & Chu, J. (1994). The critical issues committee report: Parenting skills and MPD treatment—The relationship. *International Society for the Study of Multiple Personality and Dissociation News,* 4-9.

Orenchuk-Tomiuk, N., Matthey, G., & Christensen, C. P. (1990). The resolution model: A comprehensive treatment framework in sexual abuse. *Child Welfare, 69,* 417-431.

Pearlman, K., & Saakvitne, K. (1995). Treating therapists with vicarious traumatization and secondary traumatic stress disorders. In C. Figley (Ed.), *Compassion fatigue: Coping with secondary traumatic stress disorder in those who treat the traumatized.* New York: Brunner/Mazel.

Pelletier, G., & Handy, L. C. (1986). Family dysfunction and the psychological impact of child sexual abuse. *Canadian Journal of Psychiatry, 31,* 407-412.

Penn, P. (1982). Circular questioning. *Family Process, 21,* 267-280.

Perls, F. S., Hefferline, R. F., & Goodman, P. (1951). *Gestalt therapy: Excitement and growth in the human personality.* New York: Dell.

Perry, N. (1993, November). *Therapists' experiences of the effects of working with dissociative patients.* Paper presented at the Seventh Annual Conference of the International Society for the Study of Dissociative Disorders, Chicago.

Perry, B., Pollard, R., Blakley, T., Baker, W., & Vigilante, D. (1995). Childhood trauma, the neurobiology of adaptation, and "use-dependent" development of the brain: How "states" become "traits." *Infant Mental Health Journal, 16,* 271-291.

Peterson, G. (1991). Children coping with trauma: Diagnosis of "dissociation identity disorder." *Dissociation, 4,* 152-164.

Petti, T. A. (1991). Cognitive therapies. In M. Lewis (Ed.), *Child and adolescent psychiatry: A comprehensive textbook.* Baltimore: Williams & Wilkins.

Piaget, J. (1963). *The origins of intelligence in children* (2nd ed.). New York: Norton.

Piaget, J., & Inhelder, B. (1956). *The child's conception of space.* London: Routledge & Kegan Paul.

Piaget, J., & Inhelder, B. (1969). *The psychology of the child.* New York: Basic Books.

Pierce, R., & Pierce, L. (1985). The sexually abused child: A comparison of male and female victims. *Child Abuse & Neglect, 9,* 191-199.

Porter, F. S., Blick, L. C., & Sgroi, S. M. (1982). Treatment of the sexually abused child. In S. M. Sgroi (Ed.), *Handbook of clinical intervention in child sexual abuse.* Toronto: Lexington.

Purdy, A. J. (1989). *He will never remember: Caring for victims of child abuse.* Atlanta, GA: Susan Hunter.

Putnam, F. W. (1989). *Diagnosis and treatment of multiple personality disorder.* New York: Guilford.

Pynoos, R. S., & Nader, K. (1993). Issues in the treatment of posttraumatic stress in children and adolescents. In J. P. Wilson & B. Raphael (Eds.), *International handbook of traumatic stress syndromes.* New York: Plenum.

Rogers, C. (1951). *Client-centered therapy.* Boston: Houghton Mifflin.

Russell, D. (1986). *The secret trauma: Incest in the lives of girls and women.* New York: Basic Books.

Rutter, M. (1971). Normal psychosexual development. *Journal of Child Psychology and Psychiatry, 11,* 259-283.

Santostefano, S., & Calicchia, J. (1992). Body image, relational psychoanalysis, and the construction of meaning: Implications for treating aggressive children. *Development and Psychopathology, 4,* 655-678.

Sas, L. (1995, March). *Preparing child victims of sexual abuse for courtroom testimony.* Paper presented at 27th Banff International Conference on Behavioural Science: Child Abuse, Banff, Canada.

Seligman, M. E. P. (1975). *Helplessness: On depression, development, and death.* San Francisco: Freeman.

Sgroi, S. (1982). Family treatment. In S. M. Sgroi (Ed.), *Handbook of clinical intervention in child sexual abuse.* Toronto: Lexington.

Sgroi, S. M., & Dana, N. T. (1982). Individual and group treatment of mothers of incest victims. In S. M. Sgroi (Ed.), *Handbook of clinical intervention in child sexual abuse.* Toronto: Lexington.

Sgroi, S., Porter, F. S., & Blick, L. C. (1982). Validation of child sexual abuse. In S. M. Sgroi (Ed.), *Handbook of clinical intervention in child sexual abuse.* Toronto: Lexington.

Shirar, L. (1996). *Dissociative children: Bridging the inner & outer worlds.* New York: Norton.

Sinason, V. (1991). Interpretations that feel horrible to make and a theoretical unicorn. *Journal of Child Psychotherapy, 17,* 11-24.

Sirles, E. A., Smith, J. A., & Kusama, H. (1989). Psychiatric status of intrafamilial child sexual abuse victims. *Journal of the American Academy of Child and Adolescent Psychiatry, 28,* 225-229.

Smith, H., & Israel, E. (1987). Sibling incest: A study of the dynamics of 25 cases. *Child Abuse & Neglect, 11,* 101-108.

Terr, L. (1988). What happens to early memories of trauma? A study of twenty-five children under age five at the time of documented traumatic events. *Journal of the American Academy of Child Psychiatry, 1,* 96-104.

Terr, L. (1990). *Too scared to cry.* New York: Harper & Row.

Terr, L. (1991). Childhood traumas: An outline and overview. *American Journal of Psychiatry, 148,* 10-20.

Terr, L. (1994). *Unchained memories.* New York: Basic Books.

Tobias, B., Kihlstrom, J., & Schacter, D. (1992). Emotion and implicit memory. In S. Christianson (Ed.), *The handbook of emotion and memory: Research and theory.* Hillsdale, NJ: Lawrence Erlbaum.

Trepper, T. S., & Barrett, M. J. (1989). *Systemic treatment of incest: A therapeutic handbook.* New York: Brunner/Mazel.

van der Kolk, B. (1989). The compulsion to repeat trauma: Re-enactment, revictimization, and masochism. *Psychiatric Clinics of North America, 12,* 389-411.

van der Kolk, B. (1994). The body keeps the score: Memory and the evolving psychobiology of posttraumatic stress. *Harvard Review of Psychiatry, 1,* 253-265.

Van Scoyk, S., Gray, J., & Jones, D. (1988). A theoretical framework for evaluation and treatment of the victims of child sexual assault by a nonfamily member. *Family Process, 27,* 105-113.

Visintainer, M., & Wolfer, J. (1975). Psychological preparation for surgical pediatric patients: The effect on children's and parents' stress responses and adjustment. *Pediatrics, 56,* 187-202.

Vitulano, L. A., & Tebes, J. K. (1991). Child and adolescent behavior therapy. In M. Lewis (Ed.), *Child and adolescent psychiatry: A comprehensive textbook.* Baltimore: Williams & Watkins.

Wheeler, D. (1990). Father-daughter incest: Consideration for the family therapist. In M. P. Mirkin (Ed.), *The social and political contests of family therapy.* Boston: Allyn & Bacon.

Wieland, S. (1996). *Addressing the internal trauma: Issues and techniques in abuse-focused therapy.* Manuscript in preparation.

Williamson, J., Borduin, C., & Howe, B. (1991). The ecology of adolescent maltreatment: A multilevel examination of adolescent physical abuse, sexual abuse, and neglect. *Journal of Consulting and Clinical Psychology, 59,* 449-457.

Wilson, J., Lindy, J., & Raphael, B. (1994). Empathic strain and therapist defense: Type I and II CTRs. In J. Wilson & J. Lindy (Eds.), *Countertransference in the treatment of PTSD.* New York: Guilford.

Winnicott, D. (1971a). Mirror-role of mother and family in child development. In D. Winnicott (Ed.), *Playing and reality.* London: Tavistock.

Winnicott, D. (1971b). *Therapeutic consultations in child psychiatry.* New York: Basic Books.

Wolfe, V., Gentile, C., & Wolfe, D. (1989). The impact of sexual abuse on children: A PTSD formulation. *Behavior Therapy, 20,* 215-228.

Yassen, J. (1995). Preventing secondary traumatic stress disorder. In C. Figley (Ed.), *Compassion fatigue: Coping with secondary traumatic stress disorder in those who treat the traumatized.* New York: Brunner/Mazel.

Yokley, J. M., & McGuire, D. (1990). Introduction to the therapeutic use of victim-offender communication. In J. M. Yokley (Ed.), *The use of victim-offender communication in the treatment of sexual abuse: Three intervention models.* Orwell, VT: Safer Society Press.

Younger, B. A., & Cohen, L. B. (1986). Developmental change in infant's perception of correlations among attributes. *Child Development, 57,* 803-815.

Yuille, J. (1988). The systematic assessment of children's testimony. *Canadian Psychology, 29,* 247-262.

Subject and Name Index

About the Author

Sandra Wieland, PhD, is Director and Clinical Associate of the Centre for Treatment of Sexual Abuse & Childhood Trauma in Ottawa, Ontario, Canada, and assistant clinical professor at the University of Ottawa. She has presented workshops and training sessions across Canada on working with children and adolescents who have been sexually abused.

Photograph by Rod MacIvor. Appeared in the *Ottawa Citizen* on November 17, 1995. Used by permission of the *Ottawa Citizen*.

DAT D